THIS BUSINESS OF
GLOBAL MUSIC MARKETING

TAD LATHROP

BILLBOARD BOOKS

AN IMPRINT OF WATSON-GUPTILL PUBLICATIONS / NEW YORK

Executive Editor: Bob Nirkind
Project Editor: Ross Plotkin
Production Manager: Salvatore Destro
Designer: Lisa Hamilton

© 2007 by Grayson F. Lathrop

First published in 2007 by Billboard Books,
An imprint of Watson-Guptill Publications,
Nielsen Business Media, a division of The Nielsen Company
770 Broadway, New York, NY 10003
www.watsonguptill.com

Library of Congress Control Number: 2006936442

ISBN-10: 0-8230-7788-8
ISBN-13: 978-0-8230-7788-5

Printed in the United States

First printing, 2007

1 2 3 4 5 6 7 8 9 / 14 13 12 11 10 09 08 07

ACKNOWLEDGMENTS

True to the subject matter, writing this book was something of a journey, both literally (travel abroad) and figuratively. Fortunately I didn't travel alone. Music specialists from around the globe appeared at just the right times to graciously light the way through some of the darker passageways. Without them, I couldn't have completed the trip. Thanks to:

Jim Pettigrew, for coordinating interviews and reviewing the manuscript-in-progress.

Suzanne Ciani, for sharing her insights and experience as an independent musician.

Daniel Cheung of The Orchard for shedding light on digital music strategies and on business in China.

Rob Kuilboer of Astral Music for his detailed comments on distribution.

Peter Fosso of the Global Music Project for his view from the nonprofit sector.

Mary Jurey of New West Records for talking about what her job entails.

Thanks also to: Sree Nagarajan for his conversations about marketing independent music, and for his enthusiasm about the subject; Syed Rizwan Mehdi of Music World Entertainment, Hyderabad, India, for providing invaluable research on distribution in India; Gurmeet Singh of Music Today for further clarification of Indian music sales; and Ilari Kaartinen of DD Records in Finland for taking the time to answer questions.

In addition, I'd like to thank:

Bill Krasilovsky, for his pioneering book *This Business of Music*.

The folks at Broadcast Music Inc. (BMI), for providing my first experiences with the "back end" of music commerce.

The crew at Cherry Lane Music—fellow travelers in my early music publishing days.

Nancy Carroll, for her chart designs; Audrey Celenza for editorial assistance; Brandy Jones for technical consultation; and Shelba Sellers for lending her expertise in economics.

At Billboard Books, thanks to executive editor Bob Nirkind, manuscript editor Ross Plotkin, copyeditor Michèle LaRue, designer Jay Anning, and production manager Salvatore Destro.

Finally, a tip of the hat to musicians everywhere. The magic is in your hands.

CONTENTS

Start small, expand widely, then go global. That's the well-traveled path of the music marketer. But today, the "go global" imperative is more pressing, more promising, and more possible.

Today's music audience is global. Concert tours are worldwide in scope. Internet downloads are available the world over. An artist's albums are distributed internationally. This globalization of the music audience—of the music business—represents a gold-plated opportunity for musicians and sellers of music. More income, more distribution, more worldwide awareness—these are the prizes that await the music maker who has the ambition to pursue them. And you don't have to be a large business operation to sell globally. Nowadays anyone can do it—even a one-person enterprise.

This Business of Global Music Marketing is intended as a source of practical information for those who wish to take advantage of today's global opportunities to sell music. It provides guidelines for systematically and profitably engaging in cross-border music commerce—guidelines that will be useful to the following kinds of readers:

- Independent musicians and music producers who market their own recordings
- Entrepreneurs building and expanding their own music businesses
- Music managers looking for ways to broaden their artist clients' audiences
- Marketing executives seeking ideas for entering foreign markets
- Career seekers interested in music and global business

This book is a companion volume, of sorts, to my other book on the music business, *This Business of Music Marketing and Promotion*. That book provides general principles for operating at each stage of marketing, from product development to distribution (via brick and/or click), from promotion in the media to selling on the Internet. *Global Music Marketing* takes those same principles and explains how they can apply beyond the borders of your own country. There are important differences—cultural, regulatory, administrative, legal, political, logistical—beyond the obvious language variations.

To give readers the broadest possible perspective, I've included strategies and concepts that are applied across industries, not just in music. The hardest-core music devotees may be inclined to bypass some of this material. Certainly, it's possible to focus only on the music-marketing basics and then dive into the global marketplace with some success. But more and deeper knowledge tends to result in wiser, more informed choices and reduced risk of error and loss. The information is here if you want it, and worth taking the time to think about.

As with *This Business of Music Marketing and Promotion*, *Global Music Marketing* can be read straight through from front to back, as a logically unfolding narrative of the marketing process. The book can also be "cherry picked" for information relevant to your immediate needs. Just use the Index and the Contents.

It's my hope that readers of *Global Music Marketing* will come away with an understanding of country-to-country differences and how to bridge them to reap maximum profit from music in the full, planet-spanning marketplace.

Note: This publication has been written with the aim of providing accurate and up-to-date information about the music industry. However, business customs, technologies, and monetary values change over time. Furthermore, every business situation is unique; readers' circumstances will invariably differ from those I describe, even if the circumstances appear similar. For those reasons, the author and the publisher bear no responsibility for actions taken by readers based on information provided in this book. Readers are urged to seek the current advice of appropriate professionals.

CHAPTER I

Going Global: Why It's a Good Idea

Foreign lands are closer than ever, for people considering doing business in them. The Internet, transport technology, international trade agreements, and the spread of free-market trade policies have all contributed to the opening of borders to trade and to the speed and agility with which sellers can get their products into foreign hands.

Yet during your first attempts to sell music, foreign markets may be far from your thoughts.

If you're a marketer for a record company, small or large, you're probably focusing at first on ways to sell to audiences in your own country, where you're familiar with the system of distribution, with the national media, with ways of doing business, and with the tastes, habits, and desires of music consumers.

If you're an artist trying to sell your own recording, you have a full-time job just getting local land distribution, placing the product for sale on the Web, and figuring out how to convince anyone outside your family and friends to sample and purchase your music.

A positive customer response in the artist's immediate region may be cause for celebration, for any kind of music seller. Sales on a national level may seem like the ultimate success.

But there's further opportunity, and it lies beyond your country's borders. The sheer numbers of potential customers worldwide, the variety of markets that global commerce offers, and the increasing ease of doing business around the globe make thinking globally a natural extension of any music marketing plan. For many established companies, of course, global commerce is basic to their business strategy. These companies sign artists, in many cases, with an eye to how they will appeal to listeners outside their own countries. But even for those looking at global commerce as an afterthought, many international markets may be fertile sales territories for domestically developed music.

MTV is one example of a music company that saw opportunities in global expansion and took advantage of them, to great success. Started in the 1980s, the U.S.-based network captured the essence of music-infused youth culture. It began exporting its branded programming overseas, and by 2006 was not only in 87.6 million homes in United States but also in more than 331 million homes in 164 countries and territories, broadcast in 18 languages, reaching more than 1 billion people worldwide.

Importantly, the key to MTV's international success was not in delivering its U.S. content in exact form to other countries. Instead, it combined its trademark style with local content to appeal to local tastes. As writer Johnnie Roberts described in *Time* magazine, "MTV Indonesia regularly airs 'calls to prayer' for its Muslim audience. . . . MTV Japan [provides] a sense of technology edginess; MTV Italy—style and elegance." MTV India features Indian videos and entertainers.

With the U.S. accounting for 80 percent of overall revenue of $5.2 billion in 2006, MTV stood to benefit immensely from building on the non-U.S. portion of its earnings.

Large companies like MTV aren't the only beneficiaries of global marketing opportunities. Independent record companies in Canada receive 30 to 50 percent of their revenues from outside North America, according to the Canadian Independent Record Production Association (CIRPA).

Even one-person operations, such as composer Suzanne Ciani's Seventh Wave Productions (see her interview on page 229) can profitably pursue international sales and licensing deals.

However distant the notion of international marketing may have been for you previously, you've now come to the point of considering whether and how you can put globalization to work for your music. The "whether" part of your inquiry is relatively easy to answer: With the right product packaging, the right distribution tactics, and the right promotion, virtually any musical product should be saleable somewhere outside its home country (music is something of an international language, after all), resulting in bigger audiences and increased profits. As for the "how" part, that's what this book is here to help you with.

THE CURRENT GLOBAL MARKETPLACE

It's a propitious time to do business globally. Markets are open to world trade as never before. China, with its population of 1.27 billion, has become a leading power in the international economy and increasingly active as a global trader. The same is true of the former Soviet Union, and of its divested satellite countries, now trading freely with distant partners. The creation of regional economic unions and alliances—such as the European Union (EU), the North American Free Trade Agreement (NAFTA), and MERCOSUR—has begun to facilitate trade between member countries. The emergence of global institutions and agreements—the World Bank, the World Trade Organization (WTO), the International Monetary Fund (IMF), and the General Agreement on Trade and Tariffs (GATT)—has helped bring order and management to the world marketplace.

ECONOMIC ALLIANCES AND REGIONAL TRADE AGREEMENTS

Countries in a geographic region may reach formal agreement to reduce barriers to free flow of goods and services between participating countries, theoretically bene-fiting all and opening formerly closed markets to foreign trade. These agreements create regional trade blocs, which can wield greater economic and political power than if individual countries were acting alone. There are various possible levels of economic integration between countries, from basic relaxation of intra-alliance tariffs to full harmonization of currency and tax rates (the European Union) to complete political integration (the United States). There has been a surge in regional trade agreements since the 1990s. Key RTAs include:

APEC (Asia Pacific Economic Cooperation): Australia, Brunei, Canada, Chile, China, Indonesia, Japan, Malaysia, Mexico, New Zealand, Papua New Guinea, Philippines, Singapore, South Korea, Taiwan, Thailand, United States

ASEAN (Association of South East Asian Nations): Brunei, Cambodia, Darussalam, Indonesia, Laos, Malaysia, Myanmar, Philippines, Singapore, Thailand, Vietnam

BAFTA (Baltic Free-Trade Area): Estonia, Latvia, Lithuania

CACM (Central American Common Market): Costa Rica, El Salvador, Guatemala, Honduras, Nicaragua

CAN (Andean Community): Bolivia, Colombia, Ecuador, Peru, Venezuela

CARICOM (Caribbean Community and Common Market): Antigua, Bahamas, Barbados, Belize, Dominica, Grenada, Guyana, Haiti, Jamaica, Monserrat, Trinidad, St. Kitts, St. Lucia, St. Vincent, Surinam

CEFTA (Central European Free Trade Agreement): Bulgaria, Croatia, Romania

CER (Closer Trade Relations Trade Agreement): Australia, New Zealand

EAEC (Eurasian Economic Community): Belarus, Kazakhstan, Kyrgyz Republic, Russian Federation, Tajikistan

EU (European Union): Austria, Belgium, Cyprus, Czech Republic, Denmark, Estonia, Finland, France, Germany, Greece, Hungary, Ireland, Italy, Latvia, Lithuania, Luxembourg, Malta, Netherlands, Poland, Portugal, Slovakia, Slovenia, Spain, Sweden, United Kingdom

MERCOSUR (Southern Common Market): Argentina, Brazil, Paraguay, Uruguay

NAFTA (North American Free Trade Agreement): Canada, Mexico, United States

SADC (Southern African Development Community): Angola, Botswana, Lesotho, Malawi, Mauritius, Mozambique, Namibia, South Africa, Swaziland, Tanzania, Zambia, Zimbabwe

---

For more information on regional trade agreements, visit the World Trade Organization at www.wto.org.

KEY INTERNATIONAL TRADE AGREEMENTS AND TREATIES

Berne Convention: The Berne Convention for the Protection of Literary and Artistic Works, first adopted in 1886, stipulates copyright protections for member nations—specifically that authors' copyrights are protected for the life of the author plus seventy years.

Bretton Woods: Conference in 1944 to establish international monetary system. Called for fixed currency exchange rates and established the International Monetary Fund (IMF) and the World Bank.

Digital Millennium Copyright Act: An application of copyright to digital works, signed in 1998 to bring the U.S. into compliance with two earlier digital treaties signed by more than thirty countries.

General Agreement on Tariffs and Trade (GATT): The most notable international accord under which governments agree to remove trade barriers between countries. Eight rounds of talks have been held since 1947. The Uruguay Round of 1993 gave rise to its successor, the World Trade Organization. It also focused for the first time on the cross-border protection of intellectual property, which includes music.

Geneva Convention of 1971: An agreement, signed by more than sixty countries, to protect partner states against unauthorized duplication (piracy) of sound recordings.

ORGANIZATIONS INVOLVED IN GLOBAL TRADE

World Bank: Established in 1944, the World Bank promotes general economic development by supplying low-cost loans to developing countries.

International Monetary Fund (IMF): Established in 1944, the IMF serves to maintain stability in the international monetary system.

International Chamber of Commerce (ICC): Organization promoting open international trade and providing business services.

Organization for Economic Cooperation and Development (OECD): Economic forum for discussion of members' economic problems and possible solutions.

World Trade Organization (WTO): Created in 1993 during the Uruguay Round of the General Agreement on Tariffs and Trade (GATT), and opened for business in 1995, the WTO establishes and enforces the rules of international trade. Its membership comprises more than 140 countries.

United Nations: Global association of governments working to support international law, peacekeeping, human rights, economic development, and social equity.

To the music marketer, these developments aren't just abstractions. A free-market China means a huge potential audience for music exporters to that country.

Economic unions such as the EU lower the cost of doing business between member countries—savings that may get passed down the pipeline to you, the marketer-manufacturer.

Loosening of restrictions on foreign direct investment means that it may be easier to set up production facilities abroad, in turn making it more convenient and cheaper to distribute in the host country.

The GATT agreement strengthened international intellectual property rights, addressing the issue of piracy. At stake are billions of dollars each year that legitimate music sellers have lost due to bootlegging of albums—not to mention to illegal online file sharing. Formerly risky markets are slowly becoming more attractive, though much still needs to be done to reduce if not eliminate piracy.

Music production technology has yielded the CD and now online digital files, greatly reducing the cost of product transport from the time when larger, 33⅓-rpm albums were in vogue. In the case of online song files, the cost of transport is essentially nil.

In addition to a more open global marketplace in general, there is much more immediate and far-reaching communication among countries about different music styles than ever before. Nowadays, even the most far-flung musical offshoot may have an audience on the other side of the globe, thanks to the Internet, satellite communications, and transport technology. MTV's operation in Indonesia, for example, means that not only do Indonesians get exposed to Western pop music but listeners from other countries may get a chance to hear what's happening musically in Indonesia's culture. Worldwide awareness of the vast variety that music offers has never been more acute.

With planetwide awareness of the globe's multivarious musical options has come a convergence of global taste, to an extent. Just as blue jeans are embraced everywhere, a new recording of popular music has the potential of finding friendly ears just about anywhere. At the same time, local cultures continue to flourish. Movements to reinvigorate local musical traditions and to create new variations on them are constantly emerging and morphing the world over, injecting ever new sonic spices and exotic flavors into the global music melting pot.

To the seller of music, the opportunities for getting across to foreign audiences are virtually limitless—and are made more accessible by cultivating up-to-date intelligence about what styles are currently popular in which countries, and what countries might be most likely to enjoy that style you're selling that they may not yet have heard.

As it happens, the music that you find popular in one country may be the same music that another country has grown tired of, or never much appreciated in the first place. Jazz, for example, has been embraced by audiences in Japan and parts of Europe when citizens of the United States, the country that invented the music, have as a group been largely oblivious in recent years. The existence of those Japanese and European audiences is evidence that globalization has been very good indeed for purveyors of jazz. Likewise for other styles. Here is an additional benefit of global marketing: an outlet not just for new music but for music on the far end of the product life cycle.

The pace of invention has never been more rapid, and different countries, with their unique attitudes toward technical innovation and the use of leisure time and their particular levels of disposable income, develop and serve as testing grounds for different types of innovations. Lightning-fast commerce and communication ensure that the best of those innovations soon pollinate abroad. Japan, for instance, was the site of the most rapid initial adoption of music samples used for mobile phone ringtones—segments of songs that play on your phone when someone calls. By 2005, mobile ringtones worldwide accounted for $3.5 billion in annual sales, yielding one-tenth of total recorded music sales. Such rapid innovation holds the promise of ever-evolving new ways to configure music for sale, echoing the marketing impact of the CD and the LP vinyl album in their eras. Music listening and purchase have always been tied in with gadgetry and new technological trends, and worldwide R&D ensures that this linkage will continue to provide new packages, with new revenue streams, for the owners of the raw sounds, the music content.

HOW WE GOT HERE

Prior to the twentieth century, music traveled via live performance and printed music. The invention of the phonograph record in the early twentieth century provided a new format for mass distribution and worldwide music sales, and the accompanying development of radio, television, and movies provided new, more instantaneous transmission channels. With expanded air travel came an increase in the volume of worldwide music touring and the pace of commercial activity.

As knowledge of other countries' musical offerings spread via mass communications, international demand increased. It was completely unleashed with the arrival of the Internet in the mid-1990s, when listeners all over the world began having immediate access to music catalogues from all over the world. At the same time, the development of digital music formats made international transmission even easier, leading to a two-tiered business of marketing recorded music: traditional CD and hard-copy sales on one hand and digital formats on the other.

By 2004, the music recording industry was a $32 billion industry worldwide, with myriad new ways of doing business and increased need for flexibility on the part of participants. As the head of one long-active record company put it: "If we were starting out today, would we use the same business model we have now? Not at all. The business is completely different." Where older companies built rigid, entrenched networks of manufacturing, distribution, and promotion—difficult to change—today's companies and music marketers must be nimble, flexible, and responsive to rapid market change. Ideally, they should lead the change. Perhaps the best business model is that of the think tank with minimal infrastructure and overhead, using its intelligence to continuously devise new ways to configure and market its music worldwide, while continually developing and shifting partnerships to best suit the market demands of the moment. The associated challenge is doing this without damaging the long-lasting relationships that have traditionally accompanied and fueled long-term success in music commerce.

DIGITAL DIVISIONS

In the first decade of the 2000s, passionate opinions fueled debate over whether the future of recorded music would be exclusively digital or a mixture of digital and tangible packaged products such as CDs. An exchange between two music CEOs in 2006 captured the main arguments.

CEO of a German record company: "Digital music may not go where we all hope it will go. The recent performance of iTunes in Germany was less than expected. Physical product is still the bulk of sales, and probably will be for at least the next five to ten years. My fear is that by putting all our efforts into digital we're shooting ourselves in the foot in the area of our bread-and-butter business. What our company is doing is trying to make a more attractive physical product. Today's young audiences who trade digital files don't see the value of music in the way we did back in the sixties and seventies. We're trying to create packaging that once again conveys the value of the music it holds."

CEO of a Canadian artist management company: "The future of music is digital. We have to embrace this and all the different ways kids want their music. Embrace innovation. Stop thinking in terms of 'twelve songs on a disc.' Today's music is a digital file that streams. It's like water. A single song can have an electric version, an acoustic version, a long version, a short version. Don't think about a fixed physical product. Think of an artist as a brand. And use that brand to develop multiple revenue streams. Right now digital sales may still be a small percentage of total sales, but our company is putting most of our marketing budget into digital: about sixty percent digital, forty percent physical."

BENEFITS OF GLOBAL MUSIC MARKETING

Why, specifically, should you the music seller concern yourself with marketing and promoting outside your own country? There are five main potential benefits:

Larger Audiences. If your goal is growth, then just as you'd want to expand beyond the listenership in your immediate locale and surrounding region, so will you want to eventually expand beyond your national borders. The broader the acceptance of your music, the freer you are to operate as you see fit, the more strategic options are available to you, the more creative choices you have, and on and on. And, of course, there's the sheer satisfaction of gaining acceptance by the broadest possible audience.

Increased Earnings. When you broaden your field of operation, you increase the number of potential revenue streams and, hopefully, the overall sum of revenues. In addition to domestic earnings, you can derive income from foreign retail sales, foreign licensing, foreign performances, foreign publishing, foreign merchandising, and more.

Economies of Scale. Opening up new markets can increase the size of your target audience and, if you're marketing physical products like CDs, the number of units you'll want to manufacture. The more units you manufacture, the less you pay per unit: your fixed costs, such as for recording, are spread over more units, and you get manufacturing discounts for larger orders. If your product—CDs, for example—sells out, you'll have maximized your profit margins and improved your overall return on investment.

Decreased Risk Through Diversification. With a diverse set of revenue streams, you hedge against losses incurred if one or more of the streams should dry up. Many are the big-name rock acts from past decades whose popularity waned in their original markets but who found continuing demand for their sounds on distant shores. In the mid-1980s, the band Queen found that touring foreign markets gained it a large new fan base in Latin America, Asia, and Africa, making up for the band's decreased popularity in the U.S. and England. Similarly, having a global perspective can lead you to alternative markets if the home market never proves sufficiently responsive—although domestic success is usually a prerequisite for attracting foreign business partners.

Competitive Advantage. In the competition for finite consumer dollars, the player operating in the broadest possible array of markets is often the winner of the game. Consider: Your market competitors aren't only other recordings and performers. You're also competing with other forms of entertainment: video games, movies, cable television, and the Internet, to cite a few. There may be no room in a given domestic market for what you have to offer. But targeting other countries can help you bypass the crowd.

GLOBAL CHALLENGES

Few upsides are without their downsides, and so it is with marketing music globally. Here are some of the challenges you'll need to contend with:

Localization Versus Mass Marketing. Even though there has been a convergence of international tastes in music, some local preferences remain unique. Targeting customers with specific preferences may mean customizing your product in some way to match local tastes—leaving certain tracks off a CD, changing the imagery in the packaging, altering promotional messages. Customization is costly. You'll need to do a cost-benefit analysis for every instance of marketing customization. The alternative is mass marketing: providing the same unaltered product for every market. It's cheaper per unit than customization, but you run the risk of not appealing to some audience segments.

Communication Barriers. Language differences impact both business-to-consumer marketing and business-to-business. In the B2C realm, translation of packaging elements and marketing messages, including Web site content, may be required in order to secure sales. In B2B, complexities of business deals may be difficult to communicate when one of the parties is speaking in other than his native language. Further, differences in physical communication style—hand gestures, body language—may be incorrectly interpreted, leading to misunderstandings.

Cultural and Social Differences. Attitudes toward virtually every aspect of life—family, community, work, leisure time, religion, ethics, etiquette—vary from country to country. These differences have an impact on doing business with foreign vendors and partners. Familiarity with these factors can make a great difference in your business dealings in a given country and in whether your music and marketing campaign are warmly received.

Variances in Approaches to Distribution. Developed countries may have short, efficient distribution channels: say, two or three intermediaries between the manufacturer and the customer. In the United States, for example, the manufacturer may deal with a single distributor, who places the product in a mass retail outlet that serves a large number of customers. But some less-developed countries may have much longer distribution channels. There may be a regional distributor passing product to local subdistributors, who transfer smaller quantities to one-person operations that deliver cartloads of products to local marketplaces. These longer channels are more difficult to coordinate and require payment to more channel members. Understanding these logistical variations—and the strategies for handling them—is part of the global marketer's task.

Variances in Economic Systems and Rules of Trade. Global markets are much more open than they once were. Yet significant differences exist from country to country in attitude toward free trade. Governments intervene in trade activity to varying degrees. Some seek to protect national industries by imposing quotas on imports, so as to limit the quantities of those imports that come into the countries. The French government, for example, imposed quotas requiring radio stations to play 40 percent French music—a limiting of radio time for non-French music. Or governments may impose tariffs on imports, to make them less competitive with local versions of the same product. These tariffs raise the price of the imports, making them less attractive to local consumers. Such "protectionist" arrangements make it more difficult for outsiders to succeed in the market. Additionally, some countries impose restrictions on product content, not allowing imports that contain objectionable language or undesirable political messages, for example.

Fluctuations in the Value of Currency. Values of international currencies relative to each other change on a constant basis. Understanding tactics for minimizing the risk of losing value in a given global trade is critical to successful marketing across currency zones.

Legal Systems and Corruption Index. Countries offer varying levels of legal protection against corrupt business practices and such crimes as piracy and theft of intellectual property. Similarly, countries present different levels of risk in the area of corruption in the public sector, such as the taking of bribes by public officials. Legal systems overall differ, too, affecting the way you'll need to approach drawing up contracts. Before doing business in a country, you'll be smart to research some of these issues.

Political Instability. The smooth flow of trade depends in part on stable governments. Unfortunately, many countries present a high risk of market disruption due to political instability, which can take the form of social unrest, insurgency, civil war, coups d'états, and less extreme scenarios, with outcomes ranging from changes in tax rates to government takeovers of industries to complete shutdown of external trade. The company doing business in such a country can experience interruption or cessation of payments, loss in value of earnings, loss of inventory or other assets, increased cost of doing business, and other undesirable effects.

Increased Workload. Enjoying all the benefits of doing business abroad requires close attention to the issues just discussed. To be sure, a global marketing effort demands work hours above and beyond what you devote to local, regional, and national sales.

SOURCES OF GLOBAL INCOME

Today's global marketplace offers numerous possible sources of income for the music seller. Here are some of them:

- Retail sales of downloads, CDs, DVDs, ringtones, and other formats
- Subscription fees for digital music services via the Internet and mobile phones
- Fees for live performances
- Royalties and fees earned from performances of recordings on radio and television, on the Internet, in movies, and in commercial venues such as restaurants and nightclubs
- Royalties earned from cover versions (that is, other performers' versions) of music, created for use on records, in live performances, on television and radio, and in movies
- Sales of T-shirts, jackets, tour books, and other promotional merchandise
- Subscription fees and other Internet-based income for artists and music sellers with their own Web sites, and licensing fees for use of music on others' sites

THE JOB OF THE GLOBAL MUSIC MARKETER

Just as with domestic marketing, the international seller of music needs to deal with the basics—the Four P's of marketing.

The Four P's refer to key elements of the marketing program: product, price, place, and promotion. (A detailed introduction to working with these elements in the context of music can be found in the book *This Business of Music Marketing and Promotion*.)

In global marketing, the marketer must adjust each element to maximize its effectiveness in specific countries targeted for business. This may mean changes to the music program, fine-tuning of pricing strategy, varying distribution strategies, and carefully calibrated promotion to match local tastes and preferences.

Global marketing requires the following additional initiatives:

- **Choosing Target Markets in Foreign Countries.** The music seller must research foreign markets that offer the most promise of return on investment. This requires finding out where the music may have the best reception. It also means researching such determinants as audience demographics and attributes, market accessibility, macroeconomic indicators, promotional opportunities, and performance opportunities. Note, though, that if the music is well known, the foreign markets may proactively solicit for licensing or distribution rights, making the music seller's job easier.

- **Choosing Foreign Business Partners.** Going it alone isn't an option. A marketing effort is only as good as the network of distributors, licensees, sales agents, and other entities with whom the marketer must do business. Finding them and selecting the right ones are key to international marketing planning.

- **Choosing Methods of Doing Business.** There are many options for conducting business abroad, ranging from straight export of domestically manufactured recordings, to licensing of master recordings for repackaging and distribution by a foreign licensee, to joint venturing with a foreign music company and beyond. In a given country one of these options may be more profitable than the others. Analysis and decisions will be required.

- **Planning and Executing Integrated Marketing Communications.** As with domestic marketing, choices must be made regarding the best mix of advertising, sales promotion, direct marketing, and publicity to put into play for the product being sold.

- **Planning and Executing Internet and Radio Promotion.** The Web offers readily available access to global audiences, but Web promotion requires customizing for international audiences. Radio, the traditional outlet for music promotion, is becoming more accessible; options need to be evaluated and pursued to the extent possible.

- **Planning and Executing Live Performances.** Scheduling, booking, transportation, payment, and promotion all require careful coordination.

- **Seeking and Exploiting Additional Promotional Channels and Revenue Streams.** Television, movies, and other media offer options for exposure and income. Exploring them and adding them to the marketing effort are part of the job.

- **Pursuing Opportunities in Music Publishing.** The raw musical composition—the intellectual property—can be exploited to generate income from performances on the radio, on the Internet, on television, and in films, and from a wide range of additional uses.

- **Monitoring and Managing the Global Music Marketing Program.** Once the pieces are in place and the execution has begun, careful tracking and analysis of the results must be carried out through the complete product life cycle. Where needed, adjustment of the marketing program will have to be made.

For the global music marketer, the task can be summarized as exploiting all available opportunities while striving to minimize risk. Succeeding takes energy, stamina, resourcefulness, motivation, flexibility, and intelligence. Can it be done? Thousands of others are doing it every day. Is it worth it? If you ask an American composer whose song is used on a South Korean TV commercial, or a band finding large new audiences abroad, the answer will be an enthusiastic yes.

CHAPTER 2

Choosing Foreign Markets for Music

Faced with an entire planet's worth of potential zones in which to promote a line of records, or even just one record, you might easily begin to feel overwhelmed. That's why you may want to limit your first moves toward global marketing and promotion. You might follow a guideline used by one major company in its start-up export enterprises: "Make a little, sell a little." It basically means, keep the initial effort modest, keep your risk low, and see how it goes. Success on a small scale first can pave the way for a more expansive strategy later.

It's certainly true that telecommunications and the Internet have made planetwide marketing and promotion a lot less overwhelming—if somewhat less tangible. You could, for example, start by setting up a Web site of your own with music for sale. Right away, you're in the global market, since the Internet is accessible everywhere. Use e-commerce strategies to broaden awareness of the site, make the presentation as appealing as possible, build incentives to purchase, and let the orders come in from wherever they may.

The truth is, in today's world, that would be a limited strategy. Someday, if music evolves further into digital files that people only download from the Internet or stream into portable playback devices, this faceless, virtual-world cyber approach may be the dominant mode of music commerce. But in 2004, according to the Recording Industry Association of America, the physical compact disc still accounted for 90 percent of sales of recorded music in the United States, and predictions were that five to ten more years of life could be squeezed from that format. And of those sales, the great majority occurred in the "physical world": in 2003, the Internet accounted for only 5 percent of music sold, with 86 percent of music purchases made in brick-and-mortar stores. Given these statistics and projections, chances are good that you'll continue to have the compact disc as a viable format for some years to come, you'll have stores on the street to sell them in, and you'll have countries all over the world with streets full of stores you may want to stock with your music.

So at some point you *will* need to focus on traditional, land-based, proactive, sales-generating strategies. What's more, even when you pursue sales of digital music you need to take a proactive, hands-on approach to targeting and selling to receptive audiences. Marketing digital music is in many ways analogous to marketing tangible music formats. All of which puts you right back where you were at the beginning, faced with that entire planet's worth of potential zones in which to promote a line of records. And you're still overwhelmed.

That's why, as part of a modest start-up strategy, a good first step is to narrow your focus to one foreign market. Break into it, establish ties with suppliers, build trust, develop familiarity with the business processes, gain knowledge of the market's music-buying behavior. Later you can start thinking about moving on to other points on the globe.

The question is: How do you choose which foreign market to start with? The short answer is:

- Identify groups of listeners most likely to appreciate your sound, find out where they live, and target them within the most accessible and potentially profitable region.

But the more complete answer includes the following activities:

- Learn about the leading global music markets, and find out where emerging opportunities may exist.
- Assess the music-market infrastructure, overall economic health, and potential for greatest profit with minimum risk, of countries you're considering.
- Consider the comfort level of doing business in a given market, which means familiarizing yourself with cultural and social aspects of target markets.

SHOPPING AT A GLOBAL BUSINESS SUPERMARKET

A shortcut to learning about the global music marketplace is to attend MIDEM, the annual music-business trade show held in Cannes, France, every January. Aisle after aisle of attending music merchants and marketers from all over the world meet, talk, and make deals. Not much research into a country's macroeconomics takes place. Rather, direct conversation about prospective partners' business and financial propositions rule the day. If a good deal surfaces, it's generally taken.

There's no avoiding research, however. You need to set up business appointments before appearing at Cannes, which means finding out who will attend and whether they have potential value to you.

For more information, visit www.midem.com.

IDENTIFYING LISTENER GROUPS AND THEIR LOCATIONS

In music marketing, perhaps the most difficult task of all is identifying target groups of listeners who may be inclined to like the particular kind of music you are promoting. Taste in music is so subjective, so unpredictable, so variable, so based on the most idiosyncratic of perceptions and preferences, that precisely defining a likely-to-buy segment of the music-consuming population remains a largely elusive goal. Analyze the typical music fan's collection and you're likely to find a vast variety of music genres: Nusrat Fateh Ali Khan along with the Beatles. Tom Waits alongside Harry Partch. Javanese gamelan music followed by Miles Davis. How do you segment the people who may be collectively drawn to one particular sound or genre?

Answer: You collect data that, cumulatively, begins to point you in certain directions.

The data you collect begins with your music. It then draws from association with products that are already in the market—products that have already connected with consumers. It focuses next on the consumers who have purchased those similar products: where the buyers live, what they buy, how much of it they buy, where they learn about it, and where they buy it. So the steps are these:

1. Define and characterize your music as specifically as possible.

2. Identify products on the market that are closely related.

3. Identify the people who buy those related products.

4. Identify the channels you can use to sell to those people.

An alternate approach is to research the market first and make the music later, tailoring it to market tastes. But the discussion here assumes music that already exists.

DEFINE YOUR MUSIC

Categorize the music according to any criteria that people are drawn to. People tend to prefer certain styles of music—say, jazz, classical, or certain genres of rock. So categorize your music by genre. Some people prefer the sounds of some instruments over others. So also categorize your music according to the featured instrument. Many people listen to music for the mood it creates. Thus, you should try to define the moods your music tends to emphasize.

For example, your music may fall into the category of rock. Within rock, it might fall into the subcategory of progressive rock. It's relatively easy to collect a list of established artists labeled progressive rock. But you need to narrow down the associations even more. Your music may be progressive rock, but it might also emphasize a particular instrument: say, keyboard, or guitar, or percussion. Further, the music may be identifiable according to mood: You are able to create a list of adjectives that, cumulatively, further differentiate your progressive rock from some other progressive rock. You might find, for example, that the music tends to be dark, ominous, nightmarish, bleak, apocalyptic, and sad, while some other progressive rock might be described as sunny, bright, optimistic, uplifting, and happy. Themes in lyrics, too, can help define the mood.

IDENTIFY RELATED PRODUCTS

Internet databases such as Allmusic.com allow you to search artists by categories such as genre, instrument, and mood, and find lists of artists that are closely related. With that list, or collection of lists from different sources, you've thus found associated products—that is, similar artists. To find associated nonmusic products, look at publications that deal with your kind of music and notice who the advertisers are. Notice also the message, tone, and design of the ads to determine the kind of audience they are aiming at. Children? Adults?

Educated? Affluent? Single? Married? Such factors will play a big role in your marketing communications later in the campaign.

IDENTIFY PEOPLE WHO BUY RELATED PRODUCTS, AND THE COUNTRIES IN WHICH THEY LIVE

Ideally, you have already gathered information about the domestic local, regional, or national audiences appropriate for your music. The key now is to find pockets of other listeners in countries outside your own. Start by conducting research to find where the associated products you've identified have found listeners.

- Research sales data on albums by those similar artists.
- Examine international popularity charts and playlists.
- Search Internet databases.
- Look up research papers.

The information you accumulate via these various means should point you to promising target audiences in several countries.

Research Sales Data for Related Recordings. In the ideal world you'd have ready access to sales data for albums by artists similar to yours, categorized by country and region. You could then find where the most sales occur. You might then deduce that a regional population that buys the related product would be a reasonable target for marketing your own product. But record companies don't ordinarily make their individual product sales information public. So you have to use ingenuity to obtain estimates of sales data, and then draw conclusions from it.

One way to get sales estimates is to contact and ask the nonmanufacturing sales-channel members associated with your related product—that is, distributors and retailers. There's no assurance that they will divulge the information, but they might.

Another way to estimate is to look up a product similar to yours on Amazon.com. Look it up in each country Amazon serves: United Kingdom, Japan, Germany, France, Canada, Austria, and China—and compare its sales rankings in these countries. The product may rank higher in some countries than others. From this, you can get a general sense of where your product might receive a good reception and where it might not.

Examine International Popularity Charts and Playlists. Many organizations offer listings of what's currently popular in a given country. While your related products most likely will not be on those charts, you can still get a feel for the kinds of music that are popular in specific countries.

You can start by visiting the Internet site Charts All Over the World (www.lanet.lv/misc/charts), a collection of some 700 music-popularity charts worldwide.

You can also visit the recording industry associations of individual countries. Forty-eight of them are listed at the Web site of the International

Federation of the Phonograph Industry (IFPI) at www.ifpi.com. Many of these sites provide popularity charts. IFPI Belgium (www.ifpi.be), for example, has charts for Top 50 Singles, Top 50 Albums, Top 20 Compilations, Top 30 Dance, and more, as well as analyses of previous years' popular recordings.

Another source is MTV International online (www.mtv.cm/mtvinternational), which has links to the more than twenty subsidiaries MTV operates around the world. Each country subsidiary Web site provides various kinds of information on what's popular, from popularity charts to lists of artists categorized by music genre. MTV Spain lists the genres rock 'n' roll, pop, Latino, hip-hop and R&B, electronica, indie, and metal/nu-metal. Within each are lists of artists from within the country and from other countries. Artists similar to yours may be among a country's listings, indicating a promising target for a marketing campaign.

Yet another source is *Billboard* magazine's charts for Europe, Mexico, and Canada. Online, you can key in the artist and title of a record similar to yours and find its top ranking on these charts. You can also check back issues of *Billboard* magazine for its special issues devoted to specific countries. Find them either in a public library or online through research services such as InfoTrac and ProQuest.

Search Internet Databases. There's been much innovation in designing Internet-based research tools for music. A notable source is Allmusic.com, which permits searches and categorizations by genre, mood, instrument, theme, and country. This is a good site both for identifying products similar to yours and for exploring music that's popular in various countries. Another useful database is available at www.midem.com, the site of the annual music industry convention MIDEM. On this database you can conduct a search by activity (licensing, distribution, record company, and so on) and by country and get a list of businesses. Each business listing includes the styles of music the company handles. By looking at all of a country's listings you get an overview of the kinds of music that are popular there.

Look Up Research Papers. The Internet is also a source of research studies and reports pertaining to various aspects of music in countries around the globe. A recent search yielded reports on music industry activity in Colombia, South America, and in Thailand. More comprehensive studies are also published periodically. The International Federation of the Phonograph Industry (IFPI) publishes *Recording Industry in Numbers*, an annual compilation of music industry statistics worldwide, including retail sales patterns, repertoire breakdown, top-10 albums and music DVD charts, and sales by age and genre—all together highlighting differences between the markets, as well as national and regional trends.

IDENTIFY COMMUNICATIONS AND SALES CHANNELS

With information on products similar to yours and on the audiences that purchase them, you next choose the best ways to distribute your own product to these audiences and find the best information channels through which to promote the product. Upcoming chapters detail the processes of identifying and exploiting these channels.

The following chart summarizes associative targeting—the technique of targeting audiences through comparison of your product with existing products.

ASSOCIATIVE TARGETING

BASIC

Proposed Product	Music Genre	Countries of Genre's Popularity

Example:

New Pianist	Piano Jazz	U.S., France, Japan, Canada, U.K.

REFINED

Descriptors of Proposed Product	-as in-	Proven Products	-bought by-	Product Purchasers	-who live in-	Places of Purchase
Genre		**Music**		Descriptor 1		Country A
Subgenre		Product 1				
		Product 2		Descriptor 2		Country B
Descriptor 1		Product 3				
Descriptor 2				Descriptor 3		Country C
Descriptor 3		**Nonmusic**				
Descriptor 4		Product 1		Descriptor 4		Country D
Descriptor 5		Product 2				
		Product 3		Descriptor 5		Country E

Example:

Descriptors of Proposed Product	-as in-	Proven Products	-bought by-	Product Purchasers	-who live in-	Places of Purchase
Jazz		**Music**		25–65		U.S.
Mainstream jazz		Bill Evans				
Piano jazz		Marian McPartland		Educated		Japan
Sophisticated		Oscar Peterson				
Refined		Shirley Horn		Affluent		U.K.
Romantic						
Thoughtful		**Nonmusic**		Active		France
Elegant		Evening wear				
Luxurious		Perfume		Tech-savvy		Canada
Upscale		Beverages				
High end		Luxury cars				
		Fine foods				

EXAMINING REGIONS OF MUSIC MARKETING ACTIVITY

With potential target audiences identified in several different regions around the globe, choosing which country to enter first requires knowledge of the countries themselves. Getting an overview of the global music market is a good place to begin. Look at what the leading global music markets are, and what the emerging markets are. The benefit of working with leading markets is, those markets are familiar with the industry and its practices. The business process will be relatively straightforward. The downside is, competition is heavy. Targeting smaller, emerging markets may put you in a position of "owning the playground," or at least being among the "first movers," or at the very least having a less-crowded marketplace with which to contend. (For further information on the world's regions, see *Appendix:* Music Industry World Resources.)

U.S. DEPARTMENT OF COMMERCE TIPS FOR CHOOSING COUNTRIES

- Obtain trade statistics that indicate which countries import your type(s) of products.
- Perform a thorough review of the available market research reports in the country(ies) and industries in question to determine market openness, common practices, tariffs and taxes, distribution channels, and other important considerations.
- Identify five to ten large and fast-growing markets for the firm's product(s). Analyze them over the past three to five years for market growth in good and bad times.
- Identify some smaller but fast-emerging markets where there may be fewer competitors.
- Target three to five of the most statistically promising markets for further assessment.

THE WORLD'S MAJOR REGIONS

To put the search for potential markets in context, let's start by outlining the world's major regions. The United Nations divides up the planet as follows:

Africa, subdivided into northern, southern, eastern, western, and middle sectors

Asia, further divided into eastern, western, south-central, and south-eastern sectors

Europe, divided into northern, southern, eastern, and western sectors

Latin America, comprising the Caribbean, Central America, and South America

North America, comprising Canada and the United States

Oceania, comprising Australia and New Zealand, Melanesia, Micronesia, and Polynesia

On the other hand, the U.S. Central Intelligence Agency uses the subdivisions Southeast Asia, South America, Central America and the Caribbean, and the Middle East, segmentations maintained in this book's appendix when listing regions' global music resources.

LEADING MARKETS IN THE GLOBAL MUSIC INDUSTRY

The most obvious places to start in the search for target markets are the leading markets—the places where music activity is the most robust. According to the Canadian Independent Record Production Association (CIRPA), the world's leading recorded-music markets as of 2004 were ranked as follows:

1. United States

2. Japan

3. United Kingdom

4. France

5. Germany

6. Canada

The United States is considered the leading music market. In fact, it accounts for about 37 percent of total world music sales, even with its relatively small population of about 300 million. The power, breadth, and influence of U.S. media virtually guarantees that success in the U.S. paves the way for recognition everywhere else. This is why breaking into the U.S. market remains a goal of fame-seeking musicians everywhere. Yet the U.S. is also the most difficult market to break into. Roughly 93 percent of sales comes from domestic product, with the remaining 7 percent divided up by all non-U.S. music sellers. As discussed later in the book, the way to approach the U.S. is not as a single market but as the site of many smaller markets. Nearly any musical style and genre has a pocket of popularity somewhere in the States.

Japan, with a population of 127 million, generated about 12 percent of world music sales in 2003, with about 81 percent of sales coming from domestic music. Popular music genres include anime, J-pop, traditional Japanese pop music, karaoke, classical, and independent/alternative music. (Tokyo is a bustling site of many independent record stores focusing on specialty genres.) Imports do well in Japan, in part because of the high price of domestic music. Japan has tended to be on the cutting edge technologically; its early adoption of ringtones foretold its continuing leadership in the mobile music field. It's a good location for marketing digital music.

The United Kingdom, population 60 million, accounted for about 7 percent of world music sales in 2003. Domestic music accounted for half of that amount. A great deal of cross-pollination has occurred between the U.K. and the U.S. Two of the most successful rock acts ever, the Beatles and the Rolling Stones, came from England although their styles derived from U.S. blues, R&B, and rock 'n' roll. Punk rock developed simultaneously in the U.K. and the U.S. With a shared language, the two countries are natural markets for each other's music.

France's population of 60 million accounted for more than 4 percent of world music sales in 2003, 60 percent of which came from domestic product. Rock, pop, and middle-of-the-road (MOR) are popular genres, with domestic French-language music preferred by French listeners. France has been described by foreign performers as difficult to enter.

Germany generated around $2 billion in sales in 2003, from a population of 83.3 million. Domestic music accounted for 48 percent of sales. Pop, rock, easy listening, German folk, and jazz are popular genres, with the greater portion of sales going to German language, rather than international, music.

Canada, population 32.2 million, yielded $676 million in 2003 music sales, of which 25 percent came from domestic music. Popular genres mirror those of the U.S. Canada's proximity to the U.S, and two countries' shared language make them natural music trade partners. Notable musicians from Canada include Neil Young, Joni Mitchell, and k.d. lang.

Detailed statistics about these markets can be found at the informative Web site of CIRPA (www.cirpa.ca).

GLOBAL MUSIC CORPORATIONS

Another way to look at the global music market is to divide it up by global corporations rather than by country, since it's these corporations that dominate the industry by straddling the entire globe, with their sales in separate countries accruing to a single corporate bottom line. The companies, in order of 2005 market share, are:

1. Universal Music, with 31.71% market share

2. Sony BMG Music Entertainment, 25.61%

3. Warner Music Group, 15%

4. EMI Group, 9.55%

The remaining market share, 18.13 percent, is held by independent record companies—the category in which new entrants tend to belong.

EMERGING MARKETS IN THE GLOBAL MUSIC INDUSTRY

Emerging markets in the music industry are those countries that have until recently lacked either the market infrastructure or the open-market policies to fully engage in global music trade. Now they are catching up to developed countries and offering promising opportunities.

China can hardly be deemed an emerging market in the strictest sense, yet in global terms it has only somewhat recently emerged on the scene. According to the World Trade Organization, "in 2004, China became the largest merchandise trader in Asia, and the third largest exporter and importer in world merchandise trade." With its population of 1.27 billion, the potency of its market is obvious. In the arena of mobile music, for example, China had about 745 million mobile subscribers by 2006, according to the Chinese Ministry of Information. Mobile music executive Richard Robinson, in *MIDEM* magazine, estimated that mobile music revenues would jump from $650 million to $950 million in 2006. So ripe a market for music has China become that in 2005 *Rolling Stone* magazine licensed its brand to a Chinese firm for publication of a Chinese-language edition. The four major global record companies were active in China, too, collectively holding 25 percent of recorded music sales in 2005. Yet with rampant piracy cutting into sales of tangible CDs and quotas imposed on international releases, significant trade challenges remain.

India, too, is high on the list of emerging markets, as defined by the magazine the *Economist*. With some 125 key domestic record labels and activity from the global Big Four plus the U.K.'s Virgin Records, India's music industry is estimated to be worth $260 million. Of that, 8 to 10 percent comes from international music. Some 60 percent is accounted for by music from the burgeoning Indian film industry. Since 2003, demand for English-language music has increased by about 30 percent annually. As elsewhere, India has seen increasing demand for digital music. Palash Sen, lead singer of New Delhi–based group Euphoria, reported in an article at Rediff.com that "technology has advanced considerably and expanded the listeners' base, what with people downloading music at a low cost. Music is easily heard on radio channels, music videos are shown on television, and people are happily listening to innumerable songs on their MP3 players. However, this is precisely what has led to a considerable decrease in the sales of the music albums."

Brazil, the home of some of the most sensuous and distinctive music in the world, also has the world's fifth-largest population of mobile users. Brazil is considered one of the most promising markets for digital music, hampered only by its high taxes on phone services.

Mexico, once in the top ten of the world's music markets, has seen its music sales decimated by piracy, although enforcement reportedly improved in 2004.

Helping emerging markets emerge a little faster, and in greater number, have been the regional trade agreements that have proliferated since the 1990s. According to the U.S. Department of Commerce, "Trade agreements help level the international playing field and encourage foreign governments to adopt open and transparent rulemaking procedures, as well as non-discriminatory laws and regulations. FTAs help strengthen business climates by eliminating or reducing tariff rates, improving intellectual property regulations, opening government procurement opportunities, easing investment rules, and much more."

The European Union, for example, by removing regulatory barriers to trade between its members and by instituting a common currency, the euro, streamlined and promoted trade within the bloc and more-open trade with countries outside the EU. (Difficulties still exist, however, for EU artists touring other EU countries, because artists may face double taxation.)

While most EU countries are, of course, highly developed economic leaders, the Eastern Europe members, including Estonia and Latvia, are emerging economies. Latvia's growth rate has been high, and its small but energetic economy hosts producers of symphonic, jazz, rock, folk, and traditional styles of music. Yet the area is still catching up. The 2004 global recording industry report of the IFPI notes "a growing switch from cassette to CDs in developing markets in Eastern Europe, Asia, and the Middle East." That switch occurred about five years behind the changeover in developed countries.

Additional areas of emerging opportunity include Russia, which, since the demise of the Soviet Union, has been a center of foreign investment. Southeast Asia and Indonesia, with their vast populations, offer promise for music marketing, with an important caveat being high levels of piracy risk.

Keeping an eye on some of these markets is a worthwhile way to break off from the crowd and perhaps find previously untapped sources of music demand. But keep in mind, too, that some smaller markets may truly offer only the slightest of opportunities. Iceland, for example, the home of singer Bjork, is "not a place where you seek to break new artists," according to Gunnar Gudmundsson, a member of the Icelandic Group of the IFPI. "Foreign record companies have to realize how small the market is, and how limited the possibilities are for selling even fairly small quantities of records."

A place to research emerging-market opportunities is the U.S. Department of Commerce at www.commerce.gov.

EMERGING MARKETS SPANNING COUNTRIES

Bear in mind that international emerging opportunity may not only be definable by country location. Opportunity can take many forms. One of them is new technology and the invention of new modes of delivery, providing an opportunity to repackage music for use in the new delivery mode, which then can be introduced to markets all over the world at different times and places. Mobile music is the new mode as of this writing. Opportunity is seen at different levels in different international markets, depending on the size and tech-savviness of the population and the amount of disposable income available for purchasing new music products. The United States, though far from an emerging economy, is one of the emerging markets for mobile music. In 2006, according to a report in *Wireless World Forum*, "The emerging markets of Brazil, Russia, India, China account for the vast majority of ringtone download growth—India, for example, demonstrates annual average growth of over 250 percent."

So it's important to bear in mind that opportunity has not only a place dimension but also a product dimension. The challenge is to optimize the interaction between the two.

ASSESSING THE PROFIT AND RISK POTENTIAL OF TARGET FOREIGN MARKETS

Recall the goal of exploiting available global opportunities while minimizing risk. Remember, too, the aim of starting modestly by focusing on a single market within the most accessible and potentially profitable region. Identifying leading and emerging players in the global music industry is only your introduction to the process of choosing the first regional target. The next step is to dig deeper, to examine the factors that can help you decide whether a country is a good place to make money. Working in other countries means dealing with different "political economies"—mixtures of political, economic, and legal systems that affect the benefits, costs, and risks of doing business in that country. Your inquiry into a country's profit and risk potential can focus on four main determinants:

- Market accessibility and openness
- Music-market infrastructure
- Overall economic health
- Risk and legal protections

MARKET ACCESSIBILITY

Market liberalization has been the leading worldwide trend in trade for the past half century. But what does that mean?

Start with the opposite: Imagine a country in which the government is devoted to protecting its own citizens' businesses from outside competition, to the point where it places precisely defined limits on the kind and the quantity of goods and services that other countries can sell within its borders. That would be called a *protectionist economy*—the state is protecting its own industries—or, in textbook terminology, a *command economy*. Downside: the citizenry, while secure in its jobs, would have limited choice in goods and services. They'd miss out on potentially attractive items from other lands.

Now jump to the opposite end of the regulatory spectrum: Imagine a country where the government eases restrictions in its trade with other countries and conducts trade with similarly open countries. No limits are placed on the kind and quantity of goods and services that are allowed into the country. Market demand—local desire for the outside goods and services—determines the flow of trade. Yes, some homeland manufacturers and services may face competition from the influx of traders from outside, but there are also benefits: Consumers will have more choice of goods and services to purchase. More choice means prices overall will be lower. Money will go further. Leftover money will go back into the local economy, boosting its health. Meanwhile the influx of outside trade will expose the citizenry to new ideas, different ways of doing and seeing things, which they will then adapt for their own innovation, increasing productivity and growth. Further, if outsiders set up shop within the country, they create jobs for locals, and they add to the country's economic health. Everyone wins. At least that's the theory. This scenario falls into the category of liberal trade, or free-market economics, or, another textbook term, a *market economy*. It is toward this system that the majority of global countries have been moving toward for the last sixty-some years, prodded forward by international treaties such as the General

Agreement on Tariffs and Trade (GATT) and the formation of the World Trade Organization (WTO).

Under this system, you, the music seller, would find no regulatory barriers to exporting your product to another country.

In practice, however, most countries temper their free-market tendencies with selective protectionism. They may open their borders to most goods, but they're under pressure from one domestic industry or another to keep foreign competition to a minimum, so that the government uses one or more of a variety of instruments to ensure outsiders are put at a trade disadvantage.

It is these restrictions that you may encounter in your ventures abroad, and that you should look for ahead of time to ascertain the level of difficulty of entering a market.

The restrictive instruments include tariffs, quotas, voluntary export restraints (VERs), local content requirements, taxes of other kinds, subsidies, and antidumping policies.

Tariffs. Countries have most typically protected their domestic industries by applying taxes—*tariffs*—to imports that compete with those industries. If a nation produced mobile music players, for example, and wanted to minimize competition from foreign imports of mobile music players, its government could impose a tariff on that kind of import, making it more expensive, and thus less attractive, for domestic consumers. The tariff also adds money to home government coffers. Tariffs are typically set at a specific fee, or on an *ad valorem*—percentage of value—basis.

Example: The domestic film industries of many countries benefit from the imposition of levies on foreign films shown within their borders.

An example of how tariffs have been used to benefit local music makers and sellers: Due to losses of sales revenues resulting from unauthorized duplication of recordings, some countries have imposed tariffs on imports of recordable (blank) storage media such as CDs. The money generated by these tariffs is used to reimburse local music makers for their sales losses.

The terms *tariff* and *duty* are interchangeable.

Other Taxes. Tariffs aren't the only payments sellers have to contend with. VAT (value-added tax) may be applied to specific products. If you're exporting into a country, VAT will be added to the product price, so the amount of VAT a country levies will have a big impact on whether you are able to sell at an attractive price. Sample rates in Europe include Germany's 16 percent, Sweden's 25 percent, and Switzerland's 7.5 percent.

Countries may vary their rates among products to encourage or discourage consumption. In France, for example, a VAT of 19.6 percent is applied to recorded music but not to other cultural goods; the policy has been decried as levying a "youth tax."

Various other taxes with varied purposes may be levied. In France, a 3.5 percent tax is levied on all concert box office sales. The revenue is used to support new artists. "The idea is to take money from the American artists who make a lot of money in France, and give it back to the French artists," said Marie-Agnes Beau of the French Music Bureau, a government office promoting the export of French music.

Quotas. Another import-regulating technique, called a *quota*, is a legal limitation on the quantity of selected goods allowed into a county. In music, this most often takes the form of minimums established for local content—called *local content requirements*—rather than maximums set for foreign content.

Local Content Requirements. A kind of quota, local content requirements, put controls on the quantity of foreign product produced in the local marketplace by establishing a minimum percentage of all content that must be local. France, for example, has a requirement that 40 percent of music played on French radio must be of domestic origin. This rule boosts domestic music and limits foreign producers' access to local radio, an important promotion vehicle and source of performance royalties. In the Netherlands, local orchestras are required to devote 7 percent of their performance repertoires to Dutch music. In Malaysia, 60 percent of radio programming must be of local origin. Venezuela requires foreign musical performers to share stage time with domestic entertainers, and requires that at least half the FM radio broadcasting from 7 A.M. to 10 P.M. be dedicated to Venezuelan music.

Voluntary Export Restraints (VERs). A country might voluntarily limit its exports of selected goods at the request of the target country. In one situation, imports of some CDs from Country A to Country B had been found to be bootlegs—made from pirated master recordings. When Country B requested that Country A cease selling it CDs, Country A agreed, as a measure of good faith to protect its broader trade relationship with Country B. Unfortunately, Country A's legitimate CD producers were harmed by not being able to export, along with the black-market manufacturers.

Subsidies. Countries may choose to use public money to support selected industries. The National Endowment for the Arts does this in the United States. Government subsidies of industries (and individuals) can take the form of grants, tax reductions, and other tools. A government might fund an organization's touring costs, for example. As noted above, France's tax on concert box office receipts is used to promote current French music and musicians.

Antidumping Policies. Manufacturers may want to get rid of excess inventory by selling it abroad at a price below production cost, or below "fair market value." Because this low price can undercut sales of the target country's domestic products, there are policies that protect against the practice.

To research the trade policies of target countries, visit the World Trade Organization's online Trade Topics menu (www.wto.org). Another good information source is the U.S. Department of Commerce's International Trade Administration, at www.ita.doc.gov/td/tic/tariff/index.html.

EFFECTIVENESS AND REACH OF MUSIC MARKETING
CHANNELS AND SYSTEMS

The likeliness of achieving sales in a given region depends in part on the capacity of the region's music market to absorb your product and distribute it effectively to the largest number of people, and to promote your product effectively through print and electronic media. Music-marketing capacity varies from region to region. Compare prospective countries according to such music-market criteria as per capita expenditures on recorded music, both hard-copy and downloads; penetration of cutting-edge music delivery systems (such as mobile players); number and kinds of retail music outlets; number and kinds of live-performance venues; number of local record companies; number of music importers; and number and reach of media outlets.

Expenditures on Recorded Music. Higher per capita sales of CDs, cassettes, vinyl records, and downloads indicate greater local interest in music. Higher per capita sales also indicate effectiveness of the local marketing infrastructure: distributors are successfully reaching consumers, and information about products is successfully being communicated. Entering a national market where per-consumer sales average four CDs a year is usually preferable to targeting a one-CD-per-consumer population (the exception being when the goal is to test an untapped market).

Expenditures on Music Downloads and Adoption of New Technology. Robust sales of music downloads, the regional presence of online music services (researchable at www.pro-music.org/musiconline.htm), and expenditures on the latest music playback devices indicate maturity of the digital sector of the music market. A technologically savvy populace promises the viability of multiple delivery options, and revenue streams, for selling music. A product line can include downloads along with CDs, DVDs, cassettes, vinyl, and other formats.

Number and Kinds of Retail Music Outlets. The penetration of international chains such as Virgin Megastores, HMV, and Tower and the presence of independent music stores, department stores, books-and-music stores, electronics stores, and other sales outlets provide a general indication of the options available for brick-and-mortar sales.

Number and Kinds of Live-Performance Venues. Greater numbers of concert halls, nightclubs, and other venues indicate both the extent of regional interest in performance attendance and the range of outlets available to music marketers. Information can be found in Pollstar's annual *Concert Venue Directory* and in individual city tourist and business information sites on the Internet.

Number of Local Record Companies and Distributors. While the Big Four—Universal Music, Sony BMG Music, Warner Music Group, and EMI Group—own most record labels worldwide, the presence and number of independent labels operating in a region tell us something about the vitality of the market in that locale. The number of active distributors is further indication and provides a more relevant indicator of marketing channel opportunities for out-of-country music marketers.

Number and Reach of Media Outlets. The number of radio stations and owners (more owners meaning better chances of getting your music on a station) and the music formats offered (the more the better) give you a clue to the on-air promotional opportunities a country offers. The same point applies to television stations and programming. Further, the robustness and circulation of local print media, and the presence of local Internet programming, tell you even more about how easy or difficult it may be to conduct integrated marketing communications in a prospective target market.

Comparing per capita sales with the density of retail outlets and industry businesses (outlets per capita) can tell you something about the effectiveness of the channels for selling to consumers. Few per capita sales but many business entities suggests inefficiency of marketing channels. Many sales per capita and fewer business entities suggests effectiveness of marketing channels. Since the exporter or licenser—that is, you—would have to depend on local channels, it's important to have knowledge of how well they would work for you.

COMPARATIVE MUSIC MARKET INDICATORS*

	% of World Music Sales	Recorded Music Sales Per Capita (in U.S. $)	% Growth (1 Year)	Foreign Product Sales (% of Total)	Download Sales (% of Total)	Piracy Rate (% of Country Total)
Country A	37%	$45	3.3%	7%	3.5%	10%
Country B	11.5	39.4	1.0	19	3.1	>10
Country C	7.1	49	4.9	50	3.1	15
Country D	4.2	34	−7.6	40	2	13
Country E	2.1	21	1.0	75	2.8	>10
Country F	>1	10	−6.3	83	2.5	45

* Numbers are imaginary, for illustration purposes only. Additional indicators could include: tariffs and taxes; number of retail outlets per 1,000 people; annual live performance earnings; number of performance venues per 1,000 people; % of population that owns digital music players.

So, in general, a robust music industry and high music expenditures point to a promising market for your consideration. But if sales are not high, and the industry infrastructure is not developed, your first inclination may be to reject the country. An alternative approach would be to consider whether the region might be ripe for a pioneering marketing venture. It could be that consumers there, if properly exposed to what you're offering, might be highly attracted to it. How do you decide whether to put the country in this category? One way is to look at more general economic indicators.

OVERALL ECONOMIC HEALTH

The overall economic well-being of a country—or at least the direction in which it appears to be heading economically, whether toward weakness and contraction or toward robustness and growth—makes a difference in its viability for your music marketing enterprise. Researching GDPs may not be particularly relevant if you already have a reputable foreign record label interested in licensing your product, and your risk is limited to supplying master recordings and artwork. But if you are not yet networked in a country, and you're considering expending effort to find local partners and audiences, a country's economic fundamentals—its *macroeconomic indicators*—can tell you such facts as whether the populace is affluent; whether the local currency is weak, making your product more expensive for locals to buy; and whether other countries view the market as profitable.

Those prospective marketers who have enough understanding of a country's music market to make an immediate business decision on a short-term, low-risk arrangement can skip ahead to "Risks and Legal Protections" (page 36). Macroeconomic indicators—and the "big picture" view they offer—are of more importance when the venture is to be long term, high commitment, and high risk.

Gross Domestic Product (GDP). The value of a country's domestic economic output is referred to as its *gross domestic product*. Comparing two different countries' annual GDP is not particularly meaningful unless you also look at the sizes of the respective populations and determine the GDP *per capita* for each country (by dividing the GDP by the population). This enables you to make a general conclusion about the typical purchaser's affluence—a key bit of data for the marketer. It may be useful to know, for example, that Chinese GDP per capita, when converted to U.S. dollars, is $1,300 compared to the United States' $40,000 (2004 figures). Yet GDP per capita is not completely reliable as an indicator of purchasing power, due to differences in prices and the cost of living across borders. Five dollars in one country might buy more than five dollars in another country. Further, a static number tells you little about the strength of an economy. Better to look at the *rate of growth* over time. During 2004, for example, the United States experienced growth of 4.8 percent, Latvia 8.8 percent, and China 9.6 percent.

Purchasing Power Parity (PPP). Adjusting the GDP per capita for cross-border differences in prices and cost of living yields a more accurate indicator of real purchasing power—an indicator called *purchasing power parity*. It is calculated by comparing countries' per capita GDP not on the basis of nominal currency exchange rates—which are derived from a range of macroeconomic factors—but by comparing the prices of the same "basket of goods" in different countries in local currency, finding the ratio between two different numbers, applying that ratio to the countries' respective GDPs, and then calculating the per capita GDPs.

For example, let's say a basket of goods costs €2.50 (euros) in Country A and $3 U.S. (dollars) in Country B. That puts the ratio of euros to dollars at about .833 to 1.00—that is, €1.00 equals about $1.20. Multiply Country A's GDP in euros by 1.2 to "convert" to dollars, then divide that number by Country A's population, and you have the country's GDP per capita adjusted for purchasing power parity, which you can then easily compare with Country B or another country. You can see how affordable a purchase will be in the compared countries. Of course, you don't need to execute these calculations yourself. They're presented here to give you background on the meaning of "PPP," which is all you'll need to look for in research sources.)

The difference between standard per capita GDP and the PPP-adjusted GDP can be striking. In 2004, when the Chinese GDP per capita was $1,300, adjustment for purchasing power parity yielded $5,600, compared to the United States' $40,000.

Human Development Index (HDI) Rank. The state of human development is another measure of a country's economic well-being. The human development index (HDI) attempts to quantify the quality of human life in terms of three factors: (1) health, represented by average life expectancy; (2) knowledge, represented by literacy rate and education levels; and (3) economic well-being, represented by GDP per capita adjusted for purchasing-power parity. An organization called Human Development Reports (found online at http://hdr.undp.org/default.cfm) issues annual rankings of countries according to their HDI. In 2004, out of 177, Norway ranked first, Peru ranked somewhere in the middle, and Sierra Leone came in at the bottom. Music is less likely to sell well in countries where the populace is lacking in basic necessities and decent health.

Foreign Direct Investment (FDI). Still another indicator of healthy economic prospects, and of openness to trade with other countries, can be found in the statistics for foreign direct investment. FDI refers to the value of foreign investment in a country's businesses, whether through acquisition, merger (minority or majority ownership), or a wholly new operation, referred to as a *green-field investment*. A high level of FDI (researchable at the United Nations Conference on Trade and Development [UNCTAD], www.unctad.org) suggests that outside countries view the host as a promising site for doing business. It also suggests the country's inclination toward free trade (although FDI can also be a way for outside countries to circumvent tariffs applied to exports). Further, it may suggest cultural globalization, easing cross-border business processes and communication; affluence of the populace due to job creation from FDI; and a stimulated economy in general. How do you interpret FDI numbers to decide whether they look favorable? FDI can be expressed as a percentage of gross fixed capital formation (GFCF), the total amount invested in a country's economy. It can also be viewed as a percentage of GDP. In the United Kingdom in 2002, for example, the FDI portion of the GFCF amounted to 30 percent. In 2000 in Poland, FDI represented 23 percent of GFCF and 22 percent of GDP, both considered high figures.

High FDI can also indicate a surplus in the balance of payments.

Balance of Payments. Surpluses and deficits in a country's trade accounts further fill out the economic picture. Transactions with foreign countries are recorded in two kinds of accounts: a current account and a capital account. The *current account* records exports and imports—of merchandise, services, and investment income. If the value of imported (inflowing) merchandise exceeds the value of exports (outflows), the country is said to be experiencing a negative balance of trade—a *trade deficit*. In 2004, the United States, for example, ran a current account deficit of $646.5 billion, according to the U.S. Central Intelligence Agency. Conversely, an export value exceeding the value of imports amounts to a *trade surplus*.

Whether a deficit or a surplus, the current-account balance is supposed to be counterbalanced by the *capital account*, the record of purchase and sale of assets—such as stocks, bonds, and land—outside the country and by other nations into the country. To make up for the trade deficit, the country has to borrow an equivalent amount from international capital markets and sell off assets, credited to the current account and debited to the capital account. When there's a trade deficit, and the country counterbalances it by selling off its assets to foreign countries, the overall balance of payments is in balance. Thus a trade deficit is not in itself a bad thing. The problem arises when foreign asset holders decide they've "had enough" of those assets and sell them off, potentially flooding the market with the home country's currency, which devalues it, which brings on inflation, making goods more expensive for home consumers, and which triggers an increase in interest rates, making money harder to borrow, homes and other purchases more difficult to finance, and so on. If enough countries "dump" the home country's assets, it can create a currency crisis in which the bottom falls out of the home currency's value.

Foreign direct investment, FDI, into the country helps the balance of trade by injecting money into the country, credited to the capital account. FDI also helps the balance of payments when it replaces imports, as when a country that would ordinarily import decides instead to set up a facility inside the target country, so that the import that would have debited the target country's current account is replaced by a credit to the capital account.

Chronic deficits reduce the amount of money that would otherwise be available for stimulating internal economic growth, since payments on borrowed money tie up domestic funds. Thus, when you see a pattern of deficits in a country's balance of trade, you could bundle it with other economic indicators to establish a general conclusion about the country's health and its viability as a target market.

One impact of net negative balance of trade is on the stability of the country's currency.

Currency Stability. Increased outflows of payments, as in a deficit situation, increases the quantity of the country's currency on the world market. That, in turn, devalues the currency. (When there's more of something, its value tends to go down.) If a country's currency is low-valued against the currencies of other countries, the consumers in that currency-weakened country are less likely to purchase imports, which have become more expensive.

An important factor in your decision whether and how to do trade with a country is the *exchange rate* between your own currency and that of the target country—the relative values of the currencies. If the target country's currency is growing weaker—it takes more of that currency to buy products in your currency—exporting to that country may be less profitable.

Foreign Exchange Reserves. One of the tools a country uses to maintain stability of its currency, to control its exchange rate, and to make local businesses more competitive on the world market, is to keep a stockpile—a reserve—of foreign currency. If the country's domestic currency begins to lose too much value on the world market, whether through inflation or a growing trade deficit, the government can use its reserve of foreign currency to buy up its own currency, leaving less of it on the world market and thus boosting its value. Conversely, a government can cut the value of its own currency—thus making its exports cheaper and more attractive while making imports more expensive and less attractive—by printing domestic currency and infusing it into the foreign exchange market, making it more available and less valuable. For your purposes of gathering data, the most important thing to look for is a robust foreign reserve account, expressed as a percentage of overall money supply or some other measure. It indicates government capabilities of avoiding a currency crisis and maintaining economic stability, which is what you're looking for.

Inflation. When a country's money supply increases faster than the supply of goods and services, the value of the money goes down while demand for the goods and services, and thus the prices of those goods and services, goes up. (The idea being that if people have money, they'll want to spend it. If you, for example, have a windfall of cash, you'll likely want to buy some things you've always wanted. Other people will feel the same way. More people overall are buying things. The increasing demand and dwindling supply of goods and services lead to their greater perceived value and higher prices.) This phenomenon is called *inflation*, and a high level of it, usually indicated as a rate of growth over time of the average price level of a group of products, is not a positive indicator. If the target country's inflation rate is higher than in your country, it indicates that the country's currency may be going down in value relative to yours, making your exported goods less affordable, and making your music marketing venture to that country less viable. Causes of inflation, by the way, can include the ease of borrowing money from the government—and infusing it into the economy—due to low interest rates.

Interest Rates. To counteract inflation, to decrease the money supply, a government can make it less attractive and more difficult to borrow money (and infuse it into the economy) by raising the *interest rate*, or the percentage of the borrowed money that the borrower must pay back in addition to the loan—in effect, increasing the cost of the loan. When the United States, for example, experienced an economic recovery in 2004–2005, after a period of very low interest rates, the Federal Reserve sought to hedge against the possibility of inflation by incrementally raising interest rates.

The value of an interest rate as an economic indicator is what it tells us about the strength of the target country's currency and thus the purchasing power of the consumer population. As already pointed out, if the currency is weak, foreign goods—your export CDs—become more expensive, demand falls, and the time might not be right for doing business in that country. But as an indicator of this, the interest rate, looked at alone, is ambiguous. On one hand, a high interest rate could signal strong government monetary control and thus strength—with inflation under control, prospects for currency appreciation (strengthening) are good. On the other hand, a high interest rate could imply concern about future inflation levels—a kind of warning that future currency depreciation (weakening) is possible.

So how do you use the interest rate as an indicator? Look at it in combination with other factors such as inflation and GDP to try to reach a conclusion about where the economy and the currency are headed. Probe further into the country's interest rate activity. If interest rates are rising, it reflects concern about inflation. If they have stopped rising, the implication is that currency is stable. Just bear in mind that analyzing the impact and implications of interest rate is a complex business.

Unemployment. A country's level of unemployment may indicate the purchasing power, or lack thereof, of a portion of the populace, with implications for the viability of an attempt to sell products to that population. The unemployment rate is the economic indicator to look for. In mid-2004, Japan's unemployment rate hit 4.6 percent, the U.S. rate was 5.6 percent, China's was 8.3 percent, and the European Union's was 9.1 percent.

Put all this information together with the data you've assembled about the local music industry, and a picture of a country's economic attractiveness begins to come into focus. For a more complete picture of the market, look further into such factors as transportation and telecommunications infrastructure, education levels, population characteristics, and government. Of the many sources of this kind of information, the World Bank (www.worldbank.org) and the U.S. Central Intelligence Agency's country profiles in its World Factbook (www.cia.gov) are particularly good.

Risks and Legal Protections

Imagine a situation in which you license your master recordings and artwork to a company in another country for an advance against royalty. Sometime later you learn that unauthorized copies of your music are being exported elsewhere by a company you've never heard of, and you're getting no money for it. Further, the bootleg copies are cutting into sales of your legitimate product.

Piracy, counterfeiting, and bootlegging have been a problem in the music industry for decades. In the mid-1980s the focus was on cassettes. At this writing the problem has shifted to illegal file sharing on the Internet and the unauthorized copying and manufacturing of CDs.

There have been international attempts, most notably the 1994 round of the General Agreement on Tariffs and Trade (GATT), to strengthen intellectual property regulations. But the problem is still widespread. The International Federation of the Phonographic Industry (IFPI) estimates that in 2004 "a total of 1.2 billion pirate music discs were sold . . . —34 percent of all discs sold worldwide." Also in 2004, reports the IFPI, "sales of pirate music exceed[ed] the legitimate market in a record 31 countries."

At issue for you the prospective music seller are both the levels of piracy of target countries and the legal protections in place to punish and discourage piracy. Poor enforcement of existing laws indicates an undesirable target for your marketing. A good source of information is the IFPI (www.ifpi.com), which publishes annual reports on piracy along with news about antipiracy actions being taken around the world. In 2003, for example, the IFPI reported piracy rates (as percentage of total national sales value) of 85 percent in China, 68 percent in the Ukraine, 66 percent in Russia, and 60 percent in Mexico. The IFPI also reported stepped up enforcement efforts in Mexico, Brazil, Hong Kong, Paraguay, and Spain.

Another problem of which you should be aware is the level of corruption present in a targeted country. Corruption can take many forms: payoffs and bribes for permission to operate in a country, bribes to get radio play of recordings, payment for protection against threats, and more. As with piracy, countries vary both in the level of corruption and the degree to which it is sanctioned or discouraged by industries and governments.

To research corruption levels, a place to start is Transparency International's annual Corruption Perceptions Index (www.transparency.org). This list ranks 146 countries according to the degree to which they are perceived to have corrupt public officials and politicians, with least corrupt ranking first (a position held by Finland in 2004). My guess is that where public officials go, so goes industry. TI also publishes a Bribe Payers' Index, last updated in 2002, which lists countries in which companies are thought to have bribed foreign officials.

General indication of a country's legal system can be found in the World Factbook at www.cia.gov.

COMPARATIVE GENERAL ECONOMIC AND COUNTRY INDICATORS*

Country	Pop. (mln.)	GDP Per Cap. ($ thou.)	GDP Growth (1 yr.)	FDI (Inflow, $ bn.)	Current Acct.** ($ bn.)	Foreign Res. ($ bn.)	Inflation Rate (1 yr.)	Unem. Rate (1 yr.)	HDI Rank	Corruption Index Rank
Country A	278	$40	4.8%	$107	–$537	$38.8	3.6%	5.6%	8	17
Country B	126.7	28.0	5.6	8	160.7	798.6	–0.3	4.6	9	24
Country C	59.3	24.6	3.7	78	–39.2	31.5	2.4	4.7	12	11
Country D	59.6	24.5	1.7	24.5	2.5	23.9	2.2	9.5	16	22
Country E	32.2	21	2.4	6.5	16.3	31.2	2.0	7.2	4	12
Country F	2.3	7.7	8.8	0.6	–1.4	1.5	4.1	10.5	50	57

* Numbers are imaginary, for illustration purposes only. Additional indicators could include interest rate; exchange rate (% up or down); exports and imports; population; % increase.
** Also called *balance of trade*. A negative number indicates a *trade deficit*.

To read economic-indicator charts for signs of a country's potential as a target market, look first at the GDP growth rate. Higher means "hotter." Balance this against other factors: High FDI inflow (relative to population and GDP) indicates openness and attractiveness to foreign investors; high GDP per capita indicates strong purchasing power; low numbers are better for inflation, unemployment, HDI, and corruption.

EXPLORING CULTURAL SIMILARITIES AND DIFFERENCES

Put in the simplest possible terms, it makes good sense to target an initial foreign market that is not far, culturally and socially, from the culture you're used to. With so many other critical factors to consider and juggle, it's helpful to have one area in which you're confident and comfortable: the area of human interaction. If you're "on the same page," so to speak, with your cross-border business partners, in basic interaction, communication, customs, and business etiquette, you'll be able to give your full attention to the less-certain aspects of your enterprise.

But at some point you'll be in the position of working with less-familiar cultures. That's when openness to, and comfort with, cultural differences will be essential. And it will have an impact on your business plans in two distinct ways: First, the product you market will succeed to the extent that it harmonizes with the target culture (and fails to the extent that it doesn't). Second, your business operation will succeed to the extent that your consultations, negotiations, and agreements proceed smoothly, are communicated clearly, and are conducted respectfully. For these things to happen, you'll need to learn in advance about cultural differences.

CULTURAL DIFFERENCES AND PRODUCT DEVELOPMENT

On the island of Bali, Indonesia, villagers will gather to view a shadow-puppet play that may continue for many hours. The visual element consists of two or three shadow shapes moving behind a small screen, and the action is accompanied by the narration of the *dalang*—the puppeteer. It's difficult to imagine that a Westerner conditioned by lifelong exposure to quick-edited video images, thirty-second TV commercials, and constant bombardment with electronic messages would be an ideal consumer of a lengthy shadow-puppet performance. And that points to cultural differences, in this case related to the perception of time, and to the length of attention span, and to the kinds of stimuli a culture purveys and processes. It would be reasonable to conclude that a marketer of Balinese shadow-puppet narrations might have difficulty selling the product to larger numbers of listeners in the United States.

Some market theorists—notably Theodore Levitt—have pointed to the existence of a global culture, a homogenization of worldwide tastes that opens the door to more prevalent mass marketing—selling the exact same product everywhere. Certainly there is a worldwide youth market, as MTV's operations in many different counties have shown. MTV's colorful imagery, rapid movement, and upbeat music reflect youthful energy and taste the world over, and are embraced for it. But MTV also found that local tastes for one "global" brand of music are limited. To succeed, MTV also needed to supply music geared to local tastes.

Decisions to sell an existing product abroad, modify an existing product for sale abroad, or develop an entirely new product for sale abroad should take the following into consideration:

- **Customs and beliefs.** The lyrics of your music or the persona of the artist may suggest behavior or promulgate a point of view that one country or another considers abhorrent or that defies religious beliefs. Learn something about the key taboos of a culture before spending money on a marketing campaign there.

- **Language differences.** A key word in your most marketable song may turn out to have an offensive meaning in one language. You can't learn every language, but you can check important wordings—of titles, lyric "hooks," advertising headlines and taglines—with someone familiar with the language of your target country. Change the offensive language before marketing, or don't pursue the marketing plan.

- **Source effects.** A country's acceptance of a product may be influenced by the national source of the product. Countries have positive and negative views of other countries. This sometimes influences acceptance of particular imports. If your country is at odds with another country politically, religiously, militarily, or in another way, your product might be rejected there before it's even heard. Or, conversely, your country might be associated with the best in a certain kind of music—American bluegrass, for example—so that the American label becomes a selling point.

In addition to these factors, a strong sense of national identity bears strongly on perceptions of products. Music that takes this into account—a song in the local language, a guest appearance by a regional star, covers of locally popular songs—can have an enhanced chance of gaining favor.

CULTURAL DIFFERENCES AND BUSINESS CONDUCT

Say you're used to getting right down to business. No small talk. You just want to finalize the deal, or outline the plan, and then get on with it. "Time is money." But the people you're meeting with, from a record label in another country, have a different idea. They seem to want to socialize first. They'd rather you get to know each other, spend some time breaking the social ice. Would this frustrate you? It shouldn't, since it's just one of the many normal ways the conduct of business can differ across borders. Knowing these differences ahead of time can prevent misunderstandings and can help you navigate a path around common obstacles to getting a job done.

Differences commonly appear around the following areas:

- **Values and norms.** Values refer to the basic beliefs that hold a society together. Individual freedom is an example of a value. Hedonism could be considered a value; so, too, spartanism. Contributing to society, another. Protection of life still another. Values vary widely around the world. Norms refer to the behaviors that are condoned in a society. People follow certain social conventions; others deviate from them. Issues to consider when doing business include attitudes toward work versus quality of life, and whether productivity is valued and something you can count on; speed of decision making, with some cultures inclined toward rapid action and others toward long consideration of different courses of action.

- **Beliefs and viewpoints.** Religion can play a more important role in commerce than one might initially think. The charging of interest for loans is contrary to Islamic law, for example. Thus many banks in Islamic countries do not charge interest. Beliefs also guide attitudes toward control over events (does it come from man, or is it purely a function of fate?), sexual behavior, popular culture, and adherence to law versus pride in circumvention.

- **Social structure.** Some countries are more hierarchical than others, with strict class systems as opposed to fluid borders between social and economic strata. The role of women may be viewed differently in different locales. Attitudes of foreign business contacts may surprise you, unless you know the cultural roots of their behavior.

- **Perception of time.** Punctuality may be important in some cultures, less so in others. If you find yourself frustrated at the inability to pin down a precise meeting time in a foreign country, or at a business contact's seeming nonchalance at arriving late—or, conversely, if you wonder why a contact is so determined to meet precisely on the hour, or why he is so upset at your arrival time—try to avoid conflict, since it's probably due less to the individual's behavior and more to cultural differences.

- **Communicating.** "He's a man of few words. A man of action." That's a compliment pulled from American cowboy movies, and to an extent it's come to represent a value in the United States: decisiveness, minimal discussion. But an American holding that view might be surprised to find other countries in which lengthy discussion and analyses of problem details and data are the preferred approach to decision making. Mutual recognition of these two modes of operation needs to occur in order for productive business to take place. Further communication differences occur in the realm of directness: in some cultures, a preference not to offend leads to avoidance of saying no. A vague answer or indefinite statement may indicate not confusion but rather a cultural inclination toward obliqueness. It's surprising when you first encounter it. Then you learn to work with it, to accommodate it. You have to, if you want to close the deal.

- **Etiquette.** Are you outgoing? Gregarious? Don't be shocked when you find your new foreign business partner prefers more formality, a more reserved demeanor. It's just a cultural preference. Find out before doing business whether your potential partner's culture favors conservative rather than flamboyant dress; a special approach to greeting and parting; particular rules for who "picks up the tab." Know in advance whether you should lead or follow a guest through a door, whether you risk offending the host if you don't eat your entire portion of really strange-looking meat, or whether your off-color joke might brand you as a buffoon not worthy of entrusting with new business.

An interesting set of dimensions for understanding cultural differences has been developed by Geert Hofstede, a professor at Maastricht University. At his site, www.geert-hofstede.com, you can research many countries and get their ratings in five cultural dimensions:

- **Power Distance**, indicating the degree of equality or inequality in a society in terms of power and wealth, and the potential mobility between classes. In business or social gatherings, this can manifest itself in the degree of deference and respect some participants show to others.

- **Individualism**, indicating the degree to which a culture values the individual versus the group—the family, the company, or another collective. Will a team approach work better than a unilateral one? This dimension may determine that.

- **Masculinity**, indicating the degree of gender differentiation and the degree of value placed on traditionally male goals of achievement, control, and power.

- **Uncertainty Avoidance**, indicating the level of tolerance for uncertainty and ambiguity, with low tolerance accompanied by many rules and laws. Where there's low uncertainty avoidance, long meetings that end without concrete results or "action items" may not be cause for alarm—they just reflect a cultural attitude that "things will work out eventually" and they don't have to right away.

- **Long-Term Orientation**, indicating value placed on long-term commitments and long-term rewards for hard work. Thinking innovatively might not be encouraged in a slow-to-change environment. Conversely, the United States favors short-term results in business—quarterly profits, sometimes at the expense of long-term business development. Record companies, for example, used to nurture artists through long careers of many recordings in the expectation of eventual return on investment. That practice no longer exists, as companies shoot for instant hits and reject favored artists when they stop delivering.

With knowledge of the world's leading music markets, and a short list of territories that contain likely buyers of your music, workable music distribution and promotion mechanisms, healthy and stable economies, and relatively minimal risk, you're in place to move to the next stage of your global marketing effort.

CHAPTER 3

Planning Basic Global Business Strategy

The simplest foreign-sales scenario for the producer of a record is to have the master recording "picked up"—licensed, represented, released—by a domestic record label that has foreign subsidiaries. That way, you don't have to do any of the work. The label, as a matter of ordinary business, sees to it that your recording gets distribution to foreign lands as well as across your own country. You are left free to concentrate on product development—that is, making great recorded music.

But what if you don't have that label? What if you're doing it yourself, as a producer/label owner, or an artist/label owner, or as an executive or a marketing manager at someone else's label? In such cases, you'll proactively seek out foreign opportunities and exploit them to your advantage. The logic of doing so is easy to follow and usually starts with your domestic marketing strategy.

Let's say you, as a business, have completed production on an album. You've found a manufacturer who can package CDs for you at reasonable cost. Now you're trying to decide how many copies to manufacture.

You're reasonably sure that 10,000 units can be marketed successfully in your home country. (You have advance orders for most of that, or you have sales results for your previous album from which you feel comfortable deriving estimates for the new product.) If you manufacture a few thousand extra you calculate you'll be paying less than $1 U.S. per unit. Moreover, your fixed recording cost of $25,000 will be spread over, say, 12,000 units rather than 10,000—that's $2.08 per unit rather than $2.50. So pressing the extra couple of thousand will bring down your per-unit cost, and increase your per-unit profit. (Promotion and overhead add cost, too, but we'll leave them out here for the sake of simplicity.)

The question is, how do you justify manufacturing those extra? Where will you sell them?

Your recent research has revealed potential markets in several foreign countries. One in particular seems to hold exceptional promise. If you can find a way to sell a few thousand in that market, you'll be able to add that quantity to your manufacturing run.

You decide that you'll start investigating how to sell in that country, which we'll call Country A. Your plan is to conduct a search for companies that can help you out. But before you can do this you'll need to know what kinds of business arrangements are possible, how they work, and the criteria for deciding which strategy to pursue. Then, when you contact a prospective business partner, you'll have a strong base of knowledge from which to discuss options and carry on negotiation.

POPULAR PERCEPTION

If you've developed a conservative estimate of possible foreign sales, manufacture that quantity, since you'll probably be able to sell them somewhere.

Your estimate is based on careful research, so why shouldn't you start the manufacturing process as soon as possible?

ALTERNATE REALITY

Wait to manufacture until you have an understanding of how you'll distribute abroad.

It's possible that a distributor will need a custom version of your CD, with cover text in the local language, for instance. Already manufactured units will be useless to them.

There are several different ways to get recordings to foreign markets—and for now we're talking about hard-copy products such as CDs, not Internet-based downloads. The options include:

- Exporting, which means selling your domestically manufactured product abroad, for net income on sales
- Licensing, or selling a foreign entity the right to manufacture and sell your product, paying you an advance against royalty
- Joint venture with a foreign firm to distribute and market recordings
- Setting up a foreign subsidiary, wholly owned, to handle marketing in the foreign country, providing you with net profits

These methods employ standard distribution procedures that typically involve intermediaries such as distributors and retailers to get product to consumers. Alternative methods that involve direct-to-consumer tactics are discussed in Chapter 6.

Each of the following business strategies has its advantages and disadvantages. The one you choose will depend on various sets of circumstances. An example of adapting strategy to circumstance appeared in a 2002 issue of the *Music Business Journal* when Spectralite Music founder Greg Jarvis told writer JoJo Gould, "I set up and ran the marketing and promotions operation of BMG Czech Republic for three and a half years in the early 1990s. The label then asked me to go to Russia and to do the same thing there. In Russia my role was mainly corporate development, looking at how BMG should enter the market—either as a joint venture, licensed label, or fully owned subsidiary. In the end we opted for a small import operation, and BMG ended up as one of the few labels which didn't lose money in the Russian market."

EXPORTING TO FOREIGN COUNTRIES

In a way, exporting is the same as conducting standard distribution, except with a foreign twist. Just as you'd do in your home country, you enter an agreement with a distribution company that, for a fee, gets your product into retail stores. You are paid by the distributor periodically after the distributor receives orders from stores. Costs of advertising and promoting are handled by you. But foreign distribution—exporting—has key points of difference:

- Pricing adjustments due to the structure of the foreign distribution system
- Impact of foreign tariffs and other taxes on prices
- Risks stemming from conversion of currencies
- Administrative and logistical complexities
- Uncertainty about trustworthiness of foreign business entity and payment schedules

Before getting into these differences, a summary of standard domestic distribution procedures is in order.

Retail stores are the outlets that serve music consumers directly. There are many retail stores—so many, in theory, that it would be unfeasible for a nationally focused record company to do business with each individually. It just wouldn't be practical. (I say "in theory" because in recent reality many stores have been put out of business or bought by a few conglomerates, reducing the number of "gateways" to retail, but in no way making entry any easier for the small, independent labels.) Therefore, to simplify the work of getting product to retail, the record company deals directly with intermediaries—wholesale distributors—that specialize in stocking an array of retail stores. You, the record company, deliver your product to one distributor; the distributor disperses it out to many retail stores. It's efficient.

Of course, there's a price to be paid for this efficiency. The distributor takes a portion of the earnings. In domestic United States deals, that often takes the form of a percentage of the wholesale price (the price paid by the retailer—the wholesale price tending to be something more than half of the "suggested retail list price" or SRLP). Specific arrangements vary from situation to situation.

Since distributors function as a kind of gateway to retail, they may not automatically accept your business. Many customers other than you would also like to use their services. Distributors' capacity is limited. So distributors exercise some discretion in whom they choose to take on as "distributees." The criterion for choosing is typically the potential for bringing the distributor the most income.

Foreign distribution works similarly. You'll need to identify some distributors who handle the region you're targeting. Then you'll have to convince them of your potential for bringing in profits. The procedures for promoting your music to distributors are detailed in the book *This Business of Music*

Marketing and Promotion. In summary, you'll need to prepare an information sheet (called a *one-sheet*) that lists basic product information along with details about the artist's past sales and current promotion plans. If you've been wildly successful in your home territory, it's quite likely that you won't have to do a lot of convincing. In fact the foreign distributor, rather than you, might be the one doing the contacting.

But let's assume that your past domestic sales have been modest, yet promising. For your new release you're planning that initial run of 10,000 units, and you're hoping to add 2,000 more units to sell abroad. You've made contact with a prospective distributor in Country A, you've supplied the distributor with information about the release, and he has expressed interest in handling your product. What now?

You'll need to research whether the price and cost structure will permit you to make money, and then, if profits seem possible, you'll proceed to undertake the logistics of exporting. In total, the process comprises the following issues:

- Pricing and profitability
- Distributor deal points
- Trade regulations
- Methods of financing and payment
- Packing and shipping

PRICING AND PROFITABILITY

First, you need to consider whether exporting will, in fact, work. The answer to that depends on what you can earn from the arrangement. Costs and pricing are key. Pricing will depend on three factors: (1) your costs and required markup, (2) the price sensitivity of the target market, and (3) your intended market strategy.

Cost-Plus Pricing. So you start by considering the price you'll set. In the U.S., if you were a domestic label there, you'd set a wholesale price (the price your distributor offers to the retailer) that would allow you to earn a profit after deducting costs, which include distributor percentage. Your costs would include recording, manufacturing, packaging, promotion, artist royalties, and mechanical royalties (payment, per unit sold, to the writers and publishers of each song on the album not composed by you).

Let's say that for a quantity of 12,000 manufactured CDs, your costs would add up to $5 per unit. When you sell to a distributor, the wholesale price you set has to cover that $5 plus the distributor's deduction of between 18 and 35 percent and still leave you a profit. At the same time, it can't be so high that the retailer, who buys from the distributor, can't sell it at an attractive price and still make a profit.

Let's say your wholesale price is $10—slightly more than half the top suggested retail list price (SRLP) of $18.98 in the U.S. (The SRLP, though its topmost level appears high, is rarely the price paid by the end consumer. It's more of a nominal price, subject to various discounts at points in the distribution chain.) Assume also that the distributor's share is 25 percent of that $10.

Wholesale price per unit	$10.00
Less distributor's 25%	−2.50
Manufacturer gross	7.50
Less costs	−5.00
Manufacturer profit	$2.50

You earn $2.50 per unit. This still allows the distributor to sell it to a retailer for $10 and earn $2.50, also allowing the retailer to sell at an attractive customer discount price of $12.98 and still retain a profit margin of $2.98.

The profits are not impressively large for anyone in the channel—you, the distributor, or the retailer—but they're still profits. And with large quantities they add up to respectable earnings.

But will this arrangement work in the exporting scenario?

Three factors will decide this: (1) the chain of markups that either push the retail price up or squeeze your earnings down, (2) the price that the foreign market will bear, and (3) your marketing strategy in the foreign country.

First, start with the markups. Your cost per unit is $5. You'd love to get a profit margin of around 40 percent. That would be $2 ($5 × .40). So you set the amount you'd like to receive at $7.

In a typical export deal, you also work with a distributor. Let's say the distributor wants to earn between 15 and 25 percent of the price he offers to the retailer. The exact percentage will be based in part on the services the distributor offers, from basic to extra promotion efforts. If the desired percentage is 20, then the distributor would need to set a price to retail—called the "published price to dealer," or PPD, in some territories—of $8.75. That is, the difference between the $8.75 price he offers the retailer and the $7 price he pays you is 20 percent.

So the price of your CD is now up to $8.75.

But there may be additional costs that push the price even higher. For example, the country may levy a tariff on imports. Let's say it's 10 percent, payable at customs. The $7 export price plus 10 percent equals $7.70. Now, to earn 20 percent, the distributor has to set a higher price of $9.63 to retail.

So the foreign retailer buys at $9.63 (by this time the transactions are in foreign currency, of course). The retailer factors in its own markup. This is often in the area of one-third of the retail price. (One way retailers achieve this is by multiplying their cost price by a factor of, say, 1.4 or 1.5). Now the price is up to $14.45.

Then there is sales tax, or VAT. If the country has VAT set at 15 percent, the price to the end customer will be $16.62. ($14.45 × 15% = $2.168 . . . $14.45 + 2.168 = $16.62)

VAT, by the way, is charged at each stage of supply. Each channel member pays VAT on actual earnings. The distributor, for example, pays VAT on the 20 percent markup earned. In our example, it would work as follows:

- The distributor pays $7.70 plus VAT of 15 percent, or $1.155, for a total of $8.85.
- The distributor sells for $9.63 plus VAT of 15 percent, or $1.445, to total $11.07.
- Since the distributor has already paid VAT of $1.155, it subtracts it from incoming VAT of $1.445, to equal $0.29, payable to the government. This $0.29 is the distributor's 15 percent VAT on the actual 20 percent margin on $9.63, or $1.926.
- The retailer sells for $14.45 plus VAT of 15 percent, or $2.168, for a total of $16.62.
- Since the retailer has already paid VAT of $1.445, it subtracts it from incoming VAT of $2.168, to equal $0.723, payable to the government. This $0.723 is the retailer's 15 percent VAT on the actual 33.35 percent margin on $14.45, or $4.82.

So the price of your CD is now up to $16.62.

But there may be additional costs, such as freight. These will push the price to the end customer even higher.

Bear in mind, too, that some countries have more complex distribution chains, in which more parties would be due payment. Each of those would add an additional markup to the ever-rising price. (See the chart in Chapter 5, page 97.)

Remember the SRLP—suggested retail list price—cited in the U.S. example? An SRLP does not play a significant role in territories—such as the one in the current example—where retailers base the price they charge on their cost price rather than suggested retail price.

Consumer-Based Pricing. Recall the discussion in Chapter 2 of the comparative purchasing power parity of different nations, and of China's annual per capita income of $5,600 compared to the U.S. income of $40,000.

A price of $16.62 would be considered high in the U.S. In countries with even lower per capita incomes, it would be even less likely that consumers would pay that amount. This means that in many countries, the final price of your exported recording would be out of reach for the average consumer.

Your choices would be: (1) convince other channel members to lower their markups or (2) reduce your own profit.

If channel members are not willing to adjust, and if you can't accept a smaller profit, you can conclude that this particular export deal will not work.

If your unit costs were lower, and if the distributor and the retailer each took smaller markups, and if the tariff were low or nonexistent and the VAT were lower, you could very well come out with an attractive final price for the local consumer—and a good reason to go forward with the export deal.

Marketing Strategy. The acceptability of the final price depends on your intended marketing strategy. Some strategies go hand in hand with a higher price; others with a lower price.

For example, you might want to pursue a *market-skimming* strategy. This means that you know there is high initial demand for your music release, with a hard-core following that is willing to pay whatever it takes to be an early buyer, and you can charge top price when first going to market. In this case, your price of $16.62 might be acceptable even in a market with low per capita incomes.

Or your preference might be a *market penetration* strategy. In this case, you're more concerned with selling as many copies as possible to as many people as possible as quickly as possible. That way, awareness of your music is widespread, hopefully creating a high number of people who like the music, allowing you to raise the price for the more-in-demand next CD. For this market penetration, a low price is what you need. The $16.62 price would be too high.

You might want to unload excess stock that you can't sell elsewhere. In that case, you may not care if you don't make a profit. The $16.62 wouldn't work, but you could sell *at cost*—setting your price to match your costs—to yield a lower final price to consumers.

And you might be marketing an older product—say, a reissue of a vintage artist's first album. Since recording costs may be limited to remastering old tapes, your price to the distributor might come down to $5.50, enabling a final retail price several dollars less than $16.62. This exporting scenario might be completely acceptable.

Currency-Exchange Risk. The value of an export deal can change if there are shifts in the relative values of the currencies involved.

Here's an example: Let's assume your currency is dollars and the customer's currency is euros. The customer wants to pay you in euros, after which you'll convert them into dollars. Your unit cost is $5 and your desired profit margin is 50 percent, or $2.50, making your export price $7.50. Your estimated quantity is 2,000 units, making your total expected earnings $15,000 (2,000 × $7.50). At the time of executing the deal, $1 U.S. is equivalent to €0.83. (Conversely, €1 = $1.2048.) At that exchange rate, the euro equivalent to $15,000 U.S. is €12,450. So you finalize the deal at a payment of €12,450.

But you may not receive payment for 60, 90, or 120 days. What if, during the interim, the value of the dollar appreciates relative to the euro? Let's say that at the time of payment, $1 U.S. is equivalent to €0.88. (Conversely, €1 = $1.1364.) You still get paid the €12,450. But when you convert it into dollars, the value is no longer $15,000. It has decreased to $14,148.

The opposite could also happen. The dollar could depreciate relative to the euro. Let's say that at the time of payment, $1 U.S. is equivalent to €0.80. (Conversely, €1 = $1.25.) You still get paid the €12,450. But when you convert it into dollars, the value has increased to $15,562.50. You've received a windfall above your expected earnings.

Most traders prefer to avoid the uncertainty of currency exchange fluctuations. There are four main ways to mitigate this:

The better way is to require payment in your domestic currency. The customer will have to convert his currency to yours before paying you. That way, the currency exchange risk is borne by the customer.

The other way is to arrange what is called a *forward exchange contract* with a bank. This involves arranging in advance to buy currency from the bank at a future date at an agreed-upon exchange rate. In our example, let's assume the contract stipulates payment to you of €12,450, and payment will be rendered 120 days after execution of the contract—Date X. You then arrange a forward exchange contract in which your bank agrees to sell $15,000 to you in return for euros valued at the current exchange rate, adjusted by the bank to ensure its compensation for the deal. Whatever the actual exchange rate at Date X, you are guaranteed to get your desired $15,000 for the €12,450 payment.

A related arrangement is called a *foreign currency option*. Here, you agree to buy a currency at a future date at an agreed exchange rate, with the added option of buying at the actual exchange rate at the time of sale if that rate has turned favorable to you. In other words, you're protected against the risk of losing money while having the option of taking advantage of any favorable rate fluctuation. For this option, you pay the bank a premium.

Yet another way is to set up a foreign bank account, to receive payment in local currency. You can convert to domestic currency when the exchange rate is favorable.

To see more factors to consider in setting prices, visit www.export.gov/pricing_quotes_and_negotiations/index.asp.

FOREIGN DISTRIBUTION DEAL POINTS

If the financials look to be favorable, proceed to execute an agreement with the foreign importer. Points to be specified in the written agreement include:

- Territory of distribution. Unless you know the distributor has an excellent track record in territories outside the market you've pinpointed, limit the contract to the region you're aiming at.
- Price you will receive per unit. Since you want to have some control over the final price to the music buyer, the contract should also stipulate the dealer price (the price the distributor will offer the retailer).
- Payment schedule. Will the distributor pay you in 30, 60, 90, or 120 days? Negotiate for the fastest payment turnaround. The longer you have to wait for payment, the longer you'll have to wait to pay your vendors.
- Returns policy. This refers to the window of time within which the distributor has the right to return unsold merchandise to you for full refund or credit.
- Shipping and packing instructions. Importers often have freight-forwarding companies that they prefer to work with, and specifications for meeting their requirements may be detailed in the export agreement.

- Product specifications. You may be exporting your CD as manufactured for your domestic market. Or you may have to make changes to satisfy the needs of the foreign market: different jacket artwork, translated text, and a number of potential regulation-determined packaging elements. The agreement should detail anything that's needed.

- Promotion plans. Usually you'll be doing the promotion. But there may be aspects that the distributor can help with, depending on expertise. You may build in a discount off your export price—say, 15 percent—in return for channel promotion handled by the distributor.

- Termination of rights. You don't want to be stuck in an agreement if the distributor doesn't perform well. Specify a trial period with an option to renew. And for longer agreements, indicate a point of termination—say, after six months without a new order from the distributor.

TRADE REGULATIONS

One of the downsides of exporting is researching the many regulations that countries may have set up to control the flow of goods across their borders. They can be complex, and applicability to your product can be difficult to determine.

Take France, for example. Trade regulations include tariffs; trade barriers such as local content requirements that stipulate a percentage of radio content that must be locally produced, limiting access to foreign content providers; a range of required documents; specific labeling requirements; and more.

The Middle Eastern country of Qatar charges a 15 percent tariff on records. In Jordan, all imported items pay one combined tax of not more than 30 percent (except for cars, cigarettes, and alcoholic beverages).

In Uzbekistan, as another example, in mid-2004 a 20 percent VAT was charged on exports. A tariff regime was applied, with preferential rates for some countries. Prohibitions were applied to certain imports, including "audio products, recordings, sound materials" aimed at "undermining state and social structure" among other undesirable purposes.

Information sources on specific country regulations can be found on the Internet at the U.S. Government Export Portal, www.export.gov/shipping_documentation_and_requirements/exp_regulations_standards.asp. You can also call the Trade Information Center at 1-800-USA-TRADE, or an Export Assistance Center.

FINANCING AND PAYMENTS

Your verbal and written agreement with a foreign distributor or importer may be close to complete, but if the business is new to you there is additional risk. For many reasons, you may lack full certainty of the distributor's creditworthiness. Background information may have been difficult to find. You may have learned about the business through Internet research rather than through a network of reliable sources. And your ability to communicate with the business's representatives may be hampered by the language difference and by geographical distance. Yet you'd like to proceed with the deal because the distribution capabilities look promising. What can you do to make this work?

In exporting there's a standard practice designed for just this kind of problem. It involves use of a reputable third party, usually a bank, to act as intermediary.

You may request from the importer, and then the importer may apply to its bank for, what is called a *letter of credit*. This is a document that confirms the bank will pay to the "beneficiary"—the exporter (you)—a specified amount at a specified date upon receipt and approval of a specified set of documents.

Again: The letter of credit assures you will receive your money if you comply with its specified conditions. The conditions include supplying a bill of lading (described below), a commercial invoice and a packing slip—both discussed on page 55—and other types of documents outlined by the widely accepted rules of the International Chamber of Commerce. It's all standard operating procedure, but also a lot of detailed paperwork.

The importer pays a fee to his bank for the letter of credit, unless the importer's negotiating strength is such that he can reject the deal unless the exporter pays the fee. In any event, the issuing bank sends the letter of credit to the exporter's bank, and the bank informs the exporter of the LoC's arrival.

The exporter arranges shipment of the merchandise through a freight forwarder, who issues to the exporter a *bill of lading*—a combination receipt, agreement by the freight forwarder to provide service, and a title to the goods.

The exporter presents to his bank what is called a *draft*—essentially a "you owe me" for the amount of the deal. The exporter also signs the bill of lading to transfer title of the goods over to the bank, and presents any other required documents listed in the letter of credit, indicating compliance with the letter of credit terms.

The exporter's bank sends both the draft and the bill of lading to the importer's bank. The importer's bank approves payment of the draft to the exporter's bank.

The draft may be either a *sight draft*, which is payable by the importer immediately, or a *time draft*, which specifies a later date for payment—say, 30, 60, 90, or 120 days. If it's a time draft, the exporter may still "sell" it to his bank at an earlier date, for a discount.

The importer receives the documents—bill of lading and others—and uses them to take title to the shipped merchandise.

This procedure minimizes credit risk through its use of the third-party banks to essentially "vouch" for the creditworthiness of the two parties.

For more information about this process, you can visit the U.S. Department of Commerce's *Basic Guide to Exporting* at www.unzco.com/basicguide or look up "Export Finance" at the U.S. Government Export Portal online at www.export.gov/export_finance/index.asp.

LETTER OF CREDIT

BANK OF EXPORTER
1111 EXPORT STREET
EXPORT CITY
COUNTRY OF EXPORT

Our Advice Number: 0000000   ****Amount****
Issuing Bank Reference Number: ABCD-0000   USD****$X,XXX.00
Date: 00/00/0000

To (Beneficiary):
Music Exporter, Inc.
99 Avenue of the Exporters
Export City
Country of Export

Dear Sirs:

We have been requested by Bank of Importer, City of Import, Country of Import to advise that they have opened with us their documentary credit number XYU-12345 for account of **(Applicant)** Music Importer, Inc., 55 Import Street, City of Import, Country of Import, in your favor for the amount of U.S. dollars $X,XXX.00.

Credit is available by negotiation of your draft(s) in duplicate at sight for 100 percent of invoice value drawn on us accompanied by the following documents:

1. Signed commercial invoice in 1 original and 3 copies
2. Full set 3/3 ocean bills of lading consigned to the order of Bank of Importer, Country of Import. Notify applicant and mark freight collect.
3. Packing list in 2 copies.

Evidencing shipment of: 2,000 compact discs, "Howard McGillicuddy: Strings Attached"
                        FOB Port City, Country of Export
Shipment from: Port City, Country of Export
Shipment to: Port City, Country of Import
Latest Shipping Date: 00/00/0000
Partial shipments not allowed. Transhipment not allowed.

All banking charges outside Country of Import are for beneficiary's account. Documents must be presented within 21 days from bill of lading date.

At the request of our correspondent, we confirm this credit and hereby undertake that all drafts drawn under and in compliance with the terms of this credit will be duly honored by us upon delivery of documents as specified, if presented at this office on or before [date].

Please examine this instrument carefully. If you are unable to comply with the terms or conditions, please communicate with your buyer to arrange for an amendment.

Yours truly,

Authorized Signature

PACKING AND SHIPPING

Shipping within national boundaries is one thing. But preparing merchandise for shipping abroad is quite another. In addition to setting regulations for product content and taxation, many importing countries set up quite precise rules regarding methods of packing and the kinds of information that need to be indicated on the packages. You can also go to Internet sources to find out about regulations posed by individual countries. Some information can be found at www.export.gov/shipping_documentation_and_requirements/exp_shipping_product.asp.

When you export to a foreign distributor, it is often the distributor who arranges shipping, simply because he may have access to better deals with freight specialists. For that reason, initially you may not have to concern yourself with the details of freight logistics and regulations. But as you get deeper into international music marketing, you'll need to familiarize yourself with shipping procedures to maximize your know-how and optimize your negotiating strength.

Those involved in import–export can save a lot of time, trouble, and headache by working with a shipping agent commonly known as a *freight forwarder*. Essentially, you hire them to pack, document, and ship your product, for a handling fee. You factor the handling fee—plus other shipping costs—into the per-unit price that you offer the importer (distributor). Similarly, if the importer pays for freight, that cost gets passed along to the next customer in the distribution channel and folded into the price of goods.

What services can freight forwarders provide? Here are a few:

- Recommend the best way to ship your goods, whether by land, sea, or air
- Provide access to shipping discounts
- Make arrangements with a carrier
- Provide advice on secure packing methods, or handle the packing themselves
- Advise on the import–export regulations of the country you're targeting
- Instruct you on the kinds of documentation that are needed, including the bill of lading, and file all necessary documents
- Assist you with pricing by informing you of costs of freight, insurance, documents that you'll have to factor into overall costs that eventually get passed onto the consumer—unless that cost proves to be too great to allow for a reasonable final price
- Handle the entire process

To find a freight forwarder, look in your local telephone directory or go to the Web and do a search on the keywords "freight forwarder." To ensure reputability make sure the one you choose is licensed by either the International Air Transport Association (IATA) or the Federal Maritime Commission. For more background on what freight forwarders do, visit www.export.gov/shipping_documentation_and_requirements.

Even though freight forwarders handle documentation, you should be familiar with the kinds of paperwork that exporting tends to accumulate. An earlier section discussed the letter of credit, bill of lading, and drafts. But there are others, as follows:

Commercial Invoice. This is your (the exporter's) bill to the buyer. The information it contains includes your and the buyer's names and addresses; the shipping method; package identification; description of the goods, including quantity; price, both per unit and total; and delivery and payment terms. Many countries have their own requirements for the form and content of commercial invoices, so you should check ahead of time, or ask your freight forwarder.

Packing List. This is a highly detailed accounting of the quantities and specific items you are shipping, including weights, measurements, and types of packaging.

Certificate of Origin. Some countries require this, or just recommend it. This document certifies the country of manufacture of the export, indicating its being subject to whatever tariffs and restrictions the receiving country may apply to the exporting country.

There can be more. The U.S. Department of Commerce listed the following documents required by Uzbekistan in 2004: contract, certificate of conformity, certificate of origin; passport of an import deal; certificate of availability of funds; cargo customs declaration; commercial invoice; and license (for the goods subject to licensing).

Such requirements make the services of a freight forwarder ever more attractive.

For more information about shipping, packing, and documentation, visit www.export.gov/shipping_documentation_and_requirements/exp_shipping_product.asp.

ADVANTAGES OF EXPORTING

The primary advantage of exporting is in the relative brevity of the time frame in which you get paid. With certain other types of arrangements—licensing, for one—your payments come twice yearly, every six months. In export deals, on the other hand, the payments tend to come at the shortest intervals you can negotiate, from 30 to 60, 90, or 120 days. (If you are forced to take a 180-day interval, then you may want to consider licensing since a key benefit of exporting has been erased.)

Another advantage is the relative ease of finding a trading partner. It's still not easy, but identifying and securing the services of a distributor is less difficult than trying to arrange a deal with a record company. Getting signed by Columbia Records? Not too likely. Finding a local distributor to deliver your CDs to retail? A notch or two easier.

INCOTERMS

You'll encounter odd-seeming "terms of art" that apply to exporting, knowledge of which will better equip you to understand and execute the process. Published by the International Chamber of Commerce, these are called *incoterms*—for "international commercial terms." The terms are primarily concerned with indicating the point in the shipping process at which responsibility for insurance and handling transfer from the seller to the buyer. They relate to particular modes of transportation.

Some sea transport terms:

FOB (free on board) indicates that the seller's responsibility is complete when the goods have been loaded onto the ship, and from that point on, costs of transport and insurance are assumed by the buyer.

CIF (cost, insurance, and freight) indicates that title and risk pass to the buyer when the goods have been loaded onto the ship, but the seller pays for transport and insurance to the destination port.

FAS (free alongside ship) indicates that title, risk, and cost of transport and insurance pass to the buyer after the seller delivers the goods "alongside the ship."

Some other terms:

FCA (free carrier) is the same arrangement as FOB, but applied to air transport or road or rail. Instead of transferring responsibility at point of loading on carrier, however, it transfers at a destination determined by the buyer.

CIP (carriage and insurance paid to) indicates that the buyer takes over risks and costs after the goods have been delivered to the named destination. Up to that point, the seller pays for transport and all insurance.

The terms are referenced in the written agreement between buyer and seller. Where "price" is indicated, the notation might read "$5.00 per unit (CIF, Port of New York)."

There are many more terms. To research them, you can do an Internet search on the keyword *incoterms*. Studying their definitions can provide you with a lot of insight into the many different kinds of exporting deals that can be arranged, some more favorable to you than others.

Yet another advantage: With exporting, you typically retain your label identity. Let's say you're a recording artist who has decided to create your own recording company—we'll call it Even-Three Records—and your plan is to release your own music as well as records by some other artists that you like. You want to build Even-Three into a brand, a recognizable name. If you export, the record is sold abroad under the Even-Three name. But if you license your master recording to a foreign record company, chances are that company will use its own name. If you're lucky—or have negotiating strength—the licensed record may be released under a dual label: Foreign Records/Even-Three. Short of that, there may be a small credit "Licensed from Even-Three Records, U.S.A." But with exporting, Even-Three would be the marquee label, in most cases. For an exception, see Astral Music's P&D deal in the box on page 58.

Additional advantages are specific services offered by the distributor. They vary. The value-added services of one, the Netherlands-based Astral Music, were described by CEO Rob Kuliboer to writer Magne Hoven of the *Music Business Journal*, in 2004:

> One key facility of our web site is a log-in for the vendor or the record company, so that they can monitor—24 hours a day and 7 days a week—the units we have sold, and to which territories. They can see exactly what kind of financial statements to expect (based on the sales figures we have). They can then use this to guide their marketing function. . . .
>
> We have people in our organization who listen to tracks—basically doing secondary A&R. A record label has a certain taste and feel about its music, but they usually ask the distributor for some advice. . . . So, we give advice on, for example, possibly adding remixes or changing the packaging. The record label might say, "We don't do that . . . this is what we do . . . so take it as it is!" Or they might say, "Yes, sure, you're right!" and then adapt things a little bit. So, we give advice as "consultants."

Most of all, though, distributors are compelled to work hard due to heavy competition and the fractured nature of business deals. As Astral's Kuliboer says, "The full territory deals for Benelux [the economic union of Belgium, the Netherlands, and Luxembourg], for example, are gone. The nonexclusive, 'do your best, see how good you are and what you can do with it,' is the future."

DISADVANTAGES OF EXPORTING

The cost structure that goes into determining the price of the CD can be such that it pushes the final price to customer beyond what the market will bear. All of the costs previously cited—manufacturing, freight forwarding, insurance, taxes, currency exchange, distributor's percentage, retailer's percentage, promotion—get folded into the final price. When it's sky-high, exporting becomes unworkable.

Adding to the price are any requirements to customize the product for the foreign market. You may have to burn and duplicate CDs that have a different track list than your domestic version. The packaging may need to be reworked. Your already small profit margin may not have room for the added costs of customizing.

In exporting, too, you are responsible for promoting your CDs. You may have limited resources, poor knowledge of local media, and even poorer knowledge of the kinds of messages that connect with the local populace. You'll want to customize your promotion for the local market, and to best do that you'll need the services of local promotion and advertising specialists, but your budget may constrain your ability to access those services.

There's the risk of late payments by customers, resulting in poor cash flow and inability to pay your domestic vendors on time. Or you may need working capital to fund manufacturing for export, but banks may be reluctant to provide bridge funds for this purpose due to their caution regarding customers' reliability in paying you, and thus your ability to repay the bank loan. Banks may also be concerned about currency fluctuations that may reduce the value of payments to you, squeezing your profit margin—and your ability to repay the loan. The risk-mitigating letter-of-credit financing procedure described earlier might not be available to you if your own credit is less than triple-A.

PIGGYBACK EXPORTING

You may be able to pursue exporting without dealing directly with the exporting process. You'd do this by working with a local company that exports its own products and sometimes complementary products of other manufacturers. If your product is attractive to the exporting company, it may be willing to include your CDs in its catalogue of exports. In other words, you "piggyback" on the product line of the experienced exporter. The benefits are that you don't have the headache of arranging exporting and you possibly save costs of marketing and distribution.

VARIATIONS ON DISTRIBUTION DEALS

There is rarely just one way to structure a distribution deal. Variations abound, each with its own service characteristics and pricing arrangements. The Netherlands' Astral Music, for example, offers artists and record labels a choice of three arrangements:

- **Sales and distribution.** Here, the label delivers finished products to Astral's warehouse. The label is responsible for payment of royalties, artwork, manufacturing, packaging, mechanical rights, and promotion and is the owner of the product.
- **Manufacturing and distribution.** With the M&D deal, Astral Music takes care of payment of manufacturing, packaging, and mechanical rights. The label remains the owner of the finished products.
- **Pressing and distribution.** With the P&D deal, Astral Music pays for manufacturing, packaging, mechanical rights, and promotion, and is the owner of the product (the label), with the right to press and sell the physical products.

The possibilities for distribution deals are limited only by the imaginations of the participating businesses.

LICENSING TO FOREIGN COUNTRIES

What if the financials of exporting through a foreign distributor don't work? For example, the distributor may require modifications to your standard product—translations of words on the packaging, for example. Manufacturing this will require extra cost on your part. Further, the distributor may want you to lower your price per unit, due to the high cost of doing business in that country, squeezing the distributor's earnings. The only price that will work for the distributor is one so low that it will ensure you lose money after paying for the translated version of the CD. Moreover, you'll be responsible for funding advertising costs in the foreign market, further cutting into your earnings. In a case like this, it might make more sense to cut a licensing deal.

Licensing is a kind of *strategic alliance*—an agreement between companies to pursue a common business goal while remaining independent companies.

Even major labels may pursue licensing of their music in less-developed markets, rather than setting up wholly owned subsidiaries and distributing through them. Warner Music, for example, licenses its catalogue in Turkey through the company Balet Plak. Universal Music licenses through Ukrainian Records in the Ukraine.

HOW LICENSING WORKS

You make an arrangement with a foreign record company such that you supply the master recording and the foreign company packages it to conform to local requirements, duplicates it, handles local distribution, and carries out local promotion.

In return, you receive a royalty for each unit sold. The royalty is generally the equivalent of 8 to 17 percent of the local retail list price, less taxes and packaging costs, for 90 to 100 percent of records sold. (Sometimes payment is based on 100 percent of records sold minus promotional copies and returns.)

Frequently, the royalty is computed not on the retail price but on what is called the *published price to dealer* (PPD), which is roughly equivalent to what in the United States is called the wholesale price. When this is the case, the royalty percentage is set higher so that the amount earned is equivalent to 8 to 17 percent of retail.

At the beginning of the deal you typically receive an advance—a lump-sum payment—against future royalties, usually a portion upon signature of the contract and the balance upon delivery of the master recording. The amount of the advance depends both on estimated royalties based on predicted sales and on the strength of your negotiating position—the more the foreign company wants your music, the higher an advance you can negotiate. On the foreign company's side, the advance may be computed as, say, 75 percent of expected royalties. So, if a record is expected to sell 2,000 copies at $13 U.S., and the royalty is 10 percent, the company might calculate an advance of $1,950 and round it up to an even $2,000.

ADVANCE COMPUTATION

Retail price of CD	$13.00
Licensing royalty per unit (10%)	$1.30
Estimated sales units	2,000
Estimated total royalties	$2,600
	$2,600
Multiplied by 75% advance allowance	.75
Advance Amount	**$1,950**

After the records start to sell, the foreign company will recoup the advance from actual earned royalties—that is, keep all your earned royalties until they add up to the amount already advanced to you; after that point the company begins paying you newly earned royalties, which to you is income over and above the advance.

You receive royalty statements, hopefully with a check, every six months.

A key point about advances is, they are rarely earned back. What happens then? Do you have to pay back the amount that went unearned? Not if your contract stipulates that the advance is not repayable; it is yours to keep regardless of whether the CDs sell through. You should make sure the licensing agreement contains such wording. And you should make sure that the advance is an amount you'd be comfortable with if you never saw any additional money from the deal.

Before you reject a deal with a small advance, however, consider the other potential benefits of licensing. The foreign company will be promoting your music, bringing you new audiences. The arrangement may also be a gateway to local performance venues and other businesses that can prove helpful in your global marketing campaign. If the local promotion works, and your music sells well, the company will want to renew the agreement when it reaches the end of its term. You'll be in a position to negotiate a higher advance, and you will have established a new market at the foreign company's marketing expense.

In another type of licensing deal, you provide manufactured albums to the foreign company, which buys them at your manufacturing cost and then pays a royalty on sales. This arrangement makes sense when estimated sales are not high enough to justify the foreign label's bearing the cost of local manufacturing.

Export and Licensing Sample Cost-Earnings Comparison*

Method	Unit Manu-facturing Costs	Transport Costs	Gross Promo Costs	Net Receipts Per Unit	Receipts Per Unit
Exporting	$5	Based on quantity	Payable	$7	$2
Licensing	$0	None	None	$1.50	$1.50

* Amounts are hypothetical, for purposes of illustration only.

Durations of licensing agreements are limited, often to five years. Contracts include a "sell-off" stipulation that allows the foreign company to sell off its remaining stock once the agreement reaches the end of its term.

Many firms pursue a strategy of licensing to different companies in different countries, to maximize local marketing expertise. The European label Media Records, for example, has partners throughout Spain, Germany, and Scandinavia. "We have historically sorted out label deals, or individual exclusive/nonexclusive licensing of artists and product throughout the world, actively," label executive Peter Pritchard told writer Claire O'Neill of the *Music Business Journal.*

Advantages of Licensing

Licensing offers several benefits over exporting. To some, the primary benefit might be ease of logistics. Whereas with exporting you need to handle transport, lots of paperwork, and promotion, with licensing you have no transport (other than sending the master recording), minimal paperwork, and zero or limited promotion since the foreign company handles it.

Another benefit is less up-front cost. With exporting you pay for manufacturing, transport, and promotion. With licensing you invest little since the foreign company does the manufacturing, distribution, and promotion. Instead, you get a payment—an advance.

Income from licensing may exceed what you'd get through exporting. For example, if you export to a country that levees tariffs on imports, the tariffs will add to the cost structure underlying the final price, and may require a markdown on your profit margin to enable a competitive price to the consumer. With licensing, on the other hand, you bypass tariffs since your product is manufactured locally rather than imported.

Promotion, too, might be more effective with licensing than with exporting. In licensing, the foreign company handles promotion, and because it's a local company it knows local culture, tastes, and preferences and has experience using local marketing and promotion channels. It also has an incentive—its advance to you—to make the necessary expenditures. In exporting, you're less advantaged since you don't know the culture and have to learn the local promotion network from scratch—unless you have the financial resources to hire a local firm to execute marketing and promotion. If you did, you'd still have to spend time and energy looking for a reputable firm.

DISADVANTAGES OF LICENSING

In licensing, to some extent, you lose control over your product and the marketing of it. The foreign company may be less concerned than you with quality control; it may be satisfied with subpar manufacturing. When the product goes to market, the poor quality reflects badly on you and your music. What's more, the foreign company's execution of marketing and promotion may include product messaging and positioning that run counter to the image and personality you wish to convey. Most importantly, the company may not accurately account for the number of copies it distributes, resulting in underpayment of royalties to you.

As mentioned in the section on exporting, with licensing it's often the case that your recording is issued by a foreign record company under its name, not yours. Your brand, if you have one, is not on the marquee unless you're able to negotiate dual-company labeling. If it's important to you that you establish a company name abroad, licensing and releasing under another company's name may not be the ideal strategy.

Another disadvantage is the time lag in receiving payments. Licensing royalties are typically paid twice a year. This is a long time to wait between checks. (And there may not be any checks.) If you have bargaining power, you can negotiate for quarterly, rather than biannual, royalty payment.

Finally, the global prevalence of piracy lends an element of risk to allowing your master recordings to fall into other than your own hands. Even a reputable company may have an unethical employee who sees profit in copying your master and illegitimately manufacturing copies for sale, without paying royalties to you. If this happens, you may never find out about it directly, but you can be sure that it would cut into your legitimate sales and reduce your earnings. For this reason, before entering into a licensing agreement be sure to check the host country's legal protections against theft of intellectual property.

All of these potential downsides can be mitigated by rigorous due diligence in researching the reputation of the foreign company before executing a deal. You can also include in your written agreement requirements that cover your points of concern. Stipulate, for example, that the company must get your approval of the manufactured product, the packaging, and the advertising. When *Rolling Stone* magazine licensed its brand to a Chinese firm in 2005, the licensor acknowledged to Associated Press that they "work closely together with [*Rolling Stone* staff] because we want to make sure we're faithful to the spirit of the brand."

JOINT VENTURES

What if you've gone further into the business side of music than producing and marketing your own records and maybe a few by other artists? What if you're serious about running your own label and making it a success? Moreover, what if exporting presents too many problems, with low probability of profits? And what if licensing makes you uncomfortable because you'll lose too much control over the quality and presentation of your music? Then you might consider ratcheting up your level of direct involvement in foreign marketing by engaging in a joint venture with an existing company in the target market. This way you'll have more of a say in how business will be conducted. You'll invest more, but you'll also retain a larger portion of profits.

How Joint Ventures Work

Let's say you've identified a company in Country A that meets your requirements for a business partner. It appears to be a good fit, and you may have at first considered the company as a licensee. Its other products are in similar musical genres to your own, and the company serves audiences similar to yours. It has an excellent track record of sales to local retail and play on local radio. It's an important player in the local music market, and has a great understanding of and ties with local promotional outlets. You lack all of these assets and capabilities in that country. But the foreign company also handles a lot of product, so it may not be able to devote as much marketing attention to your product as you might wish. And the quality of its CDs and its cover artwork and packaging have never been quite to your taste. You'd be uncomfortable giving it control of product quality. In such a case, licensing might not be a good idea. Instead, you set up an arrangement in which you divide up responsibilities according to your respective areas of expertise, and you share the costs. When revenues begin to flow from sales, you reimburse your expenditures and then split profits per an agreed-upon percentage, typically fifty–fifty. You set a time limitation to the contract, so that it's easy to exit from, should that be desirable.

Joint ventures can involve any kind of business transaction, any desired division of responsibilities, and any size company, including an individual. It can be for one project, or for a series of projects. A notable large-scale joint venture is that of Sony Music Entertainment and BMG, the music division of Bertelsmann AG. By joining forces as Sony-BMG, they created the second-largest music company in the world (following Universal Music). Another example: In 2005 the U.S. music downloading service Napster arranged to enter the Japanese market by setting up a joint venture with Tower Records Japan (TRJ). In the terms of the agreement, as announced in an August 2005 press release, TRJ would contribute $7 million in cash, "the majority of the management team, local music content, and extensive marketing for the new service through its network of 108 retail stores, Web sites, music magazines and other TRJ promotional vehicles" in return for a 70 percent majority stake in Napster Japan. Napster, for its part, would provide up to $3 million in cash, its brand, its technology, its music library, and operational and marketing support in exchange for a 30 percent minority interest and royalty income, plus the right to appoint directors to the company's Board.

What responsibilities might be divided up in a typical music marketing joint venture? The company in the target market might contribute its expertise in the back-end functions: local marketing and distribution, and perhaps manufacturing if it can offer cost efficiencies. The company entering the foreign market might focus on front-end functions such as recording, packaging, and payment of royalties to artists and publishers. The profits could be divided in proportion to the investments of the two partners.

JOINT VENTURE SAMPLE COST-SHARING ARRANGEMENT

Functions	Costs	Your Company's Share	Foreign Partner's Share
Recording	$25,000	25,000	0
Packaging	5,000	5,000	0
Manufacturing	15,000	0	15,000
Royalties	40,000	40,000	0
Promotion	35,000	0	35,000
Distribution	7,500	0	7,500
Total	$127,500	$70,000	$57,500
% of Total	100%	55%	45%

ADVANTAGES OF JOINT VENTURES

As a means of entering a foreign market, joint venturing represents a higher commitment than exporting and licensing and a lower commitment than setting up a wholly owned subsidiary. You put more into it than you do with licensing, but you also stand to gain greater profits: typically 50 percent rather than licensing's 8 to 25 percent of PPD. At the same time, you don't commit so much that you're stuck in the relationship: joint ventures are typically short-term strategic alliances. They offer flexibility and tax advantages (when set up as partnerships rather than corporations).

In a joint venture, you can benefit from the local company's expertise in local business practices and from its other capabilities that you don't have.

Joint ventures can remove any impact of "source effects"—negative PR due to the nation you happen to represent. The venture is seen as a local enterprise.

Finally, a joint venture may be the only option you have if you want control, flexibility, and higher profits.

Disadvantages of Joint Ventures

Many joint ventures fail. Part of the problem is conflict over control of the venture. It's key to carefully spell out roles at the beginning to reduce room for misunderstanding.

The market-entering partner (you) may lack managerial control of the operation. The logistics of distribution and promotion may be guarded by the foreign partner, and you may disagree with them. To avoid this, try to secure a role in management of the joint venture at the outset. Majority ownership of the venture (51 to 99 percent) helps ensure this.

If the joint venture is between two large companies whose merger could establish a monopoly in the market, it could run afoul of local antitrust laws. This won't be of concern to small, independent businesses, of course, but it's nice to know that there are a few checks on the activities of the market leaders, leaving the small entities some chance of survival.

To avoid the possibility of the venture's going wrong, screen prospective partners carefully and conduct due diligence by checking their credentials and references. Make sure there is clarity in the contract on the following provisions:

- Shared business objectives

- Degree of participation and the management roles of each party

- Contribution of capital and ownership rights to property

- Division of profits and losses

- Dispute mechanism

- Development of an exit strategy and terms of dissolution of the joint venture

FOREIGN SUBSIDIARIES

The ultimate step in gaining control of a foreign operation is to own it completely. Instead of a half or majority ownership of a joint venture, in which you share decisions, costs, and profits with a partner, you may want to either acquire an existing company or start up a completely new operation—either way, owning it 100 percent and using it as a foreign subsidiary of your domestic enterprise.

Admittedly, this strategy may be beyond the capabilities and desires of the small operation—whether an artist marketing self-produced music or a start-up small-label owner exploring foreign markets for the first time. But understanding the total-ownership option can bring a broad perspective to any business decisions you make.

With a wholly owned subsidiary, you make the decisions, bear the costs, and reap the profits. It is the most complete, and most expensive, commitment you can make to marketing your recordings abroad.

How Wholly Owned Subsidiaries Work

Company A has been involved in exporting and licensing in several countries, and has learned something about the process. Now it is interested in entering Country Z, where the music distribution system is poorly organized, and where licensing and joint venture opportunities are slim due to lack of effective participants. But Company A knows that its music could be highly popular there. It decides to purchase a local distributor and send managers there to run the operation.

The managers use their knowledge of logistics, marketing, promotion, and technology to build a more efficient operation. The local employees have knowledge of local customs, tastes, and practices, which helps the operation avoid making missteps. Over time, the new managers become expert at marketing to the local audience. The operation now offers the benefit of local expertise plus 100 percent share of the profits.

An alternate approach is to build a small local operation from the ground up. This is more difficult at first, since there is no existing business structure to build on. Yet it circumvents the cultural difficulty of merging home management with an entrenched local staff, who may be resistant to change. With a new operation, you can hire employees from the surrounding area, giving you the conduit to local culture that you need while having them work according to your objectives as soon as they're hired—possibly easier than retraining existing staff.

In either approach, decisions regarding distribution, marketing, and promotion are made in the local office according to local needs, rather than in response to micromanagement from domestic headquarters—although the main office will set broad guidelines for business performance.

Advantages of a Wholly Owned Subsidiary

As already indicated, wholly owned subsidiaries provide maximum control over the business. With an acquisition, you have a head start with local expertise, although integrating new management with existing staff may be difficult. With a start-up operation, you move more slowly due to lack of local expertise, but over time you gain "location and experience economies"—savings from the know-how you gain by engaging the foreign market yourself—and you operate as you see fit rather than retooling and reengineering an existing operation.

Some governments may offer incentives for your bringing business, know-how, and jobs into the country. Incentives could be in the form of tax breaks for a period of time, a grant of workspace, or some other subsidy.

Disadvantages of a Wholly Owned Subsidiary

There is no greater commitment of resources than that required for setting up a foreign subsidiary. If the operation doesn't work out, you can lose a larger investment than with other strategies. Exiting the market is not easy—it's not like terminating a short-term export or licensing agreement.

For all those reasons, this strategy should be undertaken only after careful market research, cost-benefit analysis, and assessment of resources. Do you have the staff, money, and know-how to pull it off?

Now that you have explored the available options for entering a foreign market, you return to thoughts of the 2,000 compact discs you'd like to add to your manufacturing run to push down the unit cost. Which of the market-entry strategies appears most promising for your needs? Exporting would work, although you might have to customize the product somewhat to meet the foreign market's needs, and that might prove too costly. Licensing would not dispose of the 2,000, since the licensee would manufacture its own units; but any licensing revenues could offset the costs of manufacturing your original 10,000 so you wouldn't need the extra 2,000. A limited joint venture could work. A wholly owned subsidiary would not be appropriate for such a limited objective. Your options will be further limited by whatever business opportunities are available in your primary market of interest. The next step is to investigate potential business partners in that territory.

CRITERIA FOR SELECTING BUSINESS STRATEGY

	Earnings	Workload	Level of Commitment	Level of Control	Ease of Exit
Export	Cost-Plus	Moderate	Low	Moderate	High
License	18–25% of PPD	Low	1–5 years	Low	Moderate
Joint Venture	50/50%	High	High	Shared	Low
Subsidiary	100%	Very High	High	High	Low

CHAPTER 4

Producing and Packaging Music for Global Sale

Let's assume, for the sake of illustration, that you are in talks with a distributor in Country A to export your recording of domestic Artist B. All is proceeding smoothly until one morning you receive an e-mail from the general manager at the distributorship. She has been advised by her staff that some changes to your recording would improve its sales potential in her territory. Not substantial changes, she reassures you. But her employees feel that if the first song is remixed to emphasize the rhythm, the record will have greater appeal for local radio and for dance clubs. And they also see a problem in the cover photograph. The way the singer is wearing her jacket, buttoned left to right instead of the other way around, has special symbolism in this country. Buyers might get the wrong message and decide against purchase. Can the photograph be altered or replaced? she asks.

As you mentally assess the work it would take to meet these requests— returning to the recording studio to remix and remaster; rehiring a freelance art director to revise the cover; manufacturing a quantity of CDs exclusively for export—you also think about costs and realize that this alteration could erase your profit margin. The deal, you conclude, is suddenly in jeopardy.

You have been dragged, without warning, into the real world of product development, international style.

Everyone considers music the international language. It speaks to us all. But that language has a wide variety of dialects. And in some parts of the world, certain dialects may not be favored, while others may be embraced. To extend this analogy to encompass performers and packaging, the appearance of the speaker of the dialect may or may not appeal to populations of certain regions. What is more, the speaker's message—the semantics of the communication— may resonate in some territories while offending people in others.

Translation to music marketing: the musical style, the artist image, the package design, and the song lyrics may create excitement in some countries while eliciting only puzzlement, antipathy, or indifference in others.

The reality of product development and packaging for the global marketplace is that optimum sales are sometimes achieved by customization—fine-tuning the product to meet the preferences and requirements of target foreign markets.

Recall the case of MTV cited in Chapter 1. The music network first approached globalization with the belief that it could broadcast the same basic programming worldwide. But its MTV-India venture languished until the network provided more Indian videos and personalities, at which point the venture flourished. The essential "personality" of the network remained the same—youth culture packaged in bright colors, quick editing, and catchy beats—but the content required customization for the target market.

A superstar on the Rolling Stones' level may not have to customize—although even they had to leave several songs off the Chinese version of their greatest-hits album when it was released there in 2003. Most of us will have to consider what custom product development may mean for our effort to make the most of global marketing opportunities. The points of consideration will include the product itself—the music, encompassing the performer, the performance, and the music composition—and the packaging of the music.

STANDARDIZATION, CUSTOMIZATION, AND MASS CUSTOMIZATION

Before getting into those specifics, definitions of a few key marketing terms are worth scrutinizing. When you take a product beyond your primary market, to new market segments in foreign territories, you choose from two main product design options: standardization and customization. As technology has evolved, and as marketing theory has become more refined, you've been presented with an attractive third option: mass customization.

STANDARDIZATION

Market theorist Theodore Levitt concluded that international markets are moving toward standardization—where a single product, unaltered, can be sold in many markets worldwide. Youth culture and certain kinds of music appear to prove his point. A personal anecdote, for purposes of illustration: Back in 1980 I spent some time in Indonesia, about as far away from my home country, the U.S., as you can get. My treks took me to several barely populated spots. These included a beach that seemed the epitome of escape from Western culture—until I heard the familiar sound of the disco hit "Funkytown" blaring from some unseen sound source.

It was living proof that pop music reached everywhere. And that observation is truer now. You can score a hit in a Western culture and find that it resonates worldwide. And that resonance can endure. Seventies band Deep Purple, for example, long after its popularity faded in its native U.K., found enthusiastic audiences in Southeast Asia. Those sounds can travel without alteration. Deep Purple played the same music in Singapore that it would play in Miami Beach.

Today's MP3 of an unsigned singer–songwriter based in France has a decent chance of finding fans anywhere in the world, with no alteration of sound or style. Similarly, a pair of Levi's jeans can be marketed essentially as is all over the world.

From the standpoint of cost, standardization is ideal for the marketer. You ship or upload your basic product around the world without incurring extra expense for customized features, and you enjoy a healthy profit margin.

CUSTOMIZATION

But as MTV proved, standardization sometimes hits the brick wall of local resistance. Localities may in fact have special preferences, some cultural and some technical or logistical. The cultural might take the form of antipathy to anything from a particular country. The technical or logistical might refer to a lack of Internet access, or low per capita incomes precluding ability to buy CD players. In such cases, the product has to be changed to meet local preferences.

For an example from outside the music industry: Western refrigerators may not sell in Tokyo due to that city's small-sized apartments and kitchens.

A song may not work in a country because its lyrics express a sentiment that falls outside of local concern, and its sound is considered abrasive.

The Western refrigerator maker would have to redesign a product for Tokyo needs. The record company would have to change lyrics and rework the instrumental arrangement if it wanted to sell in the target foreign market.

With customization, you more precisely meet audience preferences, but you lose economies of scale. The fewer units you manufacture, the higher the cost per unit. With customization you may be manufacturing one version of the product for Market A, another for Market B, and yet another for Market C.

COST COMPARISON, MANUFACTURING CUSTOM VERSUS STANDARDIZED CDs

Standardized Product

Compact Disc A	All Markets	10,000 units	$7,500
Total Cost		**10,000 units**	**$7,500**

Customized Product

Compact Disc V1	Market A	1,000 units	$1,200
Compact Disc V2	Market B	1,000	1,200
Compact Disc V3	Market C	1,000	1,200
Compact Disc V4	Market D	1,000	1,200
Compact Disc V5	Market E	1,000	1,200
Compact Disc V6	Market F	1,000	1,200
Compact Disc V7	Market G	1,000	1,200
Compact Disc V8	Market H	3,000	2,650
Total Cost		**10,000 units**	**$11,050**

Mass Customization

There's a solution midway between standardization and customization. You manufacture the essential form of the product for worldwide distribution. But you tailor certain features to appeal to the local market. The cost is less than for complete customization, because you are still mass-producing the basic product, gaining economies of scale.

Example: A U.S. software program is prepared for marketing worldwide. But its numbering system is changed to the metric system for the European market.

Another example: An automobile's overall design is standardized. But for a foreign market, it is adjusted to allow for the driver to sit on the right.

A song is arranged and recorded for the worldwide market. But the vocal is recorded in different languages for different markets.

That's mass customization: standardizing as much as possible, and tailoring as necessary for additional market segments.

In global music marketing, you'll be most concerned with standardization and mass customization.

TAILORING THE MUSICAL PRODUCT FOR FOREIGN AUDIENCES

One of the earliest international pop stars, Connie Francis, achieved her popularity status the obvious way: by recording foreign-language versions of her hit songs. Francis tended to record songs in many languages, including Spanish, Italian, and Japanese; her 1961 hit "Where the Boys Are," was one of the first pop songs to get a foreign-language treatment.

In a more recent example of this approach, a singer was guided by her producer to record the vocals of an entire album many times over, each in a different language. At the end of the production cycle they had multiple versions of the album tailored for different foreign markets.

Before you think about customizing your musical product, which costs money, first consider where you might sell the product unchanged, exactly as you produced it for your domestic market. The path of least resistance is a foreign market that shares your language, or a market, such as Japan, that thrives on imports. Japan has long harbored an obsession with Western popular music, for example, from pop to punk to hip-hop. The right music from outside that country might not need any special tailoring to appeal to the right Japanese listeners. With such a market, you can build the basis of a global marketing strategy with the least financial risk. Once you have made headway, you can build out to other markets, tailoring to whatever degrees you see as required for target markets.

When you do find it necessary to customize or alter, you'll generally be focusing on one of the following product dimensions:

- Product features
- Musical style

- Atmosphere, symbolism, and mood
- Form

FEATURE CUSTOMIZATION

The most straightforward customization is to provide special product features for specific markets.

For example, you might print the local translation of the song lyrics, along with translation of production notes, artist biography, and whatever other pieces of information the domestic product provides. The cost will be limited to the design and printing of however many of these kinds of inserts you feel you will need. It's a relatively inexpensive option.

More elaborate is the inclusion of bonus tracks on foreign versions of your product. Stevie Wonder's 2005 album *A Time to Love*, for example, included two songs for the foreign market. What this achieves is adding value and appeal to the album that as an import is generally priced higher than domestic products. Buyers will be more likely to pay the extra price. And they might get an extra thrill from hearing a hit song rendered in their native tongue. This customization feature incurs substantial expense above and beyond basic manufacturing costs: separate packaging and labeling is required along with the separate batch of discs and the additional music production expenses. A degree of certainty that you can sell the requisite number of units is required before you commit to this maneuver.

Local censorship practices may require the opposite of adding tracks, as observed in the above example of a Chinese-government-modified Rolling Stones greatest-hits album. (And when the group performed in Shanghai in 2006, the government banned it from performing "Let's Spend the Night Together" and four other songs.)

Other customized product features might include special cover art for the foreign market—more about which will come in the discussion of packaging.

JAPAN: COMPETING WITH IMPORTS

Japan hosts a wide selection of imported music. The country's love for Western popular culture has spawned Tokyo's array of small specialty import stores, offering just about any niche style from any era that one might seek. A similarly diverse selection, including indie releases, is offered at the large retailers such as Tower Records and Virgin Megastore.

Part of the reason for imports' popularity in Japan is that their prices are competitive with domestic releases—in contrast to their priciness in other countries. In Japan, imports are not subject to certain pricing regulations that domestic producers are.

To compete with imports, domestic record companies add value to their releases by including special features—remixes, bonus tracks, and the like. For a foreign artist doing business with a Japanese label—a licensing deal, for example—the requests from the licensee might include a couple of extra tracks to make the release more attractive to the Japanese customer than an import with fewer tracks. As a member of the U.S. band Counting Crows wrote on a fan Web site: "Some international territories ask us for extra tracks. . . . To avoid their markets being swamped by cheaper exports, they ask us for material that's not on the American version."

STYLE CUSTOMIZATION

A more invasively "surgical" strategy is to make adjustments to the recording itself. Where the preceding approach consists of adding features to an already existing product, here you make alterations to the content of the product. For many reasons, this is an expensive operation, generally undertaken by established artists and companies with the requisite financial and human capital.

What does it involve? If you're targeting a potentially huge market, and you know that local preferences include certain kinds of instruments or certain types of rhythm, you might record alternate accompaniment to your existing tracks that adds locally desirable sonic flavors. It's not unlike doing remixes for dance clubs.

If you're considering a complete overhaul of an artist's sound, you're probably going too far. You'd simply be creating a different product from the one you originally set out to sell. Better to keep that artist's fundamental style intact and start from scratch with a new artist more suitable to the foreign market.

Some artists produce music that is globally appealing to begin with; they have an intrinsic feel for multicultural styles. Colombia-born singer Shakira is one. Raised on a cultural mix drawn from Lebanese and Colombian parents and from English-language rock and disco, Shakira pours sounds from a wide range of global sources into her songs, making them international hits. Latin pop, rock 'n' roll guitars, throbbing synthesizers, Arabic vocal inflections, and Jamaican dancehall have all contributed to her pop-music mix. "My pop shoes . . . let me walk in any direction," she told writer Jon Pareles in 2005. "One day

I feel I want to do a song with reggaeton influences, I do it. The next day I feel I need to do a song with rock elements to it, I do it. And sometimes I try to see if an Argentine bandoneon can survive in a song with flugelhorns."

Shakira also pursued conscious strategies to broaden her appeal. After becoming a Latin pop star, she set out to learn English well enough to write songs in that language. Her first English-language album, *Laundry Service*, became a hit in the United States. In 2005 she released a Spanish album, *Fijación Oral Vol. 1*, with an English counterpart, *Oral Fixation Vol. 2*, serving both her original Spanish-speaking fans and a worldwide pop market. One of the songs, "How Do You Do," featured lyrics in English, Arabic, Hebrew, and Latin. These are some of the reasons *The New York Times* dubbed her "the future of global music" in 2005.

But most of us are not Shakiras. If your music is not inherently marketable across multiple cultures, there are still plenty of ways to tweak your sound to enhance foreign appeal.

SING IN ENGLISH?

With English being the closest we have to a global language, many internationally inclined artists might want to make sure vocals are in English, to appeal to the widest audience. But one producer of world music expressed a reservation: "I record a very specialized style of world music. I recorded vocals in English to attract the pop market. But in doing so I risk losing the local audience that has been my core market."

U.S. singer Shania Twain found a clever way to expand her appeal with her 2005 album *Up*, although her tailoring was for different markets within her own country. She recorded nineteen songs, releasing them in a two-disc set in which one disc featured pop arrangements and a second disc offered country arrangements—the same nineteen songs recorded two ways.

With digital recording, it's a lot easier than it once was to mix a variety of different versions of a single song. You can have one version with a standard drum set, and another version for, say, the Brazilian market, featuring added percussion instruments like *shekere*, *cuica*, *sud*, and *berimbao*. You can strip away electronic instruments and use only acoustic sounds, featuring banjo, fiddle, and dobro for an American country ambience. The key, of course, is to know who your audience is and what it likes, and to avoid providing a style that may at one time have been popular in a market but that current audiences may view as quaint and unhip.

How do you explore the styles popular in different territories? MTV's international subsidiary sites are good places to start. Check their charts to see who's locally popular, then hunt for downloads online to see what they sound like. Also, check Internet radio that airs in target countries. Yahoo Music, for example, has channels tailored for many different territories. Go to Live 365 at www.live365.com and click International. See what you find.

ATMOSPHERE, SYMBOLISM, AND MOOD

The *atmosphere* and *symbolism* of a product refer to the overall environment and worldview suggested by—if not explicitly expressed by—the artist, the music, and the total product package. The atmosphere and symbolism match the preferences of individual buyers, or buyer segments of the total market. An artist may, for example, symbolize wealth and material success through ostentatious costuming, elaborate musical production, song lyrics, and cover art. That symbolism may appeal, perhaps subconsciously, to consumers who aspire to luxury living. Another artist might symbolize social and economic dissatisfaction, connecting with legions of younger consumers still struggling to find out where they fit in society.

A product's *mood* can support the atmosphere and symbolism. The mood can be downbeat and sad, colorful and lively (or any of a long list of characteristics, from acerbic and aggressive through wry and yearning, that the fascinating Web site Allmusic.com has assembled as a criterion for conducting a music search). The mood can be established in the music, the lyrics, and the packaging, as well as in the artist's persona expressed in appearance and behavior.

In the case of an artist whose music doesn't suggest a particular worldview or character—say, a vocal virtuoso who covers a wide range of styles—the packaging would be the place to establish a sensibility or point of view.

To attribute preference toward a particular musical atmosphere or mood to the entire population of a particular territory would be greatly oversimplifying a country's "national character" and the requirements of market segmenting. Yet within countries exist subpopulations that can be defined, loosely, according to criteria that relate to atmosphere, symbolism, and mood. Understanding the characteristics of a prospective target market can help you either predict whether your artist and music will succeed with those buyers or customize your music to appeal specifically to those buyers. In effect, you can consciously connect—through product development and marketing communication channels—the attributes of your musical product with the attributes and behaviors of customer segments.

A customer's decision to buy is influenced by a wide range of factors: geographic, demographic, sociocultural, psychographic, and behavioral. Geographic factors are discussed throughout this book, so let's look at the others.

Demographic Factors Influencing Purchase. Demographics are the basic criteria by which populations are divided into clearly definable segments—groupings—that marketers can expect to behave in distinct ways. Criteria include age, sex, sexual orientation, life stage, income, occupation, education level, socioeconomic status, religion, and nationality.

People's tastes tend to change as they pass through stages of life. Sure, one might find the occasional fiftysomething "head of household" writhing along with other fans at an Insane Clown Posse concert, but as a general rule older listeners tend to prefer more mellow sounds. Similarly, the rare fifteen-year-old girl might hold special affection for the music of Frank Sinatra, but more likely the fifteen-year-old will be drawn, by hormones, metabolic rate, and peer-group preference, to pop or rock sounds of the latest frenetic role model in the mold of Madonna in her day and Britney Spears in hers. Marketing music requires knowing, in general, the preferences of age groups and where your music's atmosphere, symbolism, and mood fit in, demographically.

Age, of course, relates to life stage: whether

- In the throes of youthful abandon and singlehood, with few financial burdens and plenty of leisure pursuits to spend money on
- Just married and entering domesticity, redirecting expenditures toward household items
- Building a family and saving money for kids' school, vacations, and the like
- Alone after seeing kids off to their own lives, now directing attention back to their own interests and entertainment
- Retired, downsizing financially, staying home, reading books and watching television and listening to music

That's the mainstream nuclear-family scenario at least. There are infinite variations. (Niche marketing plays to the variations. Mass marketing caters to the statistically dominant patterns.)

Age also impacts decisions about formats, as discussed earlier. Younger buyers tend to be more technologically savvy and more comfortable with new entertainment delivery systems. Purchasers aged forty-five and up are the predominant compact disc buyers. Rule of thumb: Classic rock, nostalgia, and more mellow music offered on compact disc and purchasable in brick-and-mortar stores serve the "mature" segment of the populace. Brash, hyperenergetic, "latest thing" music packaged as cell phone ringtones and iPod downloads meets the needs—at the fleeting moment of this writing—of younger audiences.

How do sex and sexual orientation influence buying, and relate to atmosphere, symbolism, and mood? The stereotype would be that male audiences are drawn to more robust, aggressive, macho sounds, while female audiences are attracted to lower-key, more introspective, more romantic music. Does the stereotype really hold? (And does it apply all over the world?) Between Iron Maiden on the extreme male end of the spectrum and the latest teen "boy band" on the far opposite female end, there's a lot of gray area. Think all-female-rock-band Sleater Kinney's appeal to a male audience. You may reach broad conclusions about the maleness or femaleness of the music you're marketing, but pockets of deviance from the norm are inevitably out there waiting to be brought into the fold. Be open to them.

Income, education level, and socioeconomic status are interrelated. Author Richard P. Coleman has identified stratification of social classes in the United States as follows:

- Upper upper: the social elite
- Lower upper: affluent achievers; nouveau riche
- Upper middle: professionals, managerial class, quality seekers
- Middle class: white- and blue-collar workers
- Working class: lower-paid blue-collar
- Upper lower: working poor
- Lower lower: poverty stricken, recipients of government support

An audience of low-income, low-socioeconomic-status listeners may not appreciate a singer's paean to champagne, diamonds, and the good life. Similarly, a well-tended, financially secure, upwardly mobile professional might not succumb to the charms of a punk band's exhortations to blow the military-industrial complex to smithereens. But, as with age and sex, there's a continuum of tastes and preferences that can be surprisingly flexible. That upscale singer's hymns to riches and glitz may be just the dream to which the low-income listener aspires. And the punk rockers may represent the wildness of youth that the stable professional laments the loss of—and plans to revisit at some carefree moment in the future. The smart marketer looks beyond the obvious to find the aspirational motives and fantasy yearnings of particular consumer groups, and then targets them.

But those aspirations may differ from one country to the next, in part because cultures vary in terms of their social structures. The list given above for U.S. categories does not apply exactly to other countries. Nearly everywhere, though, stratification is usually based on a combination of socioeconomic status and family background. The difference is primarily in the degree of social mobility—the ability to move from one stratum to another. India, for example, is structured in a caste system in which your social position—your caste—is determined by the status of the family into which you were born, and it is not possible to move to a higher caste. In the United States, on the other hand, there is a high degree of social mobility. Someone born into poverty can achieve the material success that opens the door to higher economic strata.

Such differences matter when, for example, your symbolism or message is one of aspiring to higher stations in life. In a socially mobile culture, such messages may be embraced as inspiring. In cultures with low social mobility, where there is no chance of higher aspirations being achieved, the message might be rejected.

Sociocultural Factors Influencing Purchase. Consumer values, perceptions, and preferences are shaped by *reference groups*—social networks with which people identify. They may include family, friends, co-workers, classmates, members of trade organizations, racial groups, and religious groups. They may also include groups that people wish to be part of, and other groups that they disdain and reject. Each group imparts cultural values, beliefs, and tastes.

In marketing, you try to identify the reference groups to which your listeners might belong or aspire, and then you appeal to the preferences of the reference groups. You connect the atmosphere, symbolism, and mood of your product with the values, beliefs, and tastes of the reference groups. For a young, counterestablishment audience, for example, you might emphasize qualities that overtly run counter to socially conventional tastes: ripped T-shirts, angry-sounding music, intentionally outrageous style.

If possible, you obtain the endorsement of what are called *opinion leaders*—key figures in reference groups who influence members. This may be as obvious as getting a positive review from a journalist in a magazine read by the reference group, and then using quotes from that reviewer in promotional material. It could also involve obtaining an endorsement from a well-known personality in another field with a demographic that overlaps that of your music. For example, a positive quote from a movie personality associated with intriguing independent films—a Steve Buscemi type—might benefit intriguing, independently released music.

Psychographic Factors Influencing Purchase. A buyer's self-concept and personality traits have an impact on purchasing habits and can be useful factors in how you target audiences, package your product, and communicate messages.

Self-concept and personality traits tie into lifestyle, and into activities, interests, and opinions (AIO). Does the person see him- or herself as high-achieving? As politically astute? As socially active? As culturally cutting-edge? As anti-intellectual? The self-concepts and personality traits motivate behavior. If the behavior you want is purchase of your CD, you appeal to the underlying motivators.

There's an interesting marketing tool called VALS (online at www.sric-bi.com/VALS) that segments groups according to three primary motivations and eight subtypes. The three primary motivations are (1) ideals—guided by knowledge and principles; (2) achievement—demonstrating success to peers; and (3) self-expression—desiring social and physical activity. The eight subtypes fall under those categories and are linked to purchasing behavior, as follows:

VALS Motivation Types

Types Common to All Three Motivators (Ideals, Achievement, Self-Expression).

Innovators: Successful, sophisticated, resourceful. Purchase upscale and niche products, jazz, classical music, cutting-edge pop, high-end recordings.

Survivors: Narrow-focused, cautious, prefer the familiar to the new, concerned with safety and security, few resources. Purchase familiar brands, mainstream music.

Types Driven by Ideals (Guided by knowledge and principles).

Thinkers: Mature, satisfied, comfortable, reflective, well educated. Purchase well-regarded music but are open to considering new products that promise quality and integrity.

Believers: Conservative, conventional, traditional, family- and community-oriented. Purchase familiar and established items, mainstream and noncontroversial music, established artists.

Types Focused on Achievement (Demonstrating success to peers).

Achievers: Goal- and career-oriented, conservative, prefer predictability and stability. Purchase prestige products, established brands, "success" imagery and atmospherics.

Strivers: Trend-conscious, fun-loving, stylish, money-oriented, approval-seeking. Purchase to impress, as conspicuous consumption; trendy, "latest thing" music.

Types Focused on Self-Expression (Desiring social and physical activity).

Experiencers: Enthusiastic, impulsive, excitement-seeking, fashionable, risk-oriented, offbeat; purchase trendy music, whatever may be currently considered cool.

Makers: Practical, self-sufficient, skilled, energetic, physical, project-oriented, traditional. Purchase for practicality and function; mainstream, established music.

To put VALS to practical use, you might generalize which of these types would be most attracted to your music. Then you'd emphasize the type's desired attributes in your packaging and communications. The atmosphere, symbolism, and mood may be left as is in the music itself but highlighted in promotion.

As VALS recommends, you

- Link sales messages to motivations
- Use language and images that resonate with your targeted market segment
- Choose communication media that reach large numbers of desired target consumers

Let's say your music is already on the market and has attracted positive reviews in cutting-edge media that call it "up and coming," "style-setting," and "the talk of the cultural elite." You might target what VALS calls *strivers:* trend-conscious approval-seekers, who purchase to impress. Sales messages could give consumers the feeling they'd be ahead of the curve if they bought the item; friends would be impressed; they'd be seen as "fashionistas." Language and images could evoke "cool," "stylish," "edgy"—however those are symbolized at the time. Communication media could include trendy magazines and Web sites.

VALS is one approach to motivational segmentation. Other ways of looking at human behavior are also used by marketers seeking to encourage purchase by appealing to underlying needs and motivators.

For example, you could use Maslow's hierarchy to determine whether a particular emerging market is a promising target for your marketing effort.

Psychologist Abraham Maslow developed a list of human needs, arranged in order from the most critical to the least critical, and argued that people will not consider satisfying certain needs unless the more critical ones are satisfied first. In Maslow's hierarchy, the most critical needs are **physiological:** food and shelter. Next is **safety and security**. Once those needs are satisfied, **social needs**—for sense of belonging and love—come next. Fourth on the list are **esteem needs**, including sense of recognition and status. Finally, **self-actualization needs** are addressed, referring to self-development and growth.

Maslow's hierarchy would suggest that if a developing country were primarily focused on safety and security, chances are its population would be minimally inclined to consider art and entertainment. In contrast, if a country were largely affluent, with its needs for physiological well-being and safety largely met, it would likely be a ripe market for social-bonding products (including group social events such as live performances and new music, the discovery of which can be shared with friends), status-enhancing products (such as music approved by the consumer's reference groups), and self-actualizing products (music that can expand one's perceptions or understandings).

One can always find exceptions to these generalizations. During the Great Depression, for example, a time when economic security was at low ebb and when many were struggling to address life's basic needs, fanciful, extravagant, "escapist" Hollywood movies directed by choreographer Busby Berkeley were highly popular. This would suggest that when having difficulty meeting essential needs, some people will seek distraction and mood enhancement in the form of uplifting entertainment. If the price is right, music might still be marketable in countries tending toward low per capita incomes (adjusted for purchasing-power parity).

Conclusion: Take theories about human motivation as broad guidelines and frameworks rather than as strict rules, and then research your target market for more direct evidence of local purchasing habits, behaviors, and possible motivators.

Behavioral Factors Influencing Purchase. Some people purchase products out of habit: the daily cup of coffee or tea, for example. Unlike some products, music purchase is not typically a habitual activity. The buying process is somewhat complex, involving several stages that have been defined by such marketing experts as author Philip Kotler. Understanding these stages, you can optimize your marketing strategy to help the potential buyer move smoothly through them, as follows:

1. **Recognition of need:** The music fan has read about or heard a snippet of music by a new artist, and likes what he has read or heard enough to consider purchase. Music marketing ensures those opportunities exist—that press coverage and airplay are occurring so that people can gain awareness.

2. **Search for more information:** Before buying, the music fan wants to learn more, to see if his initial perceptions apply more broadly, not just to a snippet of music or the opinions of one reviewer. Music marketing ensures that sources of information exist, in the form of Web sites, press coverage, song excerpts, and more.

3. **Evaluation of alternatives:** The music fan has limited money to spend and must choose between buying the new artist's CD or purchasing something else: different music, a different form of entertainment, or another kind of item. Music marketing designs packaging and communication to draw attention, to "stand out in the crowd," to emphasize appeal, to stimulate interest.

4. **Decision to purchase:** The music fan is ready to buy, as long as other factors don't make the buying process difficult. Music marketing ensures that there are no barriers to availability and that purchasing can be done easily.

5. **Desire to become a return customer:** The music fan develops loyalty to the "brand" and will purchase future music by the same artist. Music marketing strives to ensure not just satisfaction with the product but all-out delight: the music is outstanding, the production is high end, the available information is abundant, and avenues to customer feedback and involvement are open.

Here are some examples of atmosphere, symbolism, and mood matched with buyer characteristics discussed above.

Music Style	Atms. Sym. Mood	Age	Gender	Married/ Single	Edu.	Income	Reference Groups	VALS Type
Country	Folksy Rural Traditional Simple emotions	18–24 (16%) 25–54 (64%)	M=34% F=66%	Mrd.=40% Sgl.=48%	College grad. 14.5%	$30–49K=23.3% $50–74K=22% $75K+ =27.6%	NASCAR fans	Believers Makers Achievers
Jazz	Sophisticated Urbane Expressive Complex	18–24 (7%) 25–62 (89%)	M=78% F=22%	Mrd.=60% Sgl.=40%	College grad. 48%	$24–44K=28% $45–64K=24% $65–84K=20% $85K+ =23%	Liberal politics	Inno- vators Thinkers Strivers

Note: Many other criteria may be applied.

How do you use this information to tailor your product for foreign audiences? Find out where the audiences go for information, and reach them through those channels. Explore their motivators, and tailor communications to appeal to them. Make sure that you emphasize, in packaging and communications, the ideas and styles that target audience's value.

FORM CUSTOMIZATION

The form of the musical product refers to its delivery medium, or format, whether physical compact disc, downloadable digital files, or some other package. The book *This Business of Music Marketing and Promotion* points out that the core product, the raw product, is musical information. This information can be transmitted in many different ways. Formats tend to change in tandem with technological innovation, with playback hardware and music software evolving simultaneously. Often the transmittal technology leads the way. The Internet, for example, spawned downloadable digital files. The current mobile phone craze, for another example, has created a market for music ringtones.

The form you choose for delivery of your music to a specific market segment will depend on the distribution channels that offer the best market penetration, in combination with the preferences of the local customers.

To summarize, current options for sale of recorded music include the following:

- Compact discs and related products such as DualDiscs
- Older hard-copy formats (cassette tapes and vinyl discs)
- Downloads for use on computers and in portable digital music players
- Streaming audio for use on computers and in portable digital music players
- Ringtones and other music-related messaging

Of the current forms of music delivery, the compact disc is expected to remain the primary choice of customers for several more years. In 2004, CDs still accounted for 90 percent of recorded music sales, down slightly from sales in 2000, up from 77 percent in 1995. The music industry is always looking for new formats to induce purchase and "repurposing" of favorite music. It has not been particularly successful in developing a hard-copy format to replace the CD. The so-called DualDisc—playing a CD on one side and a DVD-Audio (with assorted audio-video features) on the other side—attracted some buyers.

Older hard-copy formats may be used in special circumstances. Cassette-tape players, for example, are still used by consumers who have not upgraded to digital, although this status could indicate lack of discretionary income or indifference to purchasing new music, suggesting that manufacturing cassettes for this market would be inadvisable. Vinyl records are sought by certain vintage-music collectors. There are pockets of such interest in Japan, for example. In Finland in 2005, vinyl accounted for 20 percent of recorded music sales, according to a local distributor. Decisions to manufacture vinyl will usually be based on an unusual convergence of artist style and market demand: a proponent of analog recording making music for an antidigital crowd, for example.

The prediction for the future, according to some experts, is that the dominant form of music purchase will be a monthly fee for access to all music, at any time, anywhere. That will mean subscriptions to an archive or archives of all available music for playback on both portable and stationary devices, from PCs to cell phones. But because there is no precedent for an exclusively pack-ageless approach to selling recorded music, the prediction of a digital-only future remains highly speculative. Time will reveal whether it is accurate.

On the way to that possible future, digital music downloads and subscriptions, through services such as Apple's iTunes, Rhapsody, MusicNet@AOL, MusicMatch (owned by Yahoo), and Napster, are expected to capture about 12 percent of total music consumer spending by 2009. Yet they accounted for only about $150 million annual sales in the U.S. as of 2005—"small change" compared with the $11 billion total U.S. record-industry revenues, according to David Card, a senior analyst with JupiterResearch.

A movement toward convergence of cell phone technology with music downloading and subscription has gained strength since the early 2000s. There were an estimated 1.5 billion cell phone owners in 2005, a huge potential market. Phone makers included Motorola, Nokia, and Sony Ericsson. Services included Britain's Orange (charging $7.70 a month for 4 megabytes of downloads plus $2.90 a song), Czechoslovakia's Eurotel, Norway's Telenor, and Singapore's SingTel Mobile. The U.S. wireless carrier Sprint offered a $6-per-month streaming audio service for cell phones.

Many of those cell phone owners—23 percent of U.S. owners—downloaded a music ringtone in 2005. The popularity of ringtones is such that in 2004 global sales were valued at about $2.5 billion, projected to rise to 18 percent of the music market by 2008.

Some record companies are now encouraging recording artists to record versions of their music expressly for the mobile music market. Ringtone and ringback versions of songs are, at this writing, significant enough additions to the product mix to justify customization at the product creation level.

Taking a format's projected growth into consideration, you also look at the capacity of specific markets to consume the format. Compact disc technology has long been established around the world. The newer formats, on the other hand, have more favorable markets in some areas than others. Asia and Europe, for example, have been well ahead of the U.S. in the technology supporting music downloads to cell phones, and consequently the U.S. has lagged behind in providing downloads for cell phone use. In contrast, when Sony rolled out its Chaku-Uta mobile phone master ringtone download service in Japan, it earned an impressive $94 million within a year.

Similarly, the Internet has penetrated different populations at different rates. This suggests that some markets might be better for downloads and subscriptions than others.

Audience age ranges play a role in format preferences. Buyers of CDs tend to skew older. (Of eight age-range segments surveyed by the RIAA in 2003, the 45+ segment represented the largest share of total CD sales). Younger audiences, wherever they are, tend to prefer new-technology formats such as portable downloads.

Deciding on the right product mix of compact discs and new-media formats can be based on market data gathered for prospective target territories, as shown in the following chart.

MARKET FACTORS INFLUENCING CHOICE OF PRODUCT FORMAT

	Market Conditions					
Product Format	Younger Population	Older Pop.	Retail Sales Activity	Internet Penetration	Mobile Player Usage	Cell Phone Ownership
Compact Disc		F	F	F		
Desktop Downloads	F			F		
Portable Downloads	F				F	
Streaming	F			F	F	
Ringtones	F					F

PACKAGING THE PRODUCT FOR FOREIGN AUDIENCES

Packaging consists, in part, of deciding on the delivery format for the music—hard copy or download. But here we focus instead on the enclosure and wrapping in which the product and format are delivered to the market. Because digital downloads lack packaging (apart from the digital promotion discussed in Chapter 10), the packaging discussed now is that of physically delivered music. The book *This Business of Music Marketing and Promotion* details essential physical, labeling, and design requirements for all packaging, regardless of the territory in which it will be marketed. But in addition to those requirements, others exist when packaging for foreign markets. They occur in the areas of packaging/labeling regulations and aesthetics/symbolism.

FOREIGN PACKAGING/LABELING REGULATORY REQUIREMENTS

When exporting, you'll come across regulations for labeling and packaging. Your importer will usually inform you of the target country's requirements, but you should be aware of the kinds of regulations you may encounter.

Packaging. Certain countries set up limitations on the kinds of materials that can be used in packaging. The European Union, for example, requires adherence to environmentally friendly packaging and recycling rules. Manufacturers apply for an "eco-label" to print on their packages to indicate compliance with rules and to help consumers make decisions about the products they buy. Germany has a separate recycling program, compliance with which is indicated by affixing a "green dot" to packaging, obtained by paying a license fee. (The importer handles this and provides you with information.) Other EU countries, including the U.K., Austria, Belgium, France, Italy, Spain, and

Sweden, have similar programs. For information, visit http://europa.eu.int/comm/environment/ecolabel.

Japan also has implemented package recycling rules. Importers must pay fees for recycling, so they'll take those costs into consideration when determining whether to import a product. If you're exporting to Japan, you should familiarize yourself with its packaging and recycling requirements so that you can anticipate whether your packaging will be seen as problematic.

To research regulations in different countries, a good place to begin is www.export911.com, or call 1-800-USA-TRADE.

Labeling. Just as import/export paperwork requirements vary from country to country, so do on-package labeling rules differ. If you're exporting, your importer will be your first source of information about what to include. Typical requirements are country of origin, name of product, name and address of manufacturer, and labeling in the local language. The Hong Kong Trade Development Council at www.tdctrade.com/sme/ir/index.htm lists labeling and other requirements for China, Japan, the European Union, and other selected countries.

Some countries may also have requirements for "parental advisory" labels for music with explicitly sexual lyrics. For the United States' approach to this, see the Recording Industry Association of America's comments online at www.riaa.com/issues/parents.

For general information about information and labeling requirements on compact discs, see *This Business of Music Marketing and Promotion*, Revised Edition, Chapter 5.

Packaging and Labeling for U.S. Retail. Here's a checklist of procedures for readying your recorded music for retail in the world's largest music market, the United States. Many of the steps are applicable everywhere:

- Decide on the most attractive packaging. Do you want a standard jewel box? (It's cheaper.) Or a more user-friendly DigiPak? (It's more expensive.) Do you want a cheap two-panel insert or a more elaborate eight-panel, full-color insert? Before opting for cheap, keep in mind that more elaborate packaging can convey a favorable impression of the product—as high end and high quality—that can translate into better sales, more than making up for the extra packaging cost.

- Get a bar code and have it printed on the CD. This, basically, is a requirement both for appearing professional and for actually being professional, since retailers scan the bar code to record the sales transaction and need it for their business. Get a bar code either from your manufacturer (usually cheap) or from the Uniform Code Council (usually expensive), which sends you a numerical code that you then have to convert to bar-code art. Its Web site, www.uc-council.org, tells all.

- Choose a record catalogue number, for identification on all sales documentation and communications. This assumes that you have a name for the record label. If not, create one. (Check the Internet and the U.S. trademark office to be sure the name hasn't already been used.) The catalogue number should consist of a three-letter abbreviation of the record label name plus a numerical code. It's recommended that the numerical code match digits 7 through 11 of the UPC number, just for uniformity.

- Include on the CD package all the necessary copyright and manufacturing information. Take a look at other CDs to see what is standard. The book *This Business of Music Marketing and Promotion* goes into some detail about packaging requirements.

Note these basic packaging requirements:

Back of the Tray Card (the permanent insert behind the CD holder in a standard "jewel box" package):

- Bar code and UPC number
- Song titles
- Producer name(s)
- The following copyright and manufacturing wording, set in smaller type if necessary:
  - (p)(c) [Your Label Name, Label Address.] Made in [name the country]. All rights reserved. Unauthorized duplication is a violation of applicable laws. [Your catalogue number.]

Compact Disc Label:

- Artist name
- CD title
- Song titles
- The same copyright and manufacturing wording that's on the tray card, but it can be printed quite small, even curving around the outside edge of the CD.

AESTHETIC AND SYMBOLIC ASPECTS OF PACKAGING

The art used on the cover of your domestically released CD might not be appropriate for another country. You may have to use alternate art for CDs that you wish to sell outside your own country.

Different beliefs, values, norms, customs, sensibilities, and attitudes yield different responses to visual imagery. One culture's object of humor or ridicule may be another culture's sacred cow. An innocuous image in a photograph may have important meaning, positive or negative, to a foreign viewer. The symbolism of a person's mode of dress or physical positioning may be highly significant to someone of another culture.

The singer Shakira used different imagery for her partner albums *Oral Fixation, Vol. 2* and *Fijación Oral, Vol. 1*. On *Oral Fixation*, intended mainly for the American market, Shakira is shown as Eve, covered only with a few leaves and poised to bite into forbidden fruit, original-sin style. The U.S. market responds positively to sexual imagery, and Shakira felt comfortable playing to that. For the other album, intended for the Spanish market, Shakira is seen fully clothed, holding a baby—a more modest and conservative depiction that a largely Roman Catholic audience would find acceptable.

Before committing to a cover design, research your intended market to determine how the imagery may be interpreted. Find out if there are any local taboos that you should avoid depicting. Check into whether particular colors have important meanings—in China, for example, white, blue, and black are associated with death. Look into hand gestures, clothing customs, and more. Just make sure you aren't introducing an unintended meaning in what you depict.

Obviously, make sure that the words you print don't have any unfortunate connotations in the country you're targeting. A well-known mistake along these lines was perpetrated by automobile manufacturer Chevrolet when it introduced the Chevy Nova to the South American market. In Spanish, "Nova" is heard to mean "doesn't go."

CHAPTER 5

Placing and Pricing Music for Foreign Sale

Imagine it: You're marketing in your chosen foreign country. You have decided on a basic business strategy, whether licensing, exporting, pursuing a joint venture, or, if you are highly experienced and committed, operating a wholly owned subsidiary. The depth of your involvement in the logistics of getting CDs from local warehouses to retail customers—that is, in land distribution—will vary depending on the strategy you've chosen.

If you are licensing, your involvement in distribution will be minimal: the licensee will distribute through its established channels.

For exporting, the importer will use its standard channels, but your involvement may be somewhat deeper, since you'll be concerned with promotion and other marketing matters that rely on some knowledge of the local commercial infrastructure.

For a joint venture, your involvement in distribution depends on how you and the partner have divided responsibilities. It is likely that you will have chosen the partner for its expertise in local distribution and promotion, so that your role in that area will be minimal. But perhaps not. You may have decided to take a more active role in distribution.

For a wholly owned subsidiary, your involvement will be complete. Responsibility for setting up effective and profitable distribution channels will be entirely yours.

Regardless of the strategy you've chosen, an understanding of music-distribution channels, how they can differ in different regions, and how channel length and complexity can affect product pricing is important for you to have. The knowledge can help you set a reasonable export price. It can ease determining when licensing is preferable to exporting. It can improve your collaboration with a joint-venture partner. And without it, your wholly owned subsidiary will never get off the ground.

DISTRIBUTION CHANNELS

Distribution channels consist of all the business entities involved in getting a product from the manufacturer to the customer. (They are part of the broader process called the *supply chain*, which encompasses all business processes from supply of raw material to delivery of the final product to customer and post-delivery services.) In international distribution, there are two distinct segments: (1) the country-to-country segment, and (2) the internal country segment. Getting product from country to country involves the exporting manufacturer, the importing distributor, and supporting businesses such as freight shippers, banks, export agencies (if used), and import agents (if used). But it's the internal country distribution process that is this chapter's focus.

A distribution channel can be as simple—or short—as a multinational record company's delivering CDs to a receiving warehouse of an entertainment superstore. A distribution channel can also be as complex—or long—as a record company's shipping to a chain of intermediaries that divide the shipment into smaller quantities for dissemination to an array of stores. Distribution options vary vastly from country to country, but the basic concept of distribution channels is uniform. The members of the distribution channel, working backward from the end customer, include retail outlets (stores where people buy), intermediaries that supply the retail outlets, and manufacturers of the product.

PLACES WHERE PEOPLE BUY MUSIC

People have many options for buying music, with different kinds of retailers suited to different customer needs. They include multinational music and entertainment retail chains, independent music stores, and general stores that stock music.

Entertainment superstore chains such as HMV and Virgin Megastores have outlets around the world. They offer a broad selection of music at discount prices—ideal for customers who like to browse, or who have in mind a current or still-in-print vintage recording that they'd like to purchase for as little money as possible. The superstore approach offers economies of scale for all participants. For the record manufacturer, these large stores represent an outlet for bulk sales: one stop, multiple units sold; minimal cost of selling, maximum volume of sale. The stores themselves receive volume discounts, which they are able to pass along to customers. If one thinks of the international music industry as largely an oligopoly, dominated by only a handful of multinational corporations, these superstores represent the retail sector of that oligopoly. (The remaining, "independent" part of the industry—thousands of indie record labels and retail outlets—has fluctuated in size from 30 to 17 percent of the worldwide market over the past few years.)

Smaller, independent general-music stores still exist but have increasingly been driven out of business by the superstores. The independents perhaps offer more personalized service, for customers who desire help in searching for music. But for the mass-marketing record company, they represent an inefficient way to get product to the market, since they tend to buy small quantities, and reaching them tends to involve a more complex, and expensive, distribution chain.

Another kind of small, independent store, particularly prevalent in Japan, specializes in specific music genres. They are ideal for customers who are devotees of particular genres and are willing to go out of their way and to pay more for access to a deeper selection within their favored stylistic bandwidth. For mass-market record companies, these stores are outside standard distribution channels. For small, independent record labels, specialty stores can be ideal for reaching niche market segments. If you specialize in electronic dance music, for example, a store devoted to that sound is perfect for getting your music to the right customers.

Increasingly, music can be found in stores that sell other kinds of goods. Discount general-goods chains like Wal-Mart, electronics stores such as Best Buy, drugstores, and even smaller specialty stores stock CDs appropriate for their respective customer segments. The superstores, of course, serve a broad customer segment—a general audience—and consequently stock music with broad appeal: the latest hits and the most popular artists.

INTERMEDIARIES

In situations where a multinational record company is supplying a large chain retailer, product is typically shipped directly through the record label's own distribution division. But in cases where a record label is too small to do its own distribution, or where a large company doesn't have in-house distribution capability in a particular territory or to a niche segment of the market, a third party is needed to help get product into stores. This intermediary party is called a distributor.

Distributors specialize in taking shipments from record companies and gathering orders from—and shipping product to—retail stores. Distributors mitigate the problem of record companies' having to serve many retailers individually; the distributor serves as a one-stop gateway to multiple retail outlets. For independent labels, a distributor is a necessity. Being represented by one validates the quality of a record in the eyes of the retailer, who knows and has worked with the distributor but may never have heard of the record label. As the Canadian Independent Record Production Association (CIRPA) states on its Web site, "Major-chain retailers are more cautious about stocking independently produced albums, and if an album does not have a major independent distributor or is not on a known independent label, it won't be accepted by music retailers."

There are different kinds of distributors.

As mentioned previously, major record companies such as Sony and Warner Music tend to have wholly owned distribution divisions that may act as profit centers but still add to the mother company's aggregate bottom line. These arrangements are examples of vertical integration, in which a single company owns multiple links in the supply chain in order to maximize profits by avoiding having to pay external suppliers.

Such corporate distribution arms may have global reach. In France, for example, the distribution operations of the four major music conglomerates account for 96 percent of supply activity. There is very little independent music distribution in France.

On the other hand, a conglomerate may decide that it is not economically advantageous to maintain its own distribution operation in a given territory. In Canada, Warner Music, Universal Music, and BMG (pre-Sony) outsourced distribution to Cinram, a Canadian company.

Similarly, a conglomerate may decide that its own distribution works best supplying large retail chains, but not so well selling and delivering to local independent stores. Warner, for example, hired third-party distributors to handle smaller retail accounts in the U.K.

A notable aspect of conglomerate distribution operations in foreign lands is that they often include local manufacturing. In other words, "MegaMusic Inc." doesn't necessarily ship U.S. product all over the world. Instead, it may manufacture discs within a foreign territory through its local manufacturing and distribution subsidiary. Why? Three good reasons: (1) avoid unnecessary shipping costs, (2) avoid distribution delays that might occur if shipping from afar, and (3) more accurately and cost-effectively customize products to meet local tastes, as discussed in Chapter 4. Manufacturing may be cheaper in the locality, and local product managers may have a clearer understanding of the kinds of product enhancements needed to increase local appeal, from inclusion of a local singing star on a track to remixes for dancehalls.

Apart from the Big Four's in-house distributors, there are independent distributors with multinational operations. Canada's Cinram is one such, offering service in Canada, the U.S., Europe, France, and Mexico.

Smaller independent distributors, such as the ones hired by Warner and BMG in England, may specialize in certain types of retail stores, such as neighborhood independents. In the U.S., specialists called rack jobbers handle music racks in general stores such as Kmart and Wal-Mart. In Quebec, the company Distribution Select handles most of the panoply of independent French-language record labels.

Certain distributors specialize in musical genres. Japan, for example, hosts the following specialty distributors:

- Ahora Corporation: World music, country, folk, blues, Latin, hip-hop, other
- Area B: Classical, jazz, blues, Latin, other
- Blues Interactions: Dance, electronic, blues, R&B, reggae, other
- Mikasa Tsusho: Traditional, ethnic, other
- Tokyo M-Plus: Classical, jazz, blues, ethnic, world

Distributors vary in the mix of services they offer. To the basic service of taking shipment, storing inventory, selling to retail accounts, fulfilling orders, and tracking sales, some companies might add marketing consultation and promotion advice. Some offer pressing-and-distribution deals, in which they arrange for and pay for manufacturing. Netherlands-based Astral Music views itself as more hands-on, promotionally, than one typically finds in a distributor. As the company's CEO, Rob Kuliboer, explained to the *Music Business Journal*'s Magne Hoven:

> Another task is to phone and e-mail all our customers and ask, "What's selling for you? What's doing well for you?" We are fishing for feedback, which we can then relay onto the record labels. . . .
>
> We also promote. We know deejays and record companies worldwide. We can contact those deejays and say, for example: "We have something by Olav Basoski for you, are you playing it?" If they say yes, we will make a note of that on our site, and put the sign of approval on the sales note.

We don't license, but we do a lot of work in building and branding our artists—something that the majors are not willing to do much of anymore.

LENGTH OF DISTRIBUTION CHANNEL

The number of intermediaries between the record company and the customer can be few or many. A distribution channel with few intermediaries is, obviously, easier to work with—there are fewer deals to arrange, entities to count on, and pieces of the financial pie to share. Short, efficient distribution chains occur primarily in developed countries. A channel with many intermediaries, on the other hand, involves more business arrangements, more links of which one or two might be weak, and more shares of earnings to factor into the price.

A **concentrated market**, in which only a few retail outlets dominate, tends to operate with short distribution channels.

A **fragmented market**, consisting of many small retail outlets and competing participants, tends to require longer distribution channels.

The United States has a highly concentrated system that in some cases employs a two-member distribution chain consisting of record company and retailer. A music conglomerate may have its own distribution, which deals directly with buyers for large retail chains. (Warner Music does this, for example.) In other cases, a third entity—an independent distribution company—may be involved. There are numerous variations on this arrangement depending on the final retail destination, but overall the system is efficient and concentrated. The mainstream sector, in its oligopolistic structure, is largely closed to smaller companies not affiliated with one of the dominant corporations.

SHORT DISTRIBUTION SUPPLY CHAIN

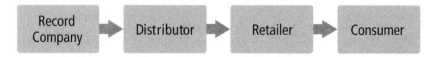

In contrast, Japan has a somewhat fragmented market. Tokyo, which along with Osaka accounts for roughly 85 percent of Japanese music sales, hosts a diverse array of independent music stores operating alongside the superstore Virgin, Tower, and HMV outlets. (As earlier noted, the smaller stores tend to specialize in particular music genres.) While the superstores such as Tower—a separate entity from the now-defunct American corporation—still dominate the distribution network, the market share of the independents has been rising. This kind of fragmentation typically involves a less efficient process of piecemeal stocking by many distribution entities rather than high-quantity inventory supplied by fewer distribution channel members.

India, as another example, has a formerly fragmented market that since around 2000 has been leaning more toward concentration. Gurmeet Singh, business director of the Indian record label Music Today, said in 2006 that until "about six years back . . . all retailers would come to warehouses of various wholesalers and buy music for their respective retail shops. Retailers who are unable to come are dispatched stocks based on telephonic orders. [Since] six years ago, two retail chains have come up with 100 stores each of various sizes (800 to 15,000 square feet). These chains—Music World and PlanetM—have taken up 50 percent of the business in metros as of now."

INDIA'S DISTRIBUTION NETWORK

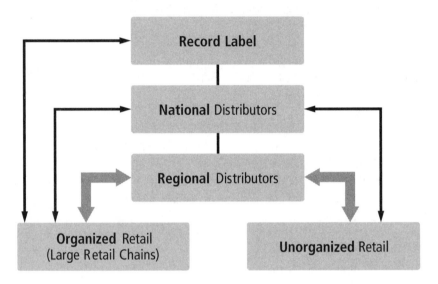

Syed Rizwan Mehdi, merchandising officer of Music World in Hyderabad, India, points out that most of the buying by "organized retail"— the large retail chains—happens through regional distributors, but "these retail majors also directly place orders with national distributors, or in some cases directly approach or get approached by record labels, depending on the universal appeal of the artist/band. By doing so the retailers avail [themselves of] bulk buying discounts and other such promotional discounts. Every city has its own set of demand, preference, and liking for artists/bands and genres of music, so the regional [local] merchandiser at the retailer holds the key in placing fresh-demand order."

The length of the distribution channel, in addition to affecting costs and logistics, also has an impact on your promotion and advertising strategy, as is discussed in Chapter 10.

Ideally, you'll have the option of choosing between markets with more or less concentrated systems, allowing you the best cost-benefit. But for a newcomer to a market, there may not be a choice. If you want to break into a market, you have to use the existing system, at least initially. The potential for sales may be so great that it outweighs the costs of a long supply chain.

PRICING STRATEGIES

With knowledge of the distribution chain, you can begin to understand the costs, above manufacturing, that contribute to the final over-the-counter price.

To put this discussion in a broader marketing context, the price of a product is one of the critical elements—along with product design, placement for distribution, and promotion—in successful marketing. The price, among other functions,

- Determines the amount of profit the manufacturer will receive over and above costs
- Affects the perception of the product's value
- Serves as a tool to achieve strategic goals
- Positions the product in relation to competitor pricing

Price has been a controversial subject in the music industry for many years, recently made more so by the advent of Internet file sharing and the resulting perception among some that music ought to be obtainable for free. Correcting that perception—communicating that makers of music, like makers of other products, are fully entitled to fair compensation—while setting a price that consumers can accept as reasonable given other product choices, has been at the core of the music industry's increasingly frenetic struggle to find a way forward.

Under domestic marketing circumstances, pricing is a precarious balancing act. International marketing can compound the difficulty due to added costs of cross-border trade. Imports are generally more expensive than domestic products, putting them at disadvantage in the marketplace.

The balancing act of pricing generally goes like this: You have fixed costs (recording, artwork) and variable costs (manufacturing) that you need to recoup. You'd also like to make a profit—an extra boost to your return on investment (ROI). You calculate that Price A will meet your ROI needs nicely—if all goes well. "All going well" depends on how the marketplace reacts to Price A. Is Price A comparable to what others charge for similar products? Is Price A realistic given the life cycle stage of the product? (If new and unknown, should the product have a lower price to induce initial sale?) If Price A is too high, are you willing to lower it and delay recoupment of your costs?

Add international factors into the balancing act, and you find yourself also dealing with whether the costs of international distribution will permit a reasonable end price, whether international audiences exhibit buying behavior different from that of your domestic market, whether your expected price will yield you more or less due to fluctuations in currency exchange rates, and more.

Overall, considerations in international pricing include the following:

- Balance between earnings needs and end-price viability
- Relationship to competitor prices (other CDs, and domestic CDs)
- Consumer perception of value (both the wholesale buyer and the end customer)

- Price discrimination
- Regulations affecting pricing
- Strategic goals, short term and long term (market penetration, early cash recovery, market skimming, predatory pricing, multipoint pricing strategy, experience-curve pricing)
- Product-line and life cycle pricing (new release, mid-price, budget)
- Promotional allowances (for free goods, promo copies, advertising)

BALANCE BETWEEN EARNINGS NEEDS
AND END-PRICE VIABILITY

The price that the exporting record company offers to the foreign distributor has to achieve several goals: (1) cover the costs of making the record plus a profit margin; (2) have enough of a margin to allow for standard discounts to the distributor for volume sales and for promotional allowances; and (3) allow for a reasonable over-the-counter price to the customer after adding costs of freight, tariffs, distribution fees, retailer profit, and sales tax or VAT.

Typically, an exporter sets an export price—the price offered to the foreign distributor—that is roughly the same as its domestic distributor wholesale price. In the United States, that would be around 50 percent of the suggested retail list price (SRLP). (The SRLP, by the way, usually represents the topmost price for a CD and is rarely the price actually paid by the customer, given retail discounts commonly applied by stores. A disc with an $18.98 SRLP might be offered to the customer for only $11.99.)

WHERE YOUR EXPORT EARNINGS GO

Your per-unit export price*	$7.00		
Less cost of recording	−2.00		
Subtotal	5.00		
Less artist royalty**		−1.14	
Subtotal		3.86	
Less mechanical royalty***			−0.91
Subtotal			2.95
Less cost of manufacturing			−1.00
GROSS MARGIN			**$1.95**

* After discount for promotion/advertising allowance. This is a hypothetical price, for illustration only.

** Assumes artist royalty is foreign rate of 6% of $18.98 SRLP (foreign rates tend to be smaller than domestic).

*** Per-unit royalty paid to songwriters and publishers. U.S. rate as of April 2007 is $.091 per song plus $0.175 per minute over five minutes. This case assumes ten songs on a recording.

If the export price covers your costs and delivers a desired profit, your attention might well stop there. But actually receiving that price depends on what happens after you transfer your goods: fees are paid and compensatory percentages are added to the price, distributor and retailer margins are factored in, and taxes are added, inflating the price to a final sum that may or may not be acceptable to the market. If it isn't, you may not receive anything.

That final price depends largely on the length and complexity of the supply chain, as discussed previously. The longer the supply chain, theoretically, the greater the price inflation, and the higher the retail price. In a short supply chain where the distributor's desired margin is 15–25 percent (of the price to retailer), the retailer's desired margin is 30–40 percent, and there's a VAT of 15 percent, an export price of $7 could add up to a retail price of over $14. In a longer supply chain with the same distributor and retailer margins and the same VAT, but with the addition of other intermediaries requiring payment, the export price of $7 could add up to a retail price of nearly $20. The following charts illustrate the differences between short and long supply chains. The first shows how the price rises through the chain; the second (next page) shows the fees that inflate the price.

The distributor can provide information about how your export price will translate into a retail price. Bear in mind, too, that freight and tariffs factor into the final price. The distributor typically pays those amounts; but as costs, they are passed along to the final customer.

COMPARATIVE PRICE STRUCTURES OF SHORT AND LONG SUPPLY CHAINS

Short Supply Chain

Record Company Price to Distributor	Distributor Price to Retailer (20% margin)*	Retailer Price (30% margin)*	VAT (15%)	Final Price to Customer**
$7.00	8.75	12.50	+1.88	= $14.38

Long Supply Chain

Record Company Price	Distributor Price (20% mgn)*	Regional Distributor Price (15% mgn)*	Local Distributor Price (15% mgn)*	Retailer Price (30% mgn)*	VAT (15%)	Final Price to Customer**
$7.00	8.75	10.30	12.12	17.32	+2.60	= $19.92

*   The channel member's share of the price he offers. Percentages vary.
** Excluding additions for tariffs, freight, and other costs.
Note: All percentages and prices are estimates for illustration only; exact amounts vary widely depending on market location.

COMPARATIVE CHANNEL COSTS OF SHORT AND LONG SUPPLY CHAINS

Short Supply Chain

Record Company Price	Distributor Share (15–25%)*	Retailer Share (30–40%)*	VAT (15%)	Final Price to Customer**
$7.00	+1.75 (20%)	+ 3.75 (30%)	+1.88	= $14.38

Long Supply Chain

Record Company Price	Distributor Share (15–25%)*	Regional Distributor Share (c. 15%)*	Local Distributor Share (c. 15%)*	Retailer Share (30–40%)*	VAT (15%)	Final Price to Customer**
$7.00	+1.75 (20%)	+1.55 (15%)	+1.82 (15%)	+ 5.20 (30%)	+2.60	= $19.92

* Desired percentage range, as percentage of the price offered to buyers.
** Excluding additions for tariffs, freight, and other costs.
Note: All percentages and prices are estimates for illustration only; exact amounts vary widely depending on market location.

DISCOUNTS FOR VOLUME SALES AND PROMOTIONAL ALLOWANCES

When deciding on a price, in addition to covering your costs you need to consider the standard practice of offering the distributor a discount for purchases of large quantities and another discount that is in effect a payment for advertising and promotion.

A volume discount of 15 to 20 percent is not unusual. Thus, you need to calculate your price such that *after* the volume discount your earnings will cover your costs to your satisfaction. (If they don't, you may still want to proceed for some other strategic reason, such as gaining entry to a new market.)

Similarly, you may need to provide the distributor with funds to pass on to the retailer for in-store promotion and advertising. The amount varies depending on what packages are offered or available. The payment is typically made in the form of a discount off the price to the distributor, who passes it on the retailer. Again, your price calculation should account for this kind of "payment."

An alternative to these kinds of discounts emerged in Canada, when Universal Music lowered its top-line SRLP to $14.98 ($12.90 U.S.) in exchange for no longer providing discounts or advertising allowances.

Competitive Pricing

When you set a price, customers evaluate it in comparison with other products vying for their money, whether other compact discs or other forms of entertainment. Whether the price of your CD is higher or lower than other products may factor into the buy-or-not-buy decision.

Music isn't like other products. Where buyers may look at two different brands of the same frozen food and choose the cheaper one, with music there is no "brand X" replica of, say, the new Bruce Springsteen album. Since the Bruce Springsteen album is unique, it stands to reason that the record company, seeing no competition, would charge as high a price as possible.

Popular Perception

A music product is unique, so it can be priced without regard for competing products.

A monopoly can charge what it wishes; similarly, a unique popular artist, with no "cheaper alternative" to his or her inimitable sound, can and should charge top price.

Alternate Reality

A music product is only one among many entertainment choices; pricing must be competitive.

Even if the artist is unique, and may be a must-buy item for hard-core fans, many other consumers may weigh it against other leisure-time products, from movie DVDs to games. An uncompetitive price may be the tipping point for a no-buy decision.

For many years, that axiom applied. But today the marketplace is flooded with entertainment choices. Nowadays, the price does matter, and buyers may look elsewhere if your product is perceived to be overpriced.

Imported music, as a prime example, tends to have higher prices than domestic music and for that reason faces a marketplace hurdle. In Japan, that relationship is turned on its head, since prices for domestic music are regulated to the point where Japan-originated CDs actually cost more than imports. Some companies, to avoid the regulations and make their price more competitive, have their artists record outside the country and sell in Japan as an import—*gray importing* is the term applied to this practice.

So the challenge in pricing music for international sale is in part one of balancing cost and desired profit against prices that are too high to compete with other products, whether domestic music or other kinds of entertainment. In 2003, music retailer Philip Robinson, director of the British online store CD

WOW!, described market-aware pricing as key to success. As he told the *Music Business Journal's* Alexis Fletcher, "We really believe that the reason why CD WOW! has done well is because it has actually met the expectations of the market, with regard to what a product is worth. We think £8.99—including free delivery—in relation to other things that are in the market, is 'the' price. Obviously, for our business model it is great if everyone else is selling higher and we are only selling at £8.99. I think that as you see now with Tesco [the British grocery home-shopping service that also sells books, DVDs, and CDs], who sells almost everything for £9.99, CD-WOW! isn't a promotion—it is a regular running thing."

CONSUMER-BASED PRICING

The preceding discussion rests on a cost-based approach, a target-return approach (setting a desired profit), and a competition-based approach. But there's a conflict between the cost of distribution and the willingness of the market to accept prices further inflated by long supply chains and high tariffs. A dedicated customer may well purchase the higher-priced import because the item is unique—it has music unavailable elsewhere. But a less-discriminating customer might just decide to purchase the cheaper domestic recording, or download a single song rather than buy an entire album, or wait until the CD price is discounted, or invest instead in a cell phone.

Here are the consumer-centric factors to consider when pricing:

• Purchasing power parity
• Perceived value
• Expected demand (for a long-awaited album)

Earlier chapters have described purchasing power parity as the relative value of per capita income—the relative wealth of comparative countries. In a country with a per capita PPP value of $40,000 U.S., a CD that sells for $11.99 is a highly affordable purchase. But in a country with PPP value of $7,500, the CD for $11.99 is more expensive relative to income. Turn that CD into an import with a tariff-and-distribution-inflated price of $22, and the earner of $7,500 per year is faced with spending nearly 0.3 percent of annual income on that CD—an unappetizing prospect. So looking at a country's PPP is a way of getting a quick, macro-level sense of how a price will be perceived by the general population. If your export's end-of-the-supply-chain price is too high to be competitive in the market, you try to bring it down by adjusting your export price and look for an upside in terms of new-market penetration, or you decide to find another way into the market, or you go elsewhere.

Don't forget that the end price will be affected by the currency exchange rate. If your domestic currency is strong against the foreign country's currency, the exported CD will be even more expensive for the foreign buyer.

Perceived value has to do with the customer's perception of the price relative to the content. In music, it's getting ever more difficult to establish value—especially of a product format, like the compact disc, that has been on the market long enough to begin to seem like "old technology." Increasingly, value is established not just by the music but also by the buzz of offering it in an exciting new form, such as a cell-phone ringtone. So how do you establish value in the crusty old compact disc? You either create an unavoidable buzz around the artist and the release, through smart, targeted messaging transmitted through accurately targeted media (more about which in Chapter 10), or you *add value* to the CD by providing something extra, from a bonus track to special packaging to a brilliantly conceived sales incentive.

If you deliver CDs to a market full of pent-up demand, as was the case in England when Kate Bush released her first album in twelve years, you're in a situation where you can comfortably choose a price to suit various strategic goals. You can skim the "cream" off the market by charging a high initial price that eager fans will pay, or sell higher initial quantities—penetrating further into the market—by charging a lower initial price.

Your decisions about pricing can be carried out based on discussion with your foreign distributor, who should fully understand the local market and customer behavior.

The distributor, by the way, is as much of a customer to you as is the record fan on the street. The price you offer the distributor has to be attractive. The distributor will want to sell records and make money, calculating what an effective end price should be, what he wants to earn in profit, what the retailer will want to earn, and what has to be paid in tariffs and other fees. If your price is too high, this first customer, the distributor, may decide not to buy.

PRICE DISCRIMINATION

The fact that the same product may be sold in different countries for different prices—a condition known as *price discrimination*—raises some interesting questions. One is: If I can buy an album for $11.99 in Country A that sells for $20 in Country B, why not buy up a quantity of them in Country A and resell them for a profit in Country B? This practice is called *arbitrage* and, when pursued under certain other circumstances, such as buying and selling currencies in the foreign exchange market to take advantage of predicted shifts in exchange rates, it is quite legitimate. If you're a manufacturer, however, you don't want to see your product subject to this kind of gray-market trading.

Before looking at disadvantages and advantages of price discrimination, it's worth looking at its scope, in numbers. What does recorded music cost in different countries, and why? Interestingly, compact discs tend to be cheaper in the United States than elsewhere. One might think that a product would be cheaper in a market where per capita income was lower. In this case, one would be wrong. The U.S. has one of the highest per capita incomes in the world. Elsewhere, in countries with lower incomes, CDs have tended to cost more.

COMPARATIVE COMPACT DISC PRICES

	1996	2003
U.S.	$16	$15
Japan	25	26
U.K.	24	17
Germany	23	19
Canada	14	13

Note: Figures are based on currency exchange rates of the given years.

The differences in pricing are based on a number of factors. One is difference in perception of the value of the item. A given country may be more culturally attuned to purchasing a certain kind of music than another country, and thus its consumers may be willing to pay more. Competition may be higher in some countries than in others, making it difficult to set a higher price. Incomes may be lower in one country than another, requiring a lower price (unless other factors, such as cultural demand, serve as a counterbalance).

Variation in demand is referred to as *elasticity*. Demand that is highly *elastic* is price conscious: change in price will trigger a significant change in demand. Raise the price, for example, and demand will drop off. This occurs typically in conditions of high competition and low disposable income, although cultural tastes can play a countervailing role. Demand that is *inelastic* is relatively unresponsive to changes in price. You can charge a higher price without a significant drop-off in sales. This condition is present where there is not much competition, where disposable incomes are higher, or where the artist has a hard-core following willing to pay a high price. If the remaining Beatles were to reunite and record a new album, demand for that CD would be said to be *in*elastic; slight price changes up or down would not really affect the number of people buying that record.

So what does this all mean to the music-pricing decision? Knowing whether the conditions for elastic or inelastic demand exist in a region or territory can determine whether you are able to use price discrimination to your advantage. If a country has low product competition, decent incomes, and cultural propensity toward your music, then demand may be inelastic, allowing you to set a higher price without necessarily worrying about losing sales. The benefit of this, of course, is that your higher profits in this territory may make up for lower profits elsewhere.

But what about that gray market mentioned earlier? A higher price in one country may open the door to arbitrage—some unethical businessperson buying your product where it's sold cheaply and reselling it in the high-price zone for profit. In the music business, of course, where all-out piracy, bootlegging, and counterfeiting are rampant, the problem of arbitrage is relatively minor.

But to prevent this sort of rip-off, the trick is to introduce regional product variations, thereby keeping markets separate and making it difficult to sell the product in different territories.

PRICING TO CONFORM TO REGULATIONS

In 2004, as reported by the law firm Pinsent Masons, British online retailer CD WOW! settled a lawsuit brought upon it by the British Phonographic Industry (BPI) and others claiming that the retailer had illegally imported cheap CDs from Hong Kong, allowing it to undersell competitors in the U.K. and Ireland. Under the settlement, CD WOW! added a surcharge of £2 to its CDs. Its formerly ultra-low prices were now raised to a less-competitive range.

This case indirectly points to the legal and regulatory restrictions placed on pricing that limit the flexibility of marketers. The stated aim in the CD WOW! case was to protect the earnings of the copyright holders. But, generally, regulatory restrictions are designed to protect domestic manufacturers against foreign competitors.

On one hand, there are indirect regulatory affects on pricing, such as those of tariffs. While the tariff doesn't specifically stipulate what the end price will be, accommodating the tariff requires an inflation of the end price. The intention is to boost the end price so that the imported product will be less competitive. Similarly, VAT adds to the price, and VAT can be adjusted by a government to achieve various ends, including encouraging sale of classes of products by lowering the tax rate on those products, or discouraging sale of products by increasing the associated tax rate. As an example of how VAT rates can be perceived, in 2002 the European independent record label association IMPALA expressed concern that high VAT levels on recorded music in Europe amounted to a tax on youth. (The organization also argued that cutting VAT on music, and thus reducing the end price, would discourage piracy.)

More-direct pricing regulations can be found in various countries, set up according to a variety of idiosyncratic rationales. As mentioned previously, Japan has a "price maintenance system," known as *saihan seido*, in which recorded music can't be discounted for a period of time after initial release. The rule has resulted in prices as high as $24–29 U.S. in 2005—almost double that of new music in other Asian countries. Fortunately for exporters, those rules apply only to Japanese domestic music, making imports much more attractive and competitive. In France, a commercial law was amended to require retailers to pass along to their customers any savings they gain from "hidden" discounts provided by distributors, such as "free goods"—noninvoiced discounts.

Keeping prices down—sometimes way down—is a way to undersell competitors. But there are various international laws against selling too low. They're called antidumping regulations, and they prevent foreign companies from selling at prices below cost or, in a vaguely expressed wording in the GATT antidumping code, "below fair value." This is to prevent predatory pricing practices such as strategically underselling a domestic product to "unfairly" capture market share.

PRICING TO MEET STRATEGIC GOALS

The predatory pricing mentioned above is an extreme form of *market penetration* pricing, one of a number of market strategies that play a role in the setting of prices.

An example of predatory pricing: Record Label A in Country A specializes in compiling vintage rock songs in stylish packages and is quite successful domestically. With surplus earnings, the company would like to expand operations. It notes that in Country B several record companies are pursuing a similar strategy and are having success, but are vulnerable to competition from products with smarter, more stylish concepts and packaging—just like the ones Record Label A manufactures. Label A decides to target Country B. Its problem is how to compete with the established labels in Country B. The only way, it decides, is to use its surplus earnings to subsidize an initial period of selling in Country B at ultra-low prices—at break-even cost or even lower—to lure buyers away from the other labels. The quality of Label A's vintage rock compilations will still be such that buyers will see them as not only cheaper but smarter and more stylish than Country B's. The strategy works: Consumers "discover" Label A and turn away from local labels. Eventually the locals go out of business. Having comfortably captured the Country B market, and with competition weakened, Label A raises its prices back up to what the market will bear.

But unfortunately for Label A, Country B's domestic labels might band together and file a complaint with a regulatory agency that Label A is guilty of illegal dumping—of selling at a price below cost or "below fair value." Label A would either voluntarily desist or await a ruling from the agency.

More typically, Label A would have pursued a less-extreme version of market penetration, combining above-cost discount pricing with creative marketing communications to make initial inroads to Country B.

This is by way of illustrating that, as mentioned in Chapter 3, marketing strategy impacts pricing. *Market penetration* involves charging low to get a higher share of the market—more buyers—as soon as possible. *Market skimming*, on the other hand, involves charging high at first to "skim the cream" of hard-core fans who have to have the record as soon as it's released no matter what the price.

An already-popular artist coming out with a long-awaited new album might be put to market with a high initial price, to profit from the high demand. On the other hand, a release by a new artist, with no substantial fan base or market demand, might require a discount price to attract more buyers and build an audience of people who hopefully will become fans willing to pay higher prices for new releases later.

PRODUCT LIFE CYCLE PRICING

A piece of recorded music, like other products, has a life cycle. One way to understand that life cycle is to view it in terms of the four stages outlined by noted marketing strategist Philip Kotler:

- **Introduction:** The recording first enters the market gleaming and new, with initial promotional buzz, its potential for capturing the hearts and ears of mass listeners practically unlimited.
- **Growth:** If some of the potential is realized, and if promotion capitalizes on it by continuing to push the product, there is a period of maximum sales. The "new artist" glow lasts as long as those involved in marketing can make it last.
- **Maturity:** The formerly new product becomes "back catalogue" as other products by the same artist, or by other artists, attract the attention of the public. The mature product is still salesworthy, but perhaps in need of some creative marketing to spur purchase.
- **Decline:** Years later, that record might still be on the market, but is of interest only to a smattering of informed listeners.

At each of those life cycle stages, pricing strategies can be employed to maximize sales.

In the introduction phase, top-line pricing might be used—that is, standard pricing for a front-line new album. If the artist is new or unknown, discounts may be applied to maximize market penetration.

In the growth phase, prices can be maximized to capitalize on popularity.

In the maturity phase, the record might be packaged as a mid-priced album, discounted to between 60 and 80 percent of the top-line price in order to encourage sales.

In the decline phase, the record might be packaged as a budget album, with a deeper discount. The price might be set at 65 percent of the top-line price or lower.

SAMPLE PRICING STRATEGIES BY PRODUCT TYPE AND LIFE CYCLE STAGE

Life Cycle Stage	Recording by Unknown New Artist	Recording by Popular Artist	Reissue of Vintage Artist/Music
Introduction	Market penetration: discount price	Market skimming: premium price	Mid-price or budget price
Growth	Nondiscounted price as demand rises	Maintain premium price	Mid-price or budget price
Maturity	As sales subside, reinstate discounts	As sales subside, introduce discounts	Budget price
Decline	Deeper discounts	Deeper discounts	Budget price

Note: Strategies vary depending on many factors; each situation is unique.

CHAPTER 6

Distributing Digital Music Globally

Digital distribution of music, through the Internet and to mobile playback devices, offers an alternative and supplement to land-based methods of reaching international audiences. The question is, how does one make sense, let alone profitable use, of the many available choices for doing digital business?

The digital sector has developed rapidly since the mid-1990s, and the business model tends to shift in shape on an ongoing basis. So be aware that any discussion of current business practices has to be viewed as a snapshot at a distinct and fleeting point in time. Yet some fundamental ways of doing business are guiding the formation of the digital music infrastructure, and they will most likely remain cornerstones.

The current explosion of activity in digital music sales—with its scattershot array of options for music promotion and sales—is only the latest example of a long-running phenomenon in music commerce. Music marketing evolves hand in hand with the evolution of technology. As new product formats emerge from new technological discoveries, old music can be resold in a new form, and new music can gain greater promotional value and distribution from presentation in a popular new format. It happened when compact discs replaced vinyl records. And it's happening now as computer-based music files and portable music playback are steadily gaining favor all over the world.

A few facts and figures, to put this discussion in context: In the year 1995, compact discs accounted for 77 percent of recorded music sales in the U.S. That share jumped to 93 percent in 2000, then down to 90 percent in 2004 and lower in 2005. That's when digital music began to have a significant impact. Downloads and mobile music accounted for almost 6 percent of record companies' global revenue in the first half of 2005, according to the International Federation of the Phonograph Industry. That was almost triple the sales of the same period in 2004. In 2005 the band Green Day alone sold 3.5 million downloaded songs.

Officials of a wireless service provider, cited in the *San Francisco Chronicle* in early 2006, estimated that mobile music would be a $3 billion market by 2009. Forrester Research projected that music downloads and subscriptions would account for $4.57 billion in music sales by 2008, up from $201 million in 2004. As an article in *The Washington Post* asserted, in 2005, "CD album sales are bright, but the downloadable digital future is blinding."

As a seller of music, you need to consider all the possible ways to distribute your product, both digital and tangible. As a global seller of music, you need to first consider the local market conditions for the various product formats and then configure a product mix—CDs, downloads, ringtones, and more—best suited to the local market.

The promotional possibilities are as limitless as your imagination. Singer Madonna, for example, promoted her album *Confessions on a Dancefloor* by making its debut single available first as a ringtone via MTV's Web site. The band the Arctic Monkeys attracted fans by allowing them to swap songs for free on the Internet. Singer Shakira offered tracks from her *Oral Fixation* album online prior to general release. Nearly all artists make their catalogues available to online retailers.

MARKETING MUSIC TO THE "MY" GENERATION

In 2006, the CEO of a Canadian artist management company hailed the advent of digital music as the perfect answer to the computer-enabled desires of music-consuming youth: "Record companies have to embrace today's audiences. They have to make music for the 'my' generation: *my* music, the way *I* want it, wherever and whenever I want to get it. Give them wallpaper, give them ringtones, give them formats they can post on their Web sites. When kids find things that are cool, they tell their friends about it. They spread the word. We had a song that sold tens of thousands of copies this way. Turn your audience into your marketing department."

How do they do it? More importantly, how can you do it? How do you get your music in the pipeline for digital distribution? The system that has developed can be viewed as two-tiered: (1) distribution channels that include multiple participating businesses, and (2) direct distribution through your own Web site. Also important are hybrid tangible-digital outlets—online stores that sell physical CDs.

ONLINE CD STORES: HYBRID DIGITAL-TANGIBLE SALES OUTLETS

Before addressing the purely digital system in which digital music files are distributed digitally, let's take a look at the sales entities that combine both digital and tangible elements. Physical compact discs, in addition to being sold at brick-and-mortar stores, are made available for purchase on the Internet. The selection and ordering are conducted digitally, at the retailer Web site. The physical CD is mailed to the customer.

Leading hybrid retailers have international reach. Amazon, for example, targets the U.S., Canada, the U.K., Japan, China, France, Germany, and Austria.

To sell through the leading hybrids you typically need to get representation by a distributor, as with standard brick-and-mortar distribution. Yet some of the retailers offer special retail programs for independent sellers. Amazon's Advantage for Music program, for example, permits independent sellers to post compact discs for sale, with Amazon retaining 55 percent of sales income.

The online retailer CD Baby is especially geared toward artist-sellers and other independents. It's quite easy to place music for sale with CD Baby, as detailed at www.cdbaby.net. And sales can come from surprisingly far-flung locations. One U.S. seller saw his initial CD sales come from Italy.

MULTIMEMBER DIGITAL DISTRIBUTION CHANNELS

The digital distribution framework is shaping up to be analogous to the brick-and-mortar model. As in the land-based system, the digital supply chain can have multiple members. Working backwards from the music fan, the chain includes retailers that directly service consumers—the music fans—all around the globe. The current term for these chain members, logically enough, is *digital music retailers*, or DMRs. (Some call them DMSs, for *digital music services*.) They get their product directly from the major record companies. DMRs also receive product from entities analogous to wholesale distributors, called *digital music aggregators*, or DMAs, which handle product by independent labels and artists not signed to one of the majors.

One aspect of the digital distribution channel that sets it apart from land distribution is the array of devices and formats that listeners use for playback. In standard CD sales, customers walk out of the store or return from the mailbox with the disc in hand, which they play through CD players either at home or portably. But in digital music distribution, the only item that is handled is the playback device, which can be one of many types. And the configuration of the music can also be one of many types.

Playback options currently include:
- Computers connected to the Internet (including desktop and laptop models)
- Portable music players (including iPods, Sony PSP, and many others)
- Mobile communication devices (cell phones of various types)

Music configurations or formats currently include:
- Downloadable songs (files of complete songs purchased over the Internet from a DMR and transferred to a computer or a portable playback device)
- Streamable songs (playable from the DMR but not kept by the user)
- Ringtones and ringbacks (segments of songs that play on cell phones when people call; assignable to different callers)
- Realtones (full-length recordings of songs playable on mobile phones)

MULTICHANNEL DIGITAL DISTRIBUTION CHAIN

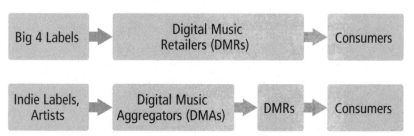

DIGITAL MUSIC RETAILERS (DMRs)
AND HOW THEY WORK

Digital music retailers provide the music, in whatever format, for the playback devices that users own. DMRs offer archives of songs from which users make choices and then purchases in a choice of several ways. DMRs tend to fall into one of two categories: (1) providers of download and streamed music for PCs and portable music players and (2) providers of mobile music for cell phones. Some providers handle both. Some providers are international in reach, and some sell primarily in their home and surrounding territory. A third important provider of digital music, Internet radio, is covered in Chapter 7.

Basic Download and Stream Providers. A basic digital music service exists as an Internet site from which users may select songs and download or stream them to personal computers with the option of transferring them to portable digital music players. Some services, like Apple's iTunes and Sony Connect, are device-centric: they exist to drive sales of the companies' music players. Other digital music services are tethered not to portable devices but to personal computers via Microsoft's Windows Media Player technology.

The first business to offer a truly consumer-friendly, clear-cut system for purchasing music online was Apple Computer's iTunes, launched in the U.S. in 2003. Its effectiveness was proven by the fact that within two years it had cornered an astounding 75 percent of the download market. By 2005, iTunes had established outlets in Australia, Canada, Japan, and seventeen European countries.

The primary offering of iTunes—the one that propelled it to the forefront of the industry—permits purchase of a song for 99¢, downloadable to a computer or to Apple's popular iPod portable music player.

The iTunes offering is obviously analogous to brick-and-mortar retail sales. But other DMRs follow different approaches. Rhapsody offers a subscription service at basic and premium levels, along with à la carte song downloads and radio stations. Napster offers a similar program, plus ringtones. These businesses compete against each other and offer variations in pricing and format structure, as shown in the chart on the next page.

The pricing structure of the DMR is also roughly comparable—in relative values—to the land-based wholesale-retail pricing model. The supplying record company (RC) sells to the DMR for a price that permits the DMR a profit. For the basic single-song download, for example, an RC-to-DMR price of 65¢ permits a roughly 35 percent markup for the retailer selling at 99¢. Of the remaining money, approximately 10 to 18 percent goes to the recording artist for royalties, about 9¢ goes to the music publisher for mechanical royalties. (Wholesale prices in the digital realm, as of this writing, range from 60 to 75 cents per song and $6 to $7.50 per album.)

Competitive Online Music Services (2006)

	Sony Connect	iTunes	Napster	Rhapsody
Number of songs	1 million	2 million	1.5 million	1.3 million
Business model	À la carte downloads	À la carte downloads	Subscription and à la carte	Subscription and à la carte
Pricing	99¢/song $9.95/album	99¢/song $9.95/album	$9.95/mth or $14.95/mth +99¢/song, $6.95/album	$9.99/mth +99¢/song or $14.99/mth + 89¢/song for portability
Positioning	More playback options	Market leader	Market creator	First legitimate service
Labels represented	4 majors; indies	4 majors; indies	4 majors; indies	4 majors; indies
Portable player compatibility	Sony NW-HD; Sony PSP	iPod	Various; not iPod	Various; not iPod
Download limits	Up to 5 PCs	Up to 5 PCs	Up to 3 PCs	Unlimited
Radio option	Yes	No; podcasts only	Yes; 50 stations	Yes; 30 stations
Advantages	Compatible with many devices; synergy with Sony electronics; owns own catalogue	First mover in à la carte market; 75% market share in 2005; iPod at 92% of device market share	High brand recognition	Early mover in subscription market; brand awareness
Disadvantages	Late entrant in market; low brand awareness in market; not compatible with iPod	Only compatible with iPod	Not compatible-with iPod	Not compatible with iPod

DIVIDING THE DOWNLOAD INCOME

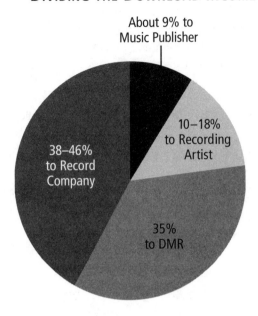

About 9% to
Music Publisher

10–18%
to Recording
Artist

38–46%
to Record
Company

35%
to DMR

Notice that the wholesale price of 65¢ is one-tenth of the wholesale price of a ten-track CD. This keeps the different sales outlets in line with each other in pricing, with no channel member favored over another. It's in the best interest of the record company to keep all distribution channel members satisfied that they are being treated equitably.

Remuneration for streaming can be about one cent per stream paid to the record label, which then sometimes splits the amount with the recording artist.

Mobile Music Providers. With the number of worldwide cell phone users estimated at 1.5 billion in 2005, and with that number showing every sign of rising, it's no wonder that the promise of selling sounds for cell phones has sparked a gold rush of business activity worldwide. New ideas for music uses, new formats for transmission, new kinds of companies—and continuing lack of agreement on how this music should be priced—have been hallmarks of the mobile boom.

The retail segment of the mobile music supply chain has been notable for its crazy-quilt collection of corporate participants. Everyone from established record companies with visions of cornering rapidly growing markets, to download service providers with appetites for new product offerings, to start-up ventures with dreams of gaining first-entry advantage, to nonmusic companies extending their brand through ringtones (just as Starbucks Coffee and Victoria's Secret have put their imprints on custom CDs with tremendous success) have jumped into the mobile market maelstrom.

Of particular interest, though, is the participation of global telecommunications companies such as Cingular, Nokia, Ericsson, AT&T, and Sprint. Normally focused on hardware or on communications systems, including mobile broadband, some of these companies see providing content as a way of building demand for the transmission technology they specialize in. Typically, they form partnerships with experienced music providers. But the relationships can get convoluted. For example, Finland's telecommunications giant Nokia makes a vast selection of mobile phones offering varying features, including ringtones supplied by Virgin Mobile. The U.K.-based Virgin, in turn, builds its own house-brand mobile phones—with the help of hardware technology partners—and provides ringtone content supplied by MTV.

Figuring out who is doing what with whom in mobile music can be quite a challenging parlor game—but, of course, a necessary one when intending to do business in the arena. And the complexities of the arrangements are actually quite to be expected in new-technology markets, where many players, uncertain of outcomes, enter with a scattershot of initiatives in hopes that one will work and pay for the rest.

ANATOMY OF A GLOBAL MOBILE MUSIC SERVICE

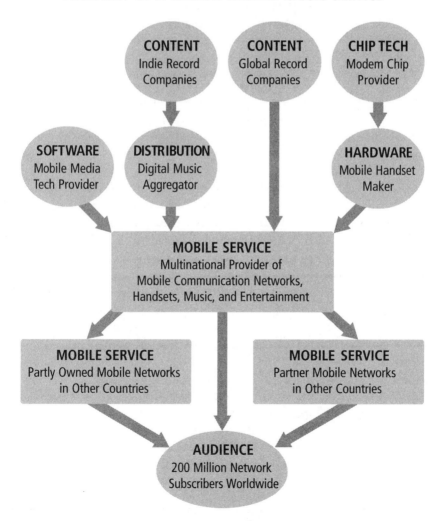

REGIONS OF MOBILE MUSIC ACTIVITY

Marketing decisions depend on knowledge of territorial music activity. In mobile music, the action began in Japan. Shortly after the turn of the millennium, primitive digital song simulations, called *chaku-mero*, gained popularity there as ringtones for mobile phones. Sony Entertainment introduced its Chaku-Uta ringtone service, with clips of actual song recordings, in about 2003, and within a year the service registered about $94 million in sales. Two years later Japan remained in the vanguard, amassing 40 percent of the world market in downloaded ringtones. Elsewhere, mobile music growth followed wireless network availability, primarily in Asia and Europe. Activity in the United States and Canada proved more tentative. By mid-2005 only a quarter of the North American population had ever downloaded to a mobile device, according to an expert quoted by UPI. In 2005, market research from TMS concluded that only 4 percent of U.S. cell phone users listened to music on their phones, compared to 19 percent worldwide. More growth potential awaited in the globe's emerging markets—especially China, India, Brazil, and Russia.

An array of mobile music products reflects the younger generation's desire to personalize their cell phone use. Ringtones provide a way of doing that, allowing the phone owner to replace a standard phone ringtone with a ringtone adapted from a favorite song, and even assign different song ringtones to different regular callers. Ringbacks, a variation, play to the caller in place of a standard ring signal. They too can be assigned to different callers.

For some market participants, the mobile phone is envisioned as far more than a ringtone player. They view it as an iPod-like portable mini-repository of music that can feed home and car stereos and anything else that has compatible connections and a set of speakers. It's the vision of any music, anytime, anywhere. For many, it's a compelling goal. For some, the sonic inadequacies of mobile phones make it unattractive.

Verizon Wireless made a move toward the any-music-anywhere goal in 2006 with its V Cast Music Service, allowing users to download entire songs directly to mobile phones rather than to PCs. This directly challenged Apple's computer- and Web-tethered iPod system, though at twice Apple's price for a single song the V Cast offering faced uncertain fate in the marketplace.

That specific uncertainty amplified the more general uncertainty in digital music's three-way competition for consumer acceptance. As each new service emerges, additional charges are added to the music consumer's monthly entertainment cost. At a certain cost-point, the consumer will not take on any new services but will begin to choose among them. Whether late-developing mobile music would prevail against highly popular PC-based downloading and satellite radio remains to be seen.

The delivery system for mobile music employs one of two channels: One channel is through the Internet to a personal computer to the cell phone. The other channel bypasses PCs and goes directly from the service provider to the cell phone.

MOBILE MUSIC DELIVERY SYSTEMS

Method	Retailer/ Source	Primary Playback Device	Secondary Playback Device
Straight to cell phone	Mobile operator	Cell phone	Computer
First to computer	Digital music service	Computer	Portable music player, cell phone

Pricing of mobile music, like that of PC-based digital music, is analogous to the brick-and-mortar structure. For a ringtone that retails for $2.50 U.S., the record company may sell it to the DMR for $1.45, allowing the DMR to receive about 40 percent against the retail price, or $1.05. Of the amount received by the record company, approximately 10 to 18 percent goes to artist royalties. Owners of musical compositions in the U.S. usually get paid the greater of 10 cents or 10 percent of the ringtone price paid by the consumer.

DIVISION OF RINGTONE INCOME

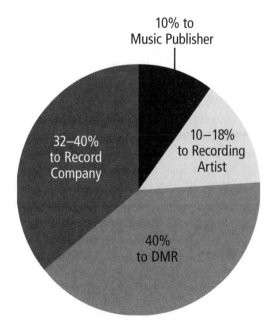

10% to Music Publisher

10–18% to Recording Artist

32–40% to Record Company

40% to DMR

International and Regional DMRs. For the global music marketer, internationally active DMRs would appear to offer an ideal conduit for passing music to distant audiences. For example, iTunes has outlets in Australia, Canada, Japan, and seventeen European countries. Mobile provider Vodafone has operations and partners in some twenty-seven countries. Inclusion in the catalogues of these kinds of DMRs and the businesses that supply them is an important part of making music available globally.

On the other hand, smaller regional DMRs such as Brazil's iMusica, Mexico's Beon, and Canada's Pure Tracks provide more-targeted audience access. Smaller DMRs, in addition to serving specific nationalities, may also attract audience subgroups with particular musical and cultural interests.

To find DMRs, conduct a quick Internet search using such keywords as *music downloads* and *music ringtones*. You'll soon find yourself confronted with more company names than you can possibly process. How do you filter the promising ones from the others?

One way is to go to the Web site of Internet distributor The Orchard (at www.theorchard.com). It lists business partners organized by service ("digital stores" versus "mobile partners") and by country.

Another interesting grouping of businesses can be found on the Web site of MIDEM (www.midem.com), the annual global music industry convention. MIDEM's online database allows you to select companies by type of activity and by country. Look up "digital/mobile service and distributor," for example, and you get some 250 results, which you can sort by country.

Bear in mind that DMRs don't want to handle small inventories of songs. They're interested in vast quantities. So if you're a one-CD operation you're not likely to merit the time and attention of content-acquisition people at the larger DMRs. You'll need to go through an entity referred to as a *digital music aggregator*.

DIGITAL MUSIC AGGREGATORS (DISTRIBUTORS) AND HOW THEY WORK

Out of two related needs has grown the distribution intermediary sometimes termed the digital music aggregator (DMA).

The first need is that of the digital music retailer. DMRs are interested in obtaining the largest possible stock of music content from the smallest number of suppliers. It makes perfect sense: getting more with less time and effort. So they go to the Big Four record labels and make large blanket deals to distribute the labels' catalogues. But that leaves the DMRs lacking the music not handled by the Big Four. For that, the DMRs are willing to deal with independent labels that have large catalogues, though they may be unwilling to deal directly with tiny indies and one-CD operations. It would be too labor-intensive.

The second need is that of the indie record label or self-distributing artist. For the reason cited above, the small label and the artist-owned imprint will meet resistance dealing directly with DMRs. Yet somehow the labels need to find ways to post their songs and albums, on all kinds of sites.

Digital music aggregators meet these needs. They deal directly with numerous small- and medium-size independent labels. They aggregate the catalogues of many of these labels into a single massive catalogue. They are then able to go with their large stock to DMRs and offer the same kind of blanket deal that the Big Four offer. DMAs offer DMRs one-stop access to a lot of indie music without having to license from many individual indie entities.

If you're a small label and you try to get on iTunes, chances are the company will send you a list of DMAs they work with. Your next move will be to arrange with one of these DMAs to handle your songs. The DMA, in turn, will make them available to iTunes and many other DMRs.

DMAs provide various selections of the following services:

- Collecting and archiving music and meta data from client record labels
- Converting clients' music into the many digital formats used by different DMRs
- Managing album data and package components
- Supplying encoded music to online retail partners (DMRs)
- Providing advice about online release scheduling and coordination
- Consulting about effective song placement and online marketing and promotion
- Collecting royalties from digital retailers
- Reporting earnings through combined sales statements and sales analysis
- Providing collective bargaining power for label clients, achieving better licensing rates
- Providing a centralized contact for all digital distribution needs
- Using standardized agreements for all DMRs

DIGITAL DISTRIBUTION CHANNEL WITH DMA

Record Label → **Digital Music Aggregator**
Music Archiving
File Conversion
Delivery to DMRs
Collective Bargaining
Royalty Collecting
Earnings Reporting
Marketing Advice
→ **Digital Music Retailers (DMRs)**

For these services, DMAs retain a percentage of sales revenue—typically 15 percent plus VAT. One indie-oriented DMA, CD Baby, charges its label clients 9 percent of the money it receives. That is, if CD Baby sells a song for 65 cents U.S., CD Baby keeps 9 percent, or 5.85 cents. CD Baby pays the record company about 59 cents, or 91 percent of the price to retail—an unusually high percentage.

Some DMAs, it should be noted, don't work with very small record labels any more than DMRs do. They prefer the larger catalogues and bigger deals. If you happen to be tiny, you'll need to shop around for a DMA that will represent you.

International and Regional DMAs. DMAs recognize the global nature of the digital distribution business. One DMA, for example, advertises a staff "fluent in French, Italian, Spanish, Japanese, Taiwanese, Chinese, and English." Many DMAs offer multilingual Web sites. When seeking a DMA to represent your music, carefully examine its list of DMR partners to make sure that they include DMRs in the country you wish to target. The German DMA Zebralution, for example, worked in 2006 with DMRs based in Denmark, the U.S., and the Netherlands in addition to such globe-trotting DMRs as iTunes, Loudeye, and 24-7 Music Shop.

One of the highest-profile online distributors for independent labels is The Orchard (www.theorchard.com.) In 2006 it had offices in the U.S., Argentina, Hong Kong, Switzerland, Spain, Italy, Israel, Kenya, Palestine, and the U.K. It maintained a catalogue of some 700,000 songs from artists spanning seventy-three countries. It supplied music to more than 100 DMRs throughout the world, including iTunes, MSN, Rhapsody, and Napster. It partnered with mobile phone carriers to provide ringtones to over 200 carriers around the globe. And it advertised marketing expertise, claiming to "make sure your priorities rise above the million other tracks, through prominent placements and close relationships with decision-makers at each service." Registration with The Orchard at that time required a one-time registration fee of $49 U.S., and The Orchard retained 30 percent of sales money received.

The Orchard provides an online interactive chart that lets you choose a wholesale price (the price offered to DMRs), then view the associated retail price and the ultimate amount that you'll receive. For example, for a wholesale price of $7.80 U.S., the retail price would be $14.98 and the "artist share"—the share you'd receive—would be $5.46 (70 percent of $7.80).

GLOBAL DIGITAL STRATEGIES—MAJOR LABEL

The most obvious strength of major labels is control of repertoire. When you own 20 percent of the world's recorded music catalogue, you are highly desirable to DMRs that need your music to sell, like lifeblood. You don't need to go through an intermediary. You cut out the middleman and go straight to the top DMRs that have the widest worldwide reach, and then you demand a favorable financial deal. With no intermediary, you have no third party to share a percentage with. If the DMR gets arrogant and demands a better deal because it believes it offers a service that can't be replaced, do what Sony did and assemble your own service.

What if you're distributing through a top DMR but it is less effective in some territories? Analagous to land distribution, you can set up your own "wholly owned foreign subsidiary"—a local or regional digital music service—or you can research and cut deals with existing local services.

GLOBAL DIGITAL STRATEGIES—INDEPENDENT LABEL

Some 18.13 percent of the world's music market share in 2005 was held by independent record companies—that is, anyone not affiliated with Universal Music (31.71%), Sony BMG (25.61%), Warner Music Group (15%), or EMI Group (9.55%). If you happen to be a member of the "indie" contingent, you're not unlike a mouse going up against a four-headed mammoth. You have to fleetingly scurry around and underneath the beast to avoid getting crushed. Fortunately, an entire sector of the music service industry has arisen to see that you survive.

As described previously, digital music aggregators can help you get to DMRs that otherwise wouldn't give you a second look. They do it by "aggregating" the music of many small indie labels into one giant catalogue that, by virtue of its size, is desirable to large DMRs. Where alone you are a mouse against a four-headed mammoth, with a DMA you are part of an army of mice; the army adds up to a force that can hold its own alongside the mammoth. That's the theory behind DMAs.

You might start by visiting the Web sites of the DMRs you desire to work with and find lists of the DMAs they buy from. Then, obviously, contact those DMAs. Be prepared to provide informational material that evidences your seriousness and your potential for sales. As outlined in *This Business of Music Marketing and Promotion*, many distributors want to see a "one sheet"—a summary of marketing data about your product, including sales track records of the artist, planned advertising and other promotion, tour plans, and more. Sell the seller on your potential for sales.

GLOBAL DIGITAL STRATEGIES—SELF-DISTRIBUTING ARTIST

There are DMAs dedicated to helping independent artists find ways to get their music to the public. As with indie labels, a full-blown sector of the music industry has emerged to handle the indie artist.

One of the leaders in this sector is the online distributor CD Baby—which specializes in selling CDs from its Web site directly to listeners as well as distributing your songs to DMRs for downloading. As mentioned previously, CD Baby retains 9 percent of the money it receives for distributing your downloads. (CD Baby sells to a retailer for around 65 cents a song, keeps 9 percent, and pays you the rest—around 59 cents.) For hard-copy CDs, CD Baby retains a flat rate of $4 for each CD sold. Prices are set by the artist-client. An example: For a retail price of $14.98 CD Baby sets a "discount" price of $10.98. Of that, the artist/label gets $6.98. (Note the difference from The Orchard. With CD Baby you earn more. But that's because CD Baby is essentially a retailer, since it sells direct-to-individual-customer.)

Something to keep in mind: as Daniel Cheung, the head of Orchard Asia, puts it, "Digital distribution provides unprecedented distribution opportunities for indie artists and record labels, and yet exacerbates competition. . . . Music from indie artists and record labels will be competing in a much larger playing field as compared with the physical distribution and traditional marketing environment."

With so many artists competing, a profitable opportunity has arisen for businesses aiming to serve the indie musicians. Put another way: today's legions of amateur and semiprofessional musicians with dreams of stardom are a cash cow for companies set up to feed their dreams. To illustrate: You have a CD master that you want to promote. Companies abound that will charge you $1,500 to $2,500 to manufacture one thousand CDs with packaging and promotion tips. Online distributors are on hand to set up an account, for a fee, with a sell-your-CD-online interface. It's entirely possible to pour all your money into this service sector to get your CDs manufactured and your inserts printed and your Web presence established. But the fantasy could easily stop right there. You might find that public interest in your music is at absolute zero, that you are lost among the 100,000-or-so indie musicians that are also trying to sell CDs on the same site.

Unlike the "song sharks" of the old days, who would promise stardom and then charge the musician for recording costs, today's services are quite legitimate and, no doubt about it, quite helpful. They are a tool for making your music available through the many open channels. Like any tool, they should be used intelligently. Before spending the money, do all the necessary advance work to make sure your music is of the highest quality. (There are services, such as Radio Paradise at www.radioparadise.com, that enable you to post MP3s and get thumbs-up or thumbs-down ratings from anonymous listeners.) Make sure you package the music to conform to retail requirements. Use professional designers and writers. Make your product stand out from the 100,000 by its professionalism, its appeal, and its production standards. And then do the follow-up to promote your music once it's being distributed by a DMA.

DIRECT DIGITAL-DISTRIBUTION CHANNELS

Of course, working with intermediaries is not the only way to distribute digitally. The Internet is open to sellers who wish to set up their own retail sites. This option amounts to direct distribution—direct from you the record seller to the individual customer.

The details of setting up a Web site are readily available elsewhere, and the book *This Business of Music Marketing and Promotion* details the available options for selling your music on a Web site, briefly summarized as follows:

- Sell hardcopy CDs by allowing users to select and pay online (by credit card), then mail them the item.
- Sell single song downloads.
- Sell subscriptions at stepped rates for different levels of service: (1) a fixed or unlimited number of streamed songs per pay period; (2) the previous plus downloads; (3) the previous plus portable downloads.

For international sites—which all Web sites essentially are—the issue of language becomes worthy of attention. Because English is the world's dominant business language, it makes sense that sites originating in non-English-speaking countries provide an English option on the site, if they wish to sell globally. You'll find this practice is quite common. The German-based download site Arvato offers both German and English options. The Swedish site inProdicon offers only English. The Latvian site Music Is Here "speaks" English.

If English is not an option, make it easy for foreign customers to purchase by using clear images, buttons, and icons. The visitor may not speak your language, but it's possible that a simple enough interface will allow him to navigate sufficiently to make a purchase.

Sales Tax Issues

If you set up a Web site that offers music for sale, must you charge and pay sales tax? It's an important question, considering the administrative headaches involved. The answer is, it depends where you are, whom you sell to, and what you're selling.

In the United States, the rule is that if your business has a "physical presence" in a state and sells to a customer located in that state, sales tax must be collected. Taxes might not apply to music downloads. In California, for example, according to its State Board of Equalization, "Your sale of electronic data products such as software, data, and digital images is generally not taxable when you transmit the data to your customer over the Internet or by modem. However, if as part of the sale you provide your customer with a printed copy of the electronically transferred information or a backup data copy on a physical storage medium such as a CD-ROM or diskette, your entire sale is usually taxable."

Selling to other countries may have sales tax requirements. The European Union, for example, requires the collection of taxes on digital goods like software and music downloads. Each of the EU member states has its own VAT rate, ranging from 15–25 percent of the price of the goods sold. The rate paid is that of the country where the customer is located.

Collecting those taxes means registering with the EU state in which you're selling, and paying the money you've collected to the EU—but only if you make at least 100,000 euros in annual sales in the country where the goods are being sold.

Other exceptions: If you're selling from outside the EU to within the EU, goods worth under U.K. £18 (about $27 U.S.) are not subject to either VAT or customs duty. That would include compact discs. Also, downloadable music sold from outside the EU to within the EU is free of tax.

Keep in mind that regulations change frequently. Be aware of current rules regarding Internet sales tax in any country in which you plan to do significant business. If you have a Web site in Country A and someone from Country B orders a download or a CD online, you generally don't have to collect or pay sales tax.

COORDINATING WITH OTHER DISTRIBUTION CHANNEL MEMBERS

If you operate your own retail Web site and have no distribution agreements with other parties—that is, if your Web site is your only sales outlet—then you have free rein to sell as you wish, setting prices and transmission formats in any configurations that you deem appropriate.

But if you also sell through other outlets, you'll need to coordinate your onsite sales strategy with that of your partners. The key is to avoid harming the partners by offering preferable deals on your site. Keep pricing in a range that matches that of your partners; don't undersell them.

Some Web site operators avoid pricing conflicts by not selling onsite at all. Instead, they provide the option to hear excerpts of songs, and for sales they link to a separate retail site, such as Amazon.

BASIC WEB SITE FEATURES

The kinds of information you need to include on a commercial Web site are well known, with detailed descriptions widely available. Here's a list of what you must not do without:

- Home page or welcome page
- Biographical information
- Current news
- Music selection and purchase mechanism
- Contact information

CONFIGURING THE DIGITAL PRODUCT MIX

Your digital marketing venture will no doubt consist of not just one kind of digital vehicle but a mix of several. You might combine online sales of hard-copy CDs with sales of individual song downloads, streamables, and cell phone configurations.

The decision factors that come into play when you decide on a digital product mix include the popularity of different formats in your target market and the standard international factors, discussed previously in this book: openness of the market, cultural differences, distribution infrastructure, and language, to cite a few.

For examples of local market factors that help you determine the right digital product mix, see the chart on page 85 (Chapter 4).

The digital music market, until recently a highly speculative experiment, has finally taken more concrete shape. But as The Orchard's promotional copy puts it: "There are still many unknowns in the digital space, from foreign markets with massive but untapped sales potential to major players who haven't entered the game yet." In other words, it is still an unexplored frontier in many respects, with as-yet-untapped opportunities for the adventurous. Think of it: Be the first to reach a country with the right technology and the music to flow through it, and you could profit from the novelty alone. To last beyond the novelty stage, of course, you'll need to make sure the music is great—and connects with the populace.

CHAPTER 7

Promoting Globally Through Radio Play and Audiovisual Performance

Once you have arranged for distribution in target foreign markets, you're only partway to the goal of gaining sales. To get all the way there, you need to promote your music, bring it attention, increase public awareness of it, and publicize its appeal. There are many ways to do this. Playing the music on radio has traditionally been the primary way to broadcast recorded sound—leading, hopefully, to purchase of the recording. Performance on television, on the Internet, and in film are associated promotion channels. Worldwide, all of these media are sources of income as well as tools of promotion.

RADIO PLAY IN FOREIGN MARKETS

The nature of radio has changed, and for artists everywhere this is a good thing. Radio was once a restrictive medium tightly controlled by gatekeepers who were in turn controlled by corporate owners who chose music playlists based on focus groups, market research, and indirect payment from record companies. Today's radio is far more open. In "old" radio most new artists had little chance of getting heard. But in today's radio, with Internet stations and satellite radio offering hundreds of music channels, the chances of a wide variety of artists being heard are much better. As one radio programmer put it, "The old radio gatekeepers have lost the keys." A new, upstart industry has grabbed them.

Radio has always been an important way for music to get heard. And now more artists have access to it. True, there will always be more performers and more music than can reasonably find room on the airwaves—Yahoo radio programmers sift through some 1,000 submissions per week—but now there's a better chance that good music will find its way to radio audiences. And those audiences could be in any part of the world.

In the upstart radio industry, the criterion for choosing music appears to be the music's quality. In contrast, entrenched commercial radio has used such criteria as whether the music is already popular, whether it fits the radio station's narrow "format," or whether the record company pays for the song to become a hit by hiring independent promoters to push key songs to key stations and clusters of stations. But as the establishment radio promotion system has come under investigation for corruption, record labels have begun taking a second look at paying large amounts of money to ensure their songs get mainstream play and a high place on popularity charts.

"I'd say the changes have only begun," radio consultant Dave Beasing told Reuters News Service in 2006. "Record labels are still extremely conscious of radio airplay charts, but becoming less so. They're learning there are many games besides the traditional charts game for promoting music."

How does the younger sector of the radio industry find out about contemporary music to play, if not from independent promoters? In a 2006 panel discussion with radio programmers from across the spectrum of current station types—terrestrial, satellite, and Internet—the programmers listed several methods of learning about current music:

- Listening to select trend-setting programs, like *Morning Becomes Eclectic* on Los Angeles's KCRW
- Noticing new music in movies and on television
- Receiving submissions from record companies
- Receiving unsolicited e-mail and snail-mail submissions from artists ("We get about four hundred a week," says KCRW's Nic Harcourt. "I listen to all of them, if only for ten seconds.")
- Hearing from listeners and playing what they want to hear
- Listening to the Web, and to what's going on in other parts of the world
- *Not* paying attention to what the big commercial stations are playing

With the current focus on quality, and with so many channels available for airplay, artists and small record labels can bypass the narrow, commercial, hit-oriented radio sector, and "do it themselves." This means conducting Internet searches to find out which stations play the artist's kind of music and then sending the music to these stations. Chances are decent that good music will rise to the surface.

Your strategies for getting music on the radio might address both sectors: the new Internet, satellite, and digital radio sector; and the more traditional, terrestrial sector, which in many countries includes state-owned stations.

TERRESTRIAL RADIO

Terrestrial is the current term for traditional radio, to differentiate it from satellite and Internet radio. Terrestrial radio, due to its limited number of channels and its consolidated ownership, whether by governments or by corporations, offers limited airplay for music. Many countries share the plight of the radio business in Turkey, as described by Nurbanu Anter, press and publicity manager for Sony Music Turkey, to the *Music Business Journal* in 2004: "Radio in Turkey mostly prefers to play just 'catchy' songs. This is the most serious problem in marketing for us, as this situation makes it harder for genres like rock, jazz, and easy listening music. Furthermore, we have just two local music channels which play foreign music."

Radio in the Netherlands echoes this problem, according to Arjen Davidse, creative managing director at the Dutch Rock and Pop Institute (NPI) in Amsterdam, in a 2001 interview with the *Music Business Journal*:

Unfortunately, most of the new commercial stations stick to popular mainstream and chart music. Late at night (and only on the public stations) you can sometimes listen to more progressive and/or alternative music. Because of the radio frequency spectrum shortage, however, it's very hard for new and different format stations to enter the broadcasting market.

Along with radio frequency spectrum limitations, ownership of many stations by a few companies further limits what can get on the air. Bob Hermon, head of regional promotions at Sony Music Entertainment (U.K.) told *Music Business Journal*'s Lara Baker in 2002 that "there are now about 250 commercial radio stations in the U.K. Most of them are playing similar types of music as they are owned collectively by a number of major groups. . . . The music policy is usually broadly similar among a group of radio stations."

Other features of terrestrial radio include a linkage to local popularity charts. The higher a song rises on the charts, the more stations notice it and add it to their playlists, making it more popular, pushing it higher up the charts, and attracting even more radio play. In the U.S., some stations function as "reporting" stations—that is, they are among a cluster of stations whose playlists are the source of data, along with retail sales, for pop charts such as *Billboard* magazine's Hot 100 Singles chart. This linkage with popularity charts is one of the reasons terrestrial radio has proven such a magnet for artists and record companies with records to push. In the U.S., companies especially aim to get music to the reporting stations, to increase the chances of getting chart "action," which triggers all kinds of promotion, from articles in print media to licensing for movies, TV commercials, and other lucrative outlets.

How does the process of promoting music to terrestrial radio work? Look at the U.K. and the U.S. as examples. In both countries, representatives of record companies regularly set up appointments with radio station programmers to "plug" their newest records. One British radio employee describes setting aside every Tuesday afternoon from 1 to 4 P.M. for fifteen-minute appointments with the pluggers—four every hour. On the other side of the transaction, a head of regional promotions at one of the Big Four music companies reports making weekly visits to radio stations—sometimes twice weekly to the reporting stations. He points out that you don't plug only to the program director; you get to know staff at every level, whether the producers, the marketers, or the receptionists. All can help connect incoming music to the right people.

Independent promoters—third-party specialists who are hired by record companies to plug their music to radio—have long been a part of the radio promotion scheme. In the U.S., some of these promoters might be paid as much as $50,000 to promote one song to key radio stations. But following investigation of corruption in this sector, independent promotion has tapered off. "The odd record is outsourced, but generally we keep everything in-house," Bob Hermon, head of regional promotions at Sony Music Entertainment (U.K.), told *Music Business Journal* in 2002. "Within our department, records only usually go out of house due to our workload."

GLOBAL TERRESTRIAL RADIO ACTIVITY

The U.S. Central Intelligence Agency's online World Factbook provides general statistics about terrestrial radio stations in the world's territories. Some sample statistics follow (data is current as of year indicated in parentheses):

Afghanistan: AM 21, FM 23, shortwave 1 (broadcasts in Pashtu, Afghan Persian [Dari], Urdu, and English) (2003)

Argentina: AM 260 (including 10 inactive stations), FM N/A (probably more than 1,000, mostly unlicensed), shortwave 6 (1998)

Brazil: AM 1,365, FM 296, shortwave 161 (of which 91 are collocated with AM stations) (1999)

Canada: AM 245, FM 582 (2004)

China: AM 369, FM 259, shortwave 45 (1998)

France: AM 41, FM about 3,500 (1998)

Germany: AM 51, FM 787 (1998)

Ghana: AM 0, FM 49, shortwave 3 (2001)

India: AM 153, FM 91, shortwave 68 (1998)

Indonesia: AM 678, FM 43, shortwave 82 (1998)

Iran: AM 72, FM 5, shortwave 5 (1998)

Iraq: approximately 80 radio stations on the air inside Iraq (2004)

Israel: AM 23, FM 15, shortwave 2 (1998)

Japan: AM 215 plus 370 repeaters, FM 89 plus 485 repeaters (2001)

Mexico: AM 850, FM 545, shortwave 15 (2003)

Nepal: AM 6, FM 5, shortwave 1 (January 2000)

Nigeria: AM 83, FM 36, shortwave 11 (2001)

Note: Each Nigerian shortwave station operates on multiple frequencies in the language of the target audience (2004).

Pakistan: AM 27, FM 1, shortwave 21 (1998)

Paraguay: AM 46, FM 27, shortwave 6 (three inactive) (1998)

Philippines: AM 369, FM 583, shortwave 5 (2004)

Russia: AM 323, FM 1,500 est., shortwave 62 (2004)

South Africa: AM 14, FM 347 (plus 243 repeaters), shortwave 1 (1998)

Syria: AM 14, FM 2, shortwave 1 (1998)

Ukraine: AM 134, FM 289, shortwave 4 (1998)

United Kingdom: AM 219, FM 431 (1998)

United States: AM 4,854, FM 8,950 (2004)

Uruguay: AM 91, FM 149, shortwave 7 (2001)

In the U.S., noncommercial college and community radio offer emerging artists and labels a workable alternative to commercial radio. College radio deejays and music directors pride themselves on finding interesting new music. If you have some and you can get it into their hands, no matter what part of the world you're from, you may get radio play. If listeners like it and respond, the airplay could increase and then attract the attention of more mainstream media. There are small independent promotion companies, contractable by music sellers, that specialize in getting music to college and community radio.

Community radio exists all over the world. The 1995 *Report on the Sixth World Conference of Community Radio Broadcasters in Dakar, Senegal* labels it:

> community radio, rural radio, cooperative radio, participatory radio, free radio, alternative, popular, educational radio. . . . their practices and profiles are even more varied. Some are musical, some militant and some mix music and militancy. They are located in isolated rural villages and in the heart of the largest cities in the world. Their signals may reach only a kilometer, cover a whole country or be carried via shortwave to other parts of the world.
>
> Some stations are owned by not-for-profit groups or by cooperatives whose members are the listeners themselves. Others are owned by students, universities, municipalities, churches or trade unions. There are stations financed by donations from listeners, by international development agencies, by advertising and by governments.

An association of international community radio broadcasters, la Asociación Mundial de Radios Comunitarias (AMARC), has almost 3,000 members and associates in 110 countries. Its Web site, at www.amarc.org, lists members located in North America, Latin America and the Caribbean, Western Europe, Eastern Europe, Maghreb and the Middle East, Central/Western Africa, Eastern/South Africa, and Asia Pacific. Listings include all contact information. The challenge is to find out which ones are open to your style of music.

Another site listing noncommercial radio stations in the United States and elsewhere can be found at www.gumbopages.com. Here's a sampling of the listings:

Australia:
Radio 4ZZZ, Brisbane—alternative music and views
ABC (Australian Broadcasting Corporation)—news, music, and arts

Europe:
Planete Indie—a Belgian radio show exclusively dedicated to independent artists/labels/music
Radio Orange—the only independent radio station in Vienna, offering mixed programming, including music
Cork Campus Radio—offering classical and indie music throughout Ireland

The point is: terrestrial radio stations are out there—all over the world—that could be open to playing your sound. The key is to find the right ones, using the Internet and other reference sources, and then to provide them your music with convincing introductory information.

When promoting songs to radio, keep in mind the station's format. Draw attention to songs that, in overall sound and tone, fit the format the station typically draws from. Think of it from the station's perspective, which was summarized by radio business development director Bobby Hain in the *Music Business Journal* in 2003: "If you're promoting [a radio network] as a *brand*; and most importantly in this commercial age, if you're representing to advertisers what a chain of radio stations sounds like, then you really need to do what you can to make sure the group stations around the country [reflect that] sound."

Well aware of the benefits of, and competition from, Internet radio, many terrestrial stations are setting up Internet extensions that offer more variety.

DIGITAL (INTERNET) RADIO

Internet music has enabled listeners to easily assemble their personalized song collections. With Internet radio, they are able to personalize their channels of music—that is, choose from hundreds of specialized, highly focused channels and choose those that match their tastes. It fits perfectly with today's young listeners' preference for having "my music, the way I want it, when and where I want it." There's much more choice—and greater openness to music of all kinds than can be found on most terrestrial radio.

Terrestrial stations have expanded their offerings to include Internet radio. Take for example, the BBC—the U.K.'s national broadcasting system. It now offers BBC-6, an Internet-based music station that offers a wide variety of sounds, as described on its Web site (www.bbc.co.uk/6music):

> Our presenters at 6 are great music lovers and we play stuff that's credible, influential and has longevity. We air tracks from the BBC's massive session archive, the 3,500 (and climbing) tunes on our core database and new releases that make it onto our playlist each week. As with other stations, daytime shows are centred more around the playlist, while evening shows have room for more obscure selections.
>
> We'll listen to your music if you want to send it in! The best thing is to send it to the producer of the show you want to get it played on. If you don't know the producer, mark the envelope "for the Producer of show X" and send it to 6 Music, BBC Broadcasting House, London, W1A 1AA.

Music download and streaming sites—that began on the Internet, not on land—also offer radio. Napster, Rhapsody, Sony Connect, and even sites that began as search engines, like Yahoo!, are among the growing ranks of Internet radio providers. Most of them offer outlets for music that may not be well known, or may be brand-new—maybe like yours.

An interesting site that links to thousands of Internet radio stations is

Live365 Internet Radio (at www.live365.com). Check the "International" category and see where your music might fit in.

INTERNET RADIO'S WIDE-RANGING MUSIC AND WORLDWIDE AUDIENCE

Web-based radio not only offers scores of different music genres but can be heard all around the world. Yahoo Music, for example, has channels tailored for Australia/New Zealand, Brazil, Canada, China, France, Germany, Hong Kong, Italy, Japan, Korea, Spain, Taiwan, and U.K./Ireland. Yahoo's separate music channels number more than 200, with lists of subgenres under such major categories as Top 10, Urban, Rock, Country, Pop/Dance, Indie/Folk, Jazz/Blues, Latin, Christian, Decades, Hits, Oldies, At Work, World Zone, Party, and Kidz Corner.

SATELLITE RADIO

In digital music, one of the great success stories of the first years of the twenty-first century, along with the rise of Apple's iTunes, was the breakout of satellite radio. Because broadcasts are beamed by communications satellite to antennas within the satellite's wide "line of sight," the geographical reach of satellite radio is much greater than that of terrestrial radio. The two leading North American satellite radio providers are Sirius and XM Radio. WorldSpace satellites provide coverage to areas across Africa, Asia, Europe, and the Middle East. By the beginning of 2007, Sirius and XM enjoyed a combined subscribership of more than 13.5 million. That's compared to around 90,000 subscribers in 2002.

With satellite radio, customers pay a monthly subscription fee (XM charged $12.95 U.S. in 2005). The service they receive consists of more than 150 channels of commercial-free, narrowly targeted music and entertainment, drawing from a vast library of tracks. Listeners cannot choose individual songs. Instead, they choose genres, represented by station channels. The formats favored by commercial radio are represented here—adult contemporary hits, alternative rock, classic rock, adult R&B, and so forth. But on the fringes of the channel list things get more interesting. XM's channels, for example, include the following:

Deep Tracks (deep classic rock)

XMU (indie/college rock)

Squizz (new hard rock)

Music Lab (jam bands/progressive)

Unsigned (unsigned artists)

Fungus (punk/hardcore/ska)

Raw (new uncut hip-hop)

Fine Tuning (eclectic/free form)

Chrome (disco/classic dance)

Alegria (reggaeton/Latin hits)

U Pop (international hits)

Obviously, choices for listeners and outlets for artists are more varied by far than what terrestrial radio has been able to offer.

The role of satellite radio is that of a start-up, according to an official of XM Radio. The role is roughly equivalent to that of FM radio when it first became popular. Before then, AM radio ruled the airwaves, offering three-minute hit songs and low-fidelity sound. In the 1970s, FM radio began offering a wider selection of music and longer tracks, reflecting the creativity of the era's music (think the Beatles' "A Day in the Life"), along with better-quality sound. Today, satellite radio is attempting to rewrite the playbook, finding the vulnerabilities of '70s-style radio and offering alternatives. The chief vulnerability, which satellite has neatly addressed, is variety.

RADIO PERFORMANCE ROYALTIES PAYABLE TO RECORDING ARTISTS AND LABELS

A key difference between satellite radio and terrestrial radio—at least in the United States—is the payment of performance royalties to recording artists and labels. In the U.S., terrestrial radio does not pay them. (It does pay royalties to songwriters and publishers, however.) Satellite radio and Internet radio, on the other hand, do pay performance royalties to recording artists. If you have a song that is being played on satellite radio, you not only get promotion due to airplay but also get periodic royalty payments.

The U.S. organization that administers these payments is SoundExchange (www.soundexchange.com). In 2005, the monthly rate SoundExchange charged satellite radio providers for the use of its catalogue of music was 10 percent of gross proceeds. The receipts are then distributed to artists and record companies registered with SoundExchange. The revenues are generally split:

- 50 percent to the sound-recording copyright holder (typically the record company)
- 45 percent to the featured artist
- 5 percent to nonfeatured musicians and vocalists

To receive money from SoundExchange, artists and record companies must register with the organization. Registration guidelines are provided at the SoundExchange Web site.

In most developed countries other than the U.S.—Europe, Japan, Canada, and Australia, for example—terrestrial radio does pay performance royalties to recording artists and record companies (for what are termed *neighboring rights*), as well as to songwriters and publishers. Hundreds of millions of dollars are paid each year to foreign record companies and their artists.

Terrestrial radio royalties in countries other than the U.S. are generally not paid for U.S.-originated recordings (just as U.S. radio does not pay royalties for recordings originating outside of the country). If you are a U.S. artist or record company, you are eligible for non-U.S. radio royalties only if the track was recorded outside the U.S. or if you reside outside the U.S.

Two U.K. royalty collection organizations are Phonographic Performance Limited (PPL), which collects for record companies and featured performers, and the Association of United Recording Artists (AURA), which represents featured recording artists, producers, and session musicians.

Some other leading markets' collection organizations are as follows:

Australia: Phonographic Performance Company of Australia (PPCA)

Canada: Neighboring Rights Collective of Canada (NRCC)

France: ADAMI

Germany: GVL (Gesellschaft zur Verwertung von Leistungsschutzrechten)

Japan: Geidankyo (Japan Council of Performers' Organizations)

For further information on international collection societies and how they work, visit Bemuso.com (www.bemuso.com/musicbiz/collectionsocieties.html), the IFPI International Federation of the Phonographic Industry site (www.ifpi.org), the Nashville Pop Songwriters Association International (www.blue-n-gold.com/halfdan/resources.htm), and David Knopfler's Royalty-Link (www.knopfler.com/Royalty-Link.html).

DO-IT-YOURSELF GLOBAL RADIO PROMOTION

Let's say you're a small recording operation—an indie artist or label—and you're targeting Country A's market. You have a finished CD, you have arranged for physical distribution in Country A, you're working with a digital music aggregator to get your songs on a Country A–accessible download site and to a locally accessible mobile service, and you have arranged live shows in Country A to coordinate with release of the CD. Now you want to get your record on that country's radio during the same time period.

Targeting Stations by Country and Genre. Start by identifying Country A radio stations that play music similar to yours. Resources are available to help you. One is Radio-Locator on the Internet (www.radio-locator.com), where you'll find a pull-down menu for "Find World Radio." Select your country from the menu of countries. You'll get a list of radio stations identified by locality and by station format. Take the time to visit the Web sites of the radio stations and get a feel for which ones might be appropriate for your music. Find the contact information for the program director and send your CD. (See sidebar, "Your Music Presentation Package," page 135.)

Targeting Radio Outlets for Emerging Music. Among the hundreds of new radio channels on satellite and Internet-based radio, and even on terrestrial radio, are programs that specialize in new music, unsigned artists, and the unusual. Among them:

- Nic Harcourt's *Morning Becomes Eclectic*, on terrestrial KCRW in Los Angeles, and on the Internet, "plays music that may not be heard anywhere else," and "has listeners all over the world on the Web," says host Harcourt.
- XM Satellite Radio has channels devoted to indie/college rock, new/emerging rock, and "The Loft," which includes 20 percent unsigned artists.
- eoRadio plays only unsigned and limited-release artists from around the world.
- Drowned In Sound Radio (www.drownedinsound.com/radio), based in the U.K., plays "generally unheard new music from around the world."
- Last.fm, also based in the U.K., offers what it describes as "the easiest and fastest way to get your music heard by the right people. Each user builds up a music profile to get custom radio stations, make personalized recommendations and hook up with people with a similar music taste. On Last.fm, unknown artists get the same exposure as those with million-pound advertising budgets and of course it's free for labels, artists and listeners."
- Swedish national radio station P3 sometimes plays emerging or unsigned artists.
- Yellow Beat Music Radio in Japan (on Shonan Beach FM 78.9) offers music by independent artists.

AUDIOVISUAL PLAY IN FOREIGN MARKETS

Music performance has always had a visual component. In the 1980s, the rise of MTV made videos and visual presentation a critical element of music marketing. Today, technological innovation has spawned many new outlets for audiovisual performance, in the same way that Internet radio and satellite radio have multiplied outlets for songs.

To get a sense of how far recorded audiovisual performance has come since the early days of videos played on MTV, consider this: In 2006, U.S. wire carrier Cingular Wireless announced Cingular Sounds Live, a "concert series that is designed to generate exclusive content specifically for the mobile environment." The company would

> create, produce, and host a series of regular music events . . . in which the taped footage from each event will be used as part of the company's exclusive video offering. Utilizing the company's soon-to-be-launched on-demand streaming video service, Cingular Video, customers will be able to use their 3G-compatible wireless phones to watch concert highlights just days after the live event.
>
> Showing video content on wireless devices is not necessarily new anymore, but what makes Cingular Sounds Live so unique is that we aren't chasing music concerts to get this footage. Instead, we are actually creating these mobile music events for the sole purpose of making the content available for our customers to access and enjoy on their wireless phones.

Your Music Presentation Package (Media Kit)

For any media, send your music in a package that shows professionalism and gives important information concisely.

You have two mailing options: (1) standard mail and (2) e-mail.

Standard mail requires a cover letter, an information sheet (often termed a *one-sheet*), and the disc or a URL to a download site.

The **cover letter** should introduce you and present a logical reason for choosing the target station:

"Because you have played tracks by [name artist similar to you], you may be interested in the song [name your most appropriate track] by [give your artist name], a talented new performer in the same vein.

Enclosed is information about the song and the artist, along with a CD [or a link to a download site].

I hope you'll consider adding the track to your playlist. Feel free to contact me if you'd like more information."

The **information sheet**, or **one-sheet**, should be an attractively designed page that contains basic facts about the artist and music along with points that will be of interest to radio programmers, such as previous radio play, tour plans, and media coverage. For general information about the content of one-sheets, refer to the book *This Business of Music Marketing and Promotion.*

E-mail submissions are your alternative to standard mail. The danger is, e-mail always runs the risk of being deleted as "spam" before it is even opened. Furthermore, you will probably need your own Web site to send people to after they open your e-mail. (For Web site guidelines, see Chapter 10.)

To avoid spam perception, provide a clear and hype-free subject line—"Music you might really enjoy"—and the name of a person in the "from" field.

The e-mail should contain the same introductory message described for the cover letter above. Grab the interest of the reader. Provide a link directly to a streamable file of your song—you'll need a Web site to host it—and another link to general information about the artist and song, also at your Web site.

For language, it's obviously ideal to provide information in the local language of the radio station. A second choice is to use English, which is widely understood. If you use your own language, make sure to use bulleted lists, not too many words, and numbers where relevant ("50,000 CDs sold," for example) to ensure the main points can be easily understood.

Wireless communication serves as only one of many video outlets. Cable and satellite television have spawned new channels and new programming for music. Internet channels, from MTV's many international sites to MSN

Music's video offerings, are further sources. Some of these channels, using a strategy dubbed *slivercasting*, target exceedingly specialized niche markets.

One of the results of this expansion has been an increase in revenues paid to video owners for play in all these new outlets. Where record companies used to supply videos free of charge to music networks, today they are paid by Internet, cable, satellite, and wireless services. "Videos have become extremely important as an asset and revenue stream. We're now seeing [record companies] putting money into them where previously they were taking it out," Adam Klein, executive vice-president of strategy and development for EMI Music, told Reuters in 2006. Today videos are sources of direct income as well as marketing tools for promoting recordings.

GLOBAL MUSIC TELEVISION PROGRAMMING

The major international music markets offer a variety of TV programming that focuses on music:

Canada: MuchMusic (rap, urban, pop), MuchMoreMusic (Adult Contemporary, Top 40 hybrid), MusiquePlus, MusiMax, CMT (Country Music Television), Bravo! (an arts specialty channel), YTV (pop music videos aired on its *Hit List* program), MTV and MTV2 (available only on digital TV).

China: Channel V Chinese, MTV China.

France: MCM, TF6, MTV, M6, 6Music, Fun TV, NRJ TV, RFMTV, and Mezzo.

Germany: Music channels include MTV Germany, MTV2 Pop, MTV Central, VH1, and Viva Media.

India: Channel V India, MTV India.

Japan: MTV Japan, Viewsic, Space Shower TV.

United Kingdom: Around thirty dedicated music channels, including MTV U.K., MTV2, MTV Base, MTV Hits, MTV Dance, TMF, VH1, VH2, The Amp, Scuzz, Flaunt, The Box, Kerrang!, Smash Hits, Kiss, and Majic. "I read the other day that the U.K. now has more music TV channels than any other country in the world," Sony Music's Bob Herman told *Music Business Journal* in 2002. "Much [of the music], though, is scheduled off-peak in the middle of the night with small audiences—apart from the very dedicated!"

United States: Music programming is found primarily on cable television channels: MTV, MTV2, VH1, The Box, CMT (Country Music Television), BET (Black Entertainment Television), the Fuse Network, and various spin-off channels. Song-length music videos are the leading format.

In addition, MTV maintains channels in Australia, Brazil, Holland, Italy, Korea, Latin America, Poland, Portugal, Romania, Russia, Southeast Asia, Spain, and Taiwan.

Do-It-Yourself Global Audiovisual Promotion

With more opportunities for video play, increased focus by musicians on creating audiovisual product would seem to be the natural response. And today, with production costs greatly reduced by the availability of digital video production tools, there is less and less reason not to create more video material. Having an artist with visual impact, and a visually compelling stage show, help a lot, of course.

Tailoring Images for Playback Hardware. When setting out to create a new video, keep in mind the hardware on which it will be viewed. Small music players and cell phones, as well as certain playback formats for the desktop computer screen, have tiny viewing frames. Imagine what your video will look like on such a screen. Complicated imagery may look cluttered and ill defined. A sprawling battle scene from *Lord of the Rings*, for example, loses impact when viewed small. Simple, large imagery—a face, a single person, an iconic image—has greater impact on a small screen. Attention-getting colors, too, may have the positive effect of jumping right out of the cell phone screen.

When deciding on the format to target, consider the country in which you will be marketing the video. What kind of playback hardware dominates in the territory? Check country data for percentages of sales devoted to particular kinds of playback—mobile versus desktop streaming or cable television. If you are targeting Japan, you can be sure that mobile players will be an important format. For Japan, you might produce the video with small screens in mind. In the United States, where consumers like their large-screen plasma and LCD television screens, thinking large may be the way to go. Of course, compromising between the two options can be done—there are production approaches that may work well on both small and large screens. Another option is to film so that the final footage can be edited and cropped in two ways, for two different viewing formats.

For concert footage, which receives airplay on wireless players, you naturally have to fit many images—an entire band's worth of images—into a single screen. What else can you do to make such imagery small-screen-friendly? Plenty of close-ups help. So do stage-set and lighting design that lean toward simplicity.

Getting Global Audiovisual Play. Let's say you're marketing a well-established performer. Chances are, production outfits will come to you for permission to use concert footage or video material. Programs such as the aforementioned Cingular Sounds Live might decide your stage show is ideal for a Cingular-funded video production. Still, as a marketer of an established performer, your job is to know what kinds of programming are available in countries you are targeting and to periodically provide their producers with promotional material on your artist and with explanations of why your artist's music would be ideal for their programming.

International trade shows such as MIDEM, which convenes every winter in Cannes, France, serve as opportunities to meet in one place many potential users of your video product (as well as straight-audio product), and possibly to cut deals on the spot. MIDEM hosts an online database of participants, which includes such categories as the following, sortable by country:

- Digital/Mobile Service and Distribution
- DVD, Film, and TV Program Production
- Online Media
- TV Program Buyers

For full access to the database, rather than only to company names, you'll need a login and password, available when you register for the convention. The advantage of using the MIDEM list rather than a general list of, for example, TV production companies, is that the MIDEM listing shows active interest in music. The MIDEM trade show is expensive, when you factor in registration fee, travel, and accommodations, but as a source of information about the worldwide music market and as a place to establish business contacts it's really quite impressive.

Now let's say you're marketing a not-so-well-established performer. Chances are, production companies and audiovisual programmers will not be coming to you with offers. Instead, you have to focus first on getting your music played and building awareness. In the meantime, shoot video of the act—onstage, in the studio, in rehearsal, even in a commercial production if you can afford it—and make video clips available for streaming or downloading on your Web site. That way, if a TV or digital producer hears your music and likes it, and then finds you on the Internet, there will be clips available to show what you can do audiovisually. The key, for all artists, is to (1) have material, and (2) make it available and easy to access.

Writer Jim Bessman, at Bandname.com, points out that you can also hire professional video promoters to try to get your product played on video outlets. Having an established professional representing you can help open doors. And promoters might offer services beyond simple placement, such as working with you to time video placements in sync with your live performance schedule. "Working in conjunction with tour dates, for instance, AristoMedia last year set up promotions for country singer Toby Keith at video outlets six weeks in advance of his tour, which involved servicing of Keith's current video, an 'electronic press kit' including a 'Barbara Walters–type' interview, and several tickets for each date for the shows to use as giveaways," Bessman writes.

If you plan to pursue video promotion, stay up to date on music programming around the world. Analyze the programming preferences of shows and networks in countries you are targeting. Web sites are emerging all the time that link to international networks and programming. At this writing, an interesting site called All Info About Music Videos (http://musicvideos. allinfo-about.com) offers links to the home pages of a handful of music TV networks, including some in Europe, Korea, Canada, and the U.S. The information changes constantly, so an ongoing effort is required.

CHAPTER 8

Promoting Globally Outside the Music Infrastructure

In clarifying the available categories of global marketing channels and vehicles, it can be helpful to distinguish music-dedicated marketing channels from those not dedicated to music.

Channels such as records, music download and streaming sites, concert halls, and many radio stations exist specifically to convey music. They're components of what can be called the music marketing infrastructure.

But music is also heard elsewhere. It is played through channels that are not primarily dedicated to music, but that benefit from the use of music. These channels may be described as being outside the main music infrastructure, but connected to it. They include brand sponsorships, advertising, television, and movies.

These outside-the-music-infrastructure channels can often be more effective than radio and records in exposing music to large numbers of listeners. A song used in a television show might easily reach three to four million viewers in one broadcast. A previously unknown band whose song is used in a TV commercial might become widely known near instantaneously. Tracks used in movies can publicize an artist even before a commercial single or album has been released. Music used in video games can become hits in their own right.

MUSIC WITHIN THE LARGER MARKETPLACE

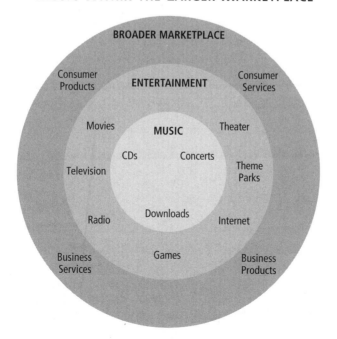

Such channels are taking on heightened importance in the marketing of music. If an artist can be considered a "brand," then it makes sense to project that brand in as many brand-enhancing ways as possible. With global products, movies, games, and more using music, these channels can be powerful ways to gain worldwide audiences.

All of this begs the question: Why should an artist deal with the entrenched record industry at all? It's a legitimate question. With the globe thriving as one giant marketplace supporting all kinds of industries and companies, many of which place value in music for a variety of reasons, an enterprising musician could simply ignore the established music industry and work with other kinds of companies with larger bank accounts and fresh ideas about engaging customers and presenting music.

Of course, selling CDs and downloads through standard channels will continue to be the main focus of most musicians, but the point here is that it's good to question the prevailing wisdom about "how things are supposed to be done." There often are options other than the standard, accepted ones.

SPONSORSHIP AND CO-BRANDING

Companies in a wide variety of industries—from automobiles to electronics to clothing to food to home decor—may share demographics with certain musical artists. This presents opportunities for mutually beneficial marketing partnerships. When the companies have global reach, or are active in the music's targeted territory, the partnership can yield an entré for the musician into a desired territory.

Two kinds of partnerships dominate: sponsorship and co-branding. *Sponsorship* refers to a business entity underwriting the costs of another party's undertaking in return for the public relations boost gained by public association with that other party. A beer company, for example, might sponsor a festival of music that fits its demographic. The firm might require that the festival bear its name. Happy festival attendees feel good about the beer company because they feel good about the festival experience.

Co-branding refers to a more equal partnership, in which each partner brings to the relationship its name recognition and established customers. The Rolling Stones and Starbucks Coffee is an example. Starbucks might agree to underwrite certain production and distribution costs of a special album of Stones rarities in return for semi-exclusive ownership. Two audiences converge: the Stones' and Starbucks'. Each company gets enhanced sales: the Stones selling more than they otherwise would because they have the added retail outlets of Starbucks' coffeeshops; Starbucks enhances its brand by association with the Stones and makes money on its sales of the Stones albums through its own channels.

The Stones–Starbucks pairing indicates one way that the nature of marketing is changing worldwide. Another example would be an artist and a wireless provider agreeing that the artist's new single will be previewed prior to retail as a ringtone offered by the wireless service.

MARKET FORCES POWERING SPONSORSHIP
AND CO-BRANDING ARRANGEMENTS

The changing global market climate is making corporate–music partnership more viable and desirable than in the past. For companies in all industries, old methods of marketing, such as traditional advertising, are working less effectively as too many messages vie for attention and ultimately drown each other out. At the same time, new technologies—the Internet, wireless systems, and more—are providing new means of communicating. These new technologies are enabling an unprecedented level of feedback from customer to marketer, and this in turn is reinventing marketing itself. To a greater degree than ever, companies can develop relationships with customers that involve finding out their needs, preferences, and habits such that products can be precisely tailored to those needs. Companies become, in effect, partners in enabling consumers to achieve their dreams. It's a far cry from the days of developing an untested product and foisting it on the public with misleading ads.

An accompanying effect of this company–customer partnership is that companies are seen as more benign and people friendly than in the past. Companies and their customers are becoming communities of common interests. (Think of Apple Computer, the maker of iPods, and its quasi-cult of adherents.) Recognizing this, and wanting to extend it, companies are increasingly associating themselves with music and musicians to enhance their brands and communicate corporate personalities to customers. Simultaneously, these companies are hungry to use every available communications tool to reach their audiences. Music, many companies have concluded, can be perfect for projecting their messaging through some of these tools.

Music also can be a tool for localizing a corporate message. A multinational company may want to tailor its offering to a specific territory. It can signal this effort by using a locally popular performer in its ads.

From the musician's perspective, the value of the corporate sponsor is fairly obvious. A corporate sponsor may have far more clout, in both media access and pure financial muscle, than any music company. How much more clout? Consider that in 2004, retail sales for the entire worldwide music industry totaled around $32 billion. Then consider that retail sales in the same year for Proctor & Gamble—one multinational company—totaled more than $54 billion. *One company earned 40 percent more than the entire music business.* No wonder that record companies are increasingly seeking commercial partners to help promote their acts.

So is born the partnership of corporation and recording artist. It's not new, of course. But today it has taken on greater importance as the costs of marketing music worldwide have increased, corporations have become more eager to underwrite the development of artists who can promote a company's values, and artists have begun viewing corporate work as less stigmatizing than in the past, when it was viewed as "selling out." (As an executive at ad agency Saatchi and Saatchi noted, "Some musicians have this distaste for ads as 'dirty' selling. But here's a bulletin: record promotion is selling, too. It's *all* about selling.")

Now artists are being encouraged by their record companies to sell their music in all possible ways, including ads and corporate co-branding.

PUTTING THE GLOBAL MUSIC BUSINESS IN PERSPECTIVE

Music Industry Total Retail Sales in 2004:	$32 billion
Procter & Gamble Total Retail Sales in 2004:	$54 billion

Some examples of musicians benefiting from use in ads, culled from the 2006 MIDEM trade-show guide: Hip-hop artist Chris Classic's track "Unleashed" was featured in ads for DaimlerChrysler's car the Dodge Charger. Afterward, some 20,000 fans contacted the record company to buy the track. Another act had a track used on a Saatchi and Saatchi ad campaign, spawning flurries of e-mails from kids asking where to buy the song.

Those examples represent fairly traditional uses of music for selling other products. Hit songs have been licensed by ad agencies for a long, long time. And star performers have rented themselves out to advertisers since the dawn of mass communication. (Remember Michael Jackson's Pepsi commercials?) But the landscape has been changing. Trends that have begun to reshape the market for sponsorship and co-branding include the following:

- New kinds of business arrangements, including joint ventures between corporate brands and music providers
- Opportunities for corporate brands to get into exclusive content creation, ownership, and exploitation
- Brands becoming media players
- The creation of agencies devoted to matching bands with brands

CONVENTIONAL WISDOM

When musicians perform in commercials they risk offending their fans.

Many musicians avoid associating themselves with product promotions for fear of appearing to "sell out."

BREAKING THE RULE

Global markets offer opportunities to work in commercials without damaging one's own brand.

In the international marketplace, you can segregate markets: Many performers who don't want to do commercials in their own market have performed in commercials in foreign markets, where the artists won't be seen by home audiences. Also, the sheer quantity of products and services around the globe increases the chances of identifying brands that closely match the musician's style, sensibility, and ethic, the promotion of which won't damage the musician's reputation.

STARBUCKS: FROM BREWING COFFEE TO BURNING CDS

The story of the Starbucks Corporation presents an intriguing look at both corporate globalization and corporate expansion into music. Musicians, by noting Starbucks' activities, can gain insight into the thinking behind corporate use of music and the kinds of marketing innovations that are possible—and occurring on an ever-more-frequent basis.

In the 1970s, Starbucks was operating as a single coffee store in Seattle. Under the marketing direction of Howard Schultz—later the CEO—the company launched its concept of multiple coffee shops offering Starbucks' own brew in tasteful, distinctively designed surroundings. Customers were able to sit and relax comfortably in a public setting and socialize, read—even work at their laptops. The coffeehouses functioned as extensions of living rooms. They caught on. By the mid 1990s Starbucks had 700 stores across the United States. Starbucks aimed beyond U.S. borders and opened shops in Japan, hewing to the coffeehouse design style used in the U.S. Successful in Japan, the company launched shops in China, Thailand, and other parts of Asia. In 2005, Starbucks could boast about 9,500 locations worldwide, with about 6,900 in the U.S., according to *The Wall Street Journal*.

Starbucks figured out that it wasn't just about coffee. The firm realized that it embodied the sense of community built around the coffeehouse lifestyle. And there were ways besides selling coffee to reinforce that Starbucks "brand." One of those ways was to draw customers into shops with music.

From that notion grew Hear Music, Starbucks' own venture into music retailing (which started as an acquisition of an existing company). The music initiative took several forms:

- Setting up a separate entertainment division of Starbucks, with a "selection team" that chooses music appropriate for Starbucks' audience
- Partnering with record companies, helping to finance the production of albums and distributing them at Starbucks shops, both in a fashion similar to that of traditional record retailers
- Producing exclusive content, with the help of established record labels
- Licensing a library of several hundred-thousand songs and letting customers at their shops burn custom CDs
- Launching a Starbucks music channel on XM Satellite Radio

In all cases, the company limited itself to music it considered "the Starbucks Sound"—the kind of music that wouldn't send older customers to a coffeeshop's exit door. That fairly broad criterion has thus far made room for jazz, pop, rock, indie, funk, and lounge music, including music by emerging artists.

The success of some of Hear Music's releases suggests that the market for corporate sponsorship of music holds some promise for the future. A nonexclusive 2004 release, Ray Charles's *Genius Loves Company*, sold about 750,000 copies in Starbucks shops—out of three million sold overall—and won eight

Grammy Awards. Hear Music also partnered with Virgin Records to release the Rolling Stones' *Rarities 1971–2003*, Starbucks contributing to manufacturing, distribution, and marketing.

The asset that Starbuck brought to the music-business table was its infrastructure of coffeehouses and the customers who regularly convened there. The company boasted a built-in distribution outlet and a long-cultivated, well-understood audience for which it could tailor releases.

Emerging artists can benefit, too. One of Starbucks' ventures involved underwriting a recording by a little-known band called Antigone Rising, which the coffee company saw as appropriate for its customer base. With help from frequent play at Starbucks' shops, the CD sold about 70,000 copies.

Now, envision Starbucks selling music out of all its 9,500 locations worldwide. And imagine it underwriting your music venture, with all those stores to sell it in. You begin to see the power of a corporate brand—if it's the right brand with the right assets—to create music success.

How Corporations and Ad Agencies Find and Choose Music

Finding a perfect match between a company's mission and a recording artist's music doesn't happen by chance. (Although chance can play a role.) Individuals with expertise in music and marketing do the searching and make the recommendations.

Where do they work? In corporations that advertise, in ad agencies, and in production houses that create music for commercials and corporate brands.

A large corporation may have an internal marketing or advertising department that provides what are called *creative services:* concepts, copy, and graphics for promotional campaigns and such marketing tools as brochures, Web pages, and advertising. Creative directors in these departments are in the business of developing creative ways to express corporate messages. An inspiration might lead to a song or performing artist that embodies the message.

Most corporations work with outside advertising agencies, which they hire to provide any component of a full range of promotional services, from message development to product packaging to commercial production to media placement. People who brainstorm and write and art-direct ad campaigns develop ideas for appropriate music. Agencies employ in-house or freelance music producers to translate the creative team's music recommendations into deliverables—whether commissioned music or existing music by old or new performers. The music producer might suggest, or the copywriter or creative director might suggest, using a song by an emerging artist. Up-and-coming artists, as opposed to superstars, have their attractions for company brands: they may help the company appear cutting-edge, for relatively little money.

Anyone on the corporation's team, whether a company staffer or an ad agency creative, might be the source of an idea to use a specific recording or performer.

How Music Sellers Get Their Music to Corporations

Just as corporate personnel scan the marketplace for appropriate music, so should music marketers scan the market for appropriate brands. In general, know which brands are active in the media. Develop an overall awareness of the marketplace. For information about companies that are currently spending money on advertising, read the U.S. journal *Advertising Age* or another of the top advertising trade publications.

If you notice a company or product that seems like a good match for your audience or for a particular song, do some homework before taking action. Gain full understanding of the message of the brand, because ultimately the message is going to come first; the music's purpose will be to help convey the message to the right people. Be certain that your song can fulfill that mission—in lyrics, musical feel, and mood.

Here's an example: Imagine you've written and recorded a song with a theme that hinges on schooling, or learning—something like "Wonderful World" ("Don't know much about history . . ."). Then let's say you hear about an educational organization—a college or an adult learning company—that's planning for a new advertising campaign including a video to run on the Internet. Right away you might consider drawing the organization's attention to your song. Its repeating chorus might be perfect for underlining the educational message. But before submitting, you should consider other factors: What about the sound? Is it upbeat and energetic? Or is it ruminative and slow? Is the musical style appropriate for the demographic the organization is targeting? If one of these aspects doesn't fit, you don't submit. But if everything aligns with the company message, it might be worthwhile to find out who works on the campaign and somehow make sure they are alerted to the potential match.

You'll hear all kinds of advice about what channels to use and what ones not to use for submitting music. None of it matters if the song is wrong. But if the song is right—really right—the only reliable piece of advice is: Get the song heard by someone with influence. One corporate music advisor, in a presentation at a music industry conference, told an audience of music professionals that they should not submit music directly to a corporation but instead should go to an ad agency. He may have been correct in a "general rule" kind of way. But rules are sometimes made to break. And nobody's going to end up in "promo prison" for bypassing standard channels. If a song is a perfect fit, get it to *anyone* who may be in a position to pass it on to decision makers. If you know someone who knows someone, get the material to that person, and point out the music's rightness for the job.

For submission guidelines, see page 135. Be sure, in the cover letter, to state clearly why the specific song is right for the company or product: "The chorus supports your message in a memorable way." "The exotic melody conveys the sensuousness of your new perfume." "The driving synthesizer pulse puts the listener right on the open road." These are the kinds of statements you can make.

Facilitating the Deal. What if a corporation or ad agency comes to you with interest in using a song? The negotiating points focus on the amount of use (how many minutes or seconds of the song), the duration of use (six months? one year?), the kinds of media (radio? television? mobile communications?), the territories of use, and exclusivity. Details of such arrangements are discussed in *This Business of Music Marketing and Promotion.*

But one way to help the deal go through successfully is to know the difficulties faced by ad agencies in contracting music, and then to go out of the way to help make the process easier.

A Saatchi and Saatchi ad executive described two key obstacles: (1) overly complex and time-consuming rights negotiations and (2) unrealistically high money demands from record companies.

The first item is understandable. Permission to use a recording involves many stakeholders: performing artist or artist's estate, artist management, legal representation, record company, songwriters, and music publishers. Any one of those entities can take a long time to respond and make demands that are difficult to meet. Exacerbating the situation is the reality that music generally comes last in a commercial production, and ad agencies have very little time to deal with all the different owners and vestees.

The second item also has valid arguments. The Saatchi executive pointed out that 90 percent of a production budget goes toward visuals. That leaves 10 percent for music. If a record company demands too high a price, the ad budget either gets scrapped or the agency looks elsewhere for music.

For the music seller who desires to work on a branding campaign, a foremost concern should be alleviating the permission, time, and cost problems (the latter within reason—don't undersell yourself; the agency's budget allotments shouldn't be your problem). Many music licensees—buyers of music rights—report that working directly with artist management is a great way to "cut through the red tape" and get a deal done. On the artist/music seller's side, try to have one person be the liaison with the ad agency, to ease the process as much as possible.

Avoiding Distribution-Channel Conflicts. Earlier discussions have pointed out the need to avoid harming participants in your distribution network; if you sell on a Web site, for example, it could hurt another outlet's sales if you offer a lower price. The same treat-your-partners-equally guideline applies when you are selling both within and outside the music infrastructure.

Pop singer Alanis Morrisette found out what can happen when channel members perceive unfavorable treatment. For one of her albums she struck a deal with Starbucks allowing them to sell the disc six weeks before anyone else. The "anyone else" included major music retail chains. One, HMV, protested by taking Morrisette's previous albums off their racks in Morrisette's native Canada.

Don't think that sales inside and outside the music infrastructure are mutually exclusive, that one has nothing to do with the other and that marketing polices can be applied separately. In most cases, the same universe of customers can buy from either sector. To most customers, it doesn't matter whether the store is a music specialist or a coffee joint; they'll buy from whichever place offers the better or more convenient deal. So unless it's possible to completely segregate market segments, treat all kinds of outlets as one giant marketplace. If you want to maintain good business relationships with all channel members, in and outside the music infrastructure, coordinate your scheduling and pricing arrangements so that no member is treated unfairly.

TELEVISION AND MOVIE USE

Both TV and cinema dwarf the music industry worldwide in sizes of audiences and earnings. And it makes sense. These forms of entertainment encompass several different forms of expression: visual, verbal, and sonic. Music is only one element. But it is an important one, and exploiting the potential for use in TV and films is an important task of music marketing.

There are two dimensions of marketing music to TV and films—as well as to other kinds of users. One dimension centers on the master recording—that is, the performance on record by a specific artist. The other dimension involves the underlying music composition, regardless of the performer. This dimension falls into the realm of music publishing and is subject to a number of distinct business practices and categories of sale including mechanical rights (standard recording by an artist for an album or single); synchronization rights (use in an audiovisual work, such as TV programming or a film); and performance rights (presentation in concert, play on radio, and other performance contexts). The following discussion emphasizes the first dimension, that of the recording and the performing artist.

TELEVISION OPPORTUNITIES WORLDWIDE

Where television's early days were characterized by only a handful of networks, today's industry includes hundreds of channels transmitted via cable and satellite technology. While MTV focuses primarily on music, other television channels worldwide may focus on other specialties—animals, fashion, history, science—or provide more general programming. Of course, some of the programming may use music for themes, background, or interludes. It could be music written expressly for the program, or it could be a preexisting recording that the producers feel would be suitable for a program's theme or mood.

Any music marketer determined to project an artist "brand" through as many sales and performance outlets as possible takes into consideration the potential for use on television, including nonmusic programming that nonetheless uses music.

TYPES OF PROGRAMMING

The globalization of industry, culture, and communications has brought about a standardization of the kinds of television programs offered all over the world. Virtually every country makes available a mixture of news, drama, comedy, action-adventure, talk shows, cartoons, game shows, cartoons, musical variety shows, reality shows, sports, Hollywood movies,and documentaries. But there are differences as well. Japanese audiences enjoy watching sumo wrestling and Kabuki drama. In Latin America, telenovelas are popular. Local tastes dictate the content and flavor of the programming, and this extends to music.

THE RECORD COMPANY OF THE FUTURE?

The traditional model, or stereotype, of a record company tends to center around a music-loving entrepreneur who records and distributes music he or she believes in and then parlays success into a commercially viable venture. Think: Sam Phillips and Sun Records; Berry Gordy and Motown; Ahmet and Nesuhi Ertegun and Atlantic Records; Germany's Manfred Eicher and his ECM Records.

But the financial model of those ventures has always been based partly on serendipity: out of twenty releases, only one may prove sufficiently appealing to generate enough revenues to subsidize the failures. Survival has often been ensured by absorption into one of the several leading global entertainment conglomerates. And even there, poor financial performance can lead to shutdown or sale.

Another model could take hold—a model that follows the corporate sponsorship concept to its logical conclusion.

Imagine a nonmusic company—say, a multinational fast-food chain—partnering with a record company to produce CDs under the food chain's brand. (A not unusual arrangement, by the way. Victoria's Secret, the Pottery Barn, and many others have done it.) The CDs would be sold in the restaurants as well as in standard music retail stores. The music targets the same demographic as the food chain. It reinforces the bond between the food chain and its customers. The music proves successful and sells more than it would without the food chain, because it has the additional retail outlets (the eateries) and a larger audience.

Now imagine that the food chain gets comfortable with this operation and decides it doesn't need the record company partner anymore. It hires experts in music production, marketing, and distribution and launches its own 100-percent-owned record company. It now sees its business as more than just food—it's "lifestyle enhancement," and music is a part of that. Unlike old-style record companies, the newly launched entity has vast amounts of capital and marketing muscle—as well as its own outlets through which it can sell. And the new company has an already existing audience to sell to. Hopefully for the company, the music will bring in new audiences.

Could this be the model record company of the future? Positive indicators exist in the form of music services launched by Apple Computer and Coca-Cola. And look at Sony—originally a hardware company—getting into the music and movie creation business.

But the key question for these companies remains, would their time, effort, and capital be better spent on their more predictably profitable core products?

More-specialized, targeted programming can be found on cable and satellite television. The niche programs are generally far more accessible to marketers of lesser-known music than are mainstream network programs and channels.

The uses of music in television are similar across borders. But the kinds of music used depend on local tastes. Youth music tends to easily cross borders. However, a high percentage of music used on programming will be of local origin.

GLOBAL GENERAL TELEVISION STATIONS AND PROGRAMMING

The major international markets offer a variety of programming. A selection of leading networks and programmers follows.

Australia: ABC (Australian Broadcasting Corporation, entertainment, news, documentary, movies, education, sports), National Nine Network (general entertainment, news), Network Ten Australia (general entertainment, news), Seven Network (comedy, drama, news, films)

Canada: Bravo!, TV for BC (British Columbia Television), CBC (Canadian Broadcasting Corporation), CTV (Canadian Television, general interest), Showcase Television (fiction network), TSN (The Sports Network), TV Ontario (public broadcaster, Toronto)

France: Arte (cultural programming), France 2 (general entertainment), France 3 (general entertainment, news), France 4 (music and arts), La Cinquième (education and science), M6-Metropole 6 (youth programming, general entertainment), TF1 (general entertainment)

Germany: ARD (public channel one), Deutsche Welle Radio and TV International (news and information), Pro-7 (American and British content), RTL Deutschland (comedy, soap operas), Sat.1 (homemade series and TV films), VOX (general entertainment, news), ZDF (public channel two)

Hong Kong: ATV (Asia Television, general entertainment and news), ATV World (in English), RTHK (Radio Television Hong Kong)

India: Doordarshan (or "DD," with national and regional service; drama, comedy, movies, sports, news, music), Star Plus (cable), Sun TV (serials, soap operas), Zee TV (general entertainment), Star One (Hindi entertainment), Sony Entertainment Television (Bollywood films), Gemini TV (game shows, children's programming)

Japan: TV Asahi Broadcasting Corporation (news and information), Fuji Network System (FNN, news), Nippon Hoso Kyokai (Japan Broadcasting Corporation: NHK 1, general entertainment; NHK 2, education), Nippon Television Network (NTV, news and information), Tokyo Broadcasting System (TBS, news and information)

Latin America: Univision (telenovelas), Telemundo (talk shows), Rede Globo (news, entertainment, sports, films), Televisa (international entertainment), Venevisión (drama, game shows), Showbiz (varied programming), Globovisión (news)

New Zealand: TVNZ (Television New Zealand; national state-owned network), C4 (music channel), TV3 (national network; news, sports, entertainment), Saturn Communications (subscription service), Sky TV (eclectic content), The Juice (music channel), Triangle Community Television (noncommercial access television)

United Kingdom: BBC (British Broadcasting Corporation, including World Service, News, beeb@ the BBC), Bravo, Carlton Select (cable), Cartoon Network, Disney Channel, ITN (Independent Television News), ITV (Independent TeleVision), Landscape Channel, Live TV, London News Network, NASTA (National Student Television Association), The Preview Channel, Sky including Sky News and Sky Digital, TCC (The Children's Channel), Television X (The Fantasy Channel), Travel (Landmark Travel Channel), Trouble TV (teenage entertainment)

United States: Network television stations include ABC, CBS, and NBC. The Public Broadcasting System (PBS) is the noncommercial network, offering a variety of news, educational, and entertainment programming. Cable networks are numerous and include Fox Network, CNN, MSNBC, HBO, Showtime, MTV. Programming that makes use of music includes dramas, comedies, made-for-TV movies, and much more.

MOVIE OPPORTUNITIES WORLDWIDE

Calculating worldwide revenues for the movie industry can be a challenge, due to the variety of outlets that generate revenues. But for 2002, Datamonitor Industry Market Research estimated total global movie revenues of about $86.5 billion—almost three times that of music.

Hollywood productions, according to the European Film Exhibition Industry Report (www.factbook.net), accounted for around 35 percent of global revenues in 2000. Given that, along with the fact that about 50 percent of global entertainment revenues are earned by only a handful of media conglomerates, the first thought for music marketers seeking to get their product in front of movie audiences worldwide would be to focus on Hollywood productions and the leading corporate content producers, which have global reach.

Yet territorial film activity has always been strong. Countries with the most internationally recognized cinema traditions include the following:

- **Australia:** With the films of director Peter Weir, starting in the 1970s, Australian productions began drawing global attention. Peter Jackson's *Lord of the Rings* trilogy (2002–2005), and his 2005 version of *King Kong*, placed Australian talent on the globe's center stage.

- **Brazil:** Film from Brazil has played roughly the same global role as its music: providing a distinctive aesthetic—sensuous, sexy, down-to-earth, sometimes gritty. *Black Orpheus*, movies featuring actress Sonia Braga, and tales from the street such as *Pixote* and *City of God*, have been exemplary.

- **China:** Over the past several decades, with such high-profile actors as Gong Li; works by Zhang Yimou (*Raise the Red Lantern*) and Chen Kaige (*Farewell My Concubine*); and crowd-pleasers such as *Crouching Tiger, Hidden Dragon* and *House of Flying Daggers*, Chinese film has achieved broad popularity.

- **France:** French film has long been at the forefront of the art form, with such renowned directors as François Truffaut, Jean Renoir, Jean-Luc Godard, Alain Resnais, Louis Malle, and Robert Bresson. Light comedy has also proven a staple of French film.

- **Germany:** German filmmakers have played a key role in international film, starting with the 1920s expressionist works *The Cabinet of Dr. Caligari* and Fritz Lang's *Metropolis*, and revitalized in the 1970s by Rainer Werner Fassbinder, Werner Herzog, Wim Wenders, and Volker Schlöndorff.

- **India:** The globe's most prolific producer of films, India is currently best known for its Bollywood productions characterized by song and dance, melodrama, comedy, and romance. With a film tradition anchored by such globally revered directors as Satyajit Ray, India now boasts numerous regional film industries.

- **Italy:** Federico Fellini, Michelangelo Antonioni, Roberto Rossellini, and Vittorio de Sica were the principle architects of Italy's respected film tradition. A series of 1960s films starring Sophia Loren and Marcello Mastroianni demonstrated Italy's affinity for comedy.

- **Japan:** Films from Japan have had a global impact since Akira Kurosawa's *Seven Samurai* of 1954 and *Yojimbo* of 1961, and Yasujiro Ozu's *Tokyo Story* of 1953. Still a leader in global film, its horror films including *Ringu*, *Ju-on*, and *Audition* have proved particularly influential, as have anime movies.

- **Sweden:** Ingmar Bergman, influential director of *The Seventh Seal*, *The Magician*, *Cries and Whispers*, *Persona*, and many more, personifies the international impact of Swedish film.

- **United Kingdom:** The actors Peter Sellers, Julie Christy, and Albert Finney were just a few who led the roster of U.K. stars post-1960, along with such directors as David Lean and Richard Attenborough. Epic spectacle (*Lawrence of Arabia*), edgy drama (*Alfie*), Hammer Studios' horror films, and the James Bond series made for popular global imports. More recent works such as *The Crying Game* and *The English Patient* have ensured continuing impact.

- **United States:** The world's leading market in box office receipts, the U.S. offers mainstream, big-budget Hollywood productions, fueled by the country's culture of celebrity worship; as well as an independent film movement that tends to lead the way in style, story, and sensibility, if not film-making technology and box office clout.

In 2001, UNESCO (United Nations Educational, Scientific, and Cultural Organization; www.unesco.org) issued data on the international film market, yielding some surprises. For example, the United States in the years 1988–1999 was *not* the most productive country in the film industry. Its volume of films was exceeded by India, China and Hong Kong, and the Philippines, which averaged 839, 469, and 456 films per year, respectively.

Just as in other industries, international trade in film is subject to the trade policies and regulations of individual countries. Such trade-inhibiting policies include national protection quotas, government censorship, and large government aid plans to encourage domestic productions. For example, China has set up some regulatory obstacles to film importers. As reported in the Associated Press in 2006, China's state-owned film distributor limits the length of time foreign films can be exhibited, to limit competition with domestic productions.

Yet with the increase in regional trade blocs and the signing of global treaties encouraging free trade, outlets for global distribution of territorial productions are multiplying. Film rental opportunities on the Internet are expanding. Large transplanted populations worldwide, such as Asians living in the U.S., offer growing markets for home-country movies and other entertainment. So broadening efforts to include territorial film production should be a significant part of any global marketing-music-to-film effort.

Use of music in films—other than scoring for the complete film—involves either new recordings used as a theme or background, or existing recordings used as a theme or background. Fees for the use of recordings tend to be "buy out" fees, covering all uses of the film, including theatrical, DVD rental, pay-per-view, and other TV uses. Music supervisors—the decision makers for movie uses of music—sometimes contract with a single record label to provide all the songs for a film. Labels, in turn, sometimes use this opportunity to include a recording by a not-yet-known artist. If you are on such a label, your recording could be the one chosen. If you're not on such a label, there are other avenues to movie use.

In terms of reaching large audiences, movies are more potent than ever. This is because a film is delivered to audiences in many more ways than just in a physical movie theater. If your song is in a movie and the movie has commercial backing, chances are good that your song will reach audiences through DVD sales and rentals, pay-per-view television, premium pay television stations, free network and cable television, syndicated TV, and ancillary uses such as airline play and video game use. These multiple outlets for film have been very good for the movie industry, which no longer has to rely on box office sales for the bulk of earnings; revenues are now more diversified. At the same time, the promotional value of movies to providers of theme or background songs has increased.

COUNTRIES RANKED BY AVERAGE FILM PRODUCTION PER YEAR

UNESCO issued the following rankings of countries according to the average numbers of films they produced per year in the period 1988–1999:

High Production			
India	839	Greece	25
China + Hong Kong SAR	469	Singapore	25
Philippines	456	Canada	24
United States of America	385	Austria	22
Japan	238	Nigeria	20
		Poland	20

Moderate Production		Low Production	
Thailand	194	Australia	18
France	183	Ireland	17
Italy	99	Netherlands	16
Brazil	86	Viet Nam	16
Myanmar	85	Denmark	15
United Kingdom	78	Czech Republic	14
Bangladesh	77	Indonesia	14
Egypt	72	Israel	14
Pakistan	64	Portugal	14
Germany	63	Switzerland	13
Republic of Korea	63	Hungary	12
Turkey	63	Malaysia	12
Islamic Republic of Iran	62	Norway	12
Sri Lanka	58	Albania	11
Argentina	47	Bulgaria	11
Russia	46	Kazakhstan	10
Spain	45	Mexico	10
PDR of Korea	37	Uzbekistan	10
Sweden	30		

Source: UNESCO, 2001

The movie industry's success in rolling out the presentation of films across multiple platforms, and segmenting those uses to maximize earnings from each, has been instructive for the music business, which is attempting to find ways to do this with music. Here's how the movie industry divides a movie release into timed "windows of exhibition":

Theatrical Release: The film is first released in physical theaters. There are some 205,000 theaters worldwide, with total seating capacity of 13.6 million, according to a UNESCO report. A film's theatrical release runs from several weeks up to about four months, with the early weeks generally being of critical importance to the film's success.

DVD/Video Sales and Rentals: Following the initial period of theatrical release, the film is released as a DVD and video for sale and rental. This occurs in a "protected window" of time—an exclusive period—that lasts around six weeks. Customers can view the film during this time period only by purchasing or renting, or by finding the straggling theatrical showing, say, in a small neighborhood cinema.

Television Pay-per-View (PPV): The next distribution platform is pay-per-view television on cable and satellite TV. Availability continues for two to six weeks.

Television Premium Pay Channels (Pay TV): The movie is next shown on premium cable and satellite channels, to which viewers subscribe. Pay-per-view and pay TV initially overlap, then the PPV availability ends and the film continues on pay TV for approximately eighteen months.

Network and Cable TV: The movie then shows on free network and cable television in one or more runs of twelve to eighteen months.

Syndicated TV: Following the broadcast premiere and second run (or however many runs the network/cable channel has bought the rights to broadcast), the movie then goes into syndication, again either on network television or a cable network, or even both. This period lasts for about five years.

The movie industry has thus stretched out the commercial run of a film for many years, maximizing earnings and audiences along the way by strategically shifting viewing platforms and viewerships.

It is for this reason, as much as for direct earnings, that marketing songs to the movie industry is a good idea. Fees for songs used in movies may not be as high as one might expect. They can range from zero to $250,000 U.S., depending on the fame of the musician, the budget of the film, and the prominence of the song in the film. Interestingly, movie fees are "buy out"—they cover all uses of the film, from DVD to TV. You don't get extra when the movie moves from the box office to DVD to television screen. Take this into consideration when negotiating the fee, and if you have bargaining leverage cite the potential for multiple uses as an argument for a higher fee. Regardless, having a song travel with a film through all its presentation modes to all its millions of viewers can only help a song, leading to additional earnings from other sources as demand peaks.

GETTING MUSIC INTO TELEVISION AND FILM

The standard approach for gaining access to global opportunities in television and film is to gain representation by a talent agent that has worldwide reach and a reputation for successfully placing its clients across media. Agencies increasingly assemble and propose "packages" of talent for projects, including their client actors, directors, and—if attractive—music talent. Being on the roster of an agency like this puts you in a position to be part of such a package deal. The William Morris Agency and Creative Artists Agency (CAA) are the best known of these full-service agencies.

Aligning with one of these agencies requires previous success or referral by a respected professional. What if you don't fit into this category? What if you are—or are representing—an "emerging artist"? The first piece of business is to start becoming familiar with the television and cinema landscape. Learn about the leading production studios, decision-making personnel, and music supervisors. Use all available means to get an "inside track" on productions in the planning stages.

Certain trade publications provide information along these lines. *The Hollywood Reporter* (www.hollywoodreporter.com) offers listings of U.S. and international film and TV projects that are in various stages of production: preproduction, preparation, and development. The listings are updated several times a week. Scan these listings for projects that may look like promising outlets for your music. *The Hollywood Reporter* covers international activity through news, box office charts, production listings, international people, and more. Access to databases requires subscription.

Screendaily.com lists international production news. Subscription is required for access.

See also Informa Telecoms & Media's *Television Business International* (TBI) *Yearbook*, which lists broadcasters, channels, producers, ad distributors, and more in Western Europe, Eastern Europe, North America, Central America, South America, Asia Pacific, Africa, and the Middle East. Information includes programming. Like many trade directories, the *TBI* is expensive, whether purchased in the print or the online version. A magazine version published six times per year includes "pre-market previews of new programming."

There's an international trade show for the audiovisual content industry called *MIPTV featuring MILIA* (on the Web at www.MIPTV.com). Like the music industry trade show MIDEM, it's offered annually in Cannes, France. Attendees represent television, video/DVD, cinema, digital media, Internet, and mobile sectors of the audiovisual industry. Some 12,000 participants attend, from about 100 countries. Attendance isn't cheap—around €1,000 ($1,192 U.S.) for the five-day event. But it's a valuable way to scan, over a short period of time, who is doing what in television all over the world. If you plan ahead you can use the trade show's Internet database to identify target companies and then set up appointments to discuss your work. Arrive armed with promotional material (such as one-sheets, discussed on page 135) and plenty of music samples to give away. But be sure to carefully study the trade show's Web site before registering, to make sure that you see real potential for finding interested buyers of your music. You don't want to waste time and money for a show with little business potential for you.

Attracting the interest of some of the trade show's established participants can be difficult, as writer Stuart Cunningham points out at www.museum.com: "Not all players in this club are equal. The most powerful are the U.S. networks; the representatives of the Hollywood studios; the major broadcasters, both commercial and public service, from the richest regions—Japan and Europe; . . . New participants will need to find ways to place themselves within the structures of power and exchange already controlled by these more established institutions and individuals."

ADVANTAGES OF BEING INDEPENDENT

The earlier discussion about working with ad agencies raised the issue of the difficulties of "clearing" music for advertising use—the complexities and delays and expenses of getting permission from artists, record companies, composers, and publishers to use a master recording. The same problem applies to clearing music for use in television and film. And here is where the independent artist/marketer has a distinct advantage. TV and movie production companies value the fact that working with indie artists is easier, faster, and cheaper than dealing with established stars and their representatives. In many cases, indie artists own the rights to their recordings, own the rights to the compositions, are happy to take smaller fees for movie or TV exposure, and are ready and able to grant permission virtually on the spot.

But indie artists should not allow themselves to be taken advantage of. In return for the advantages they offer film or TV producers on tight budgets and deadlines, indie artists should ensure themselves a fair deal. If the money up front is minimal, try to arrange the deal so that if the production is successful, according to whatever criteria seem relevant, payment will be triggered at certain milestones. Let's say the artist limits the initial license to domestic distribution. Then, if the production is successful and the producer wants to take it abroad, he'll have to come back to that artist to request international rights, and the artist will be in a strong position to demand substantial payment.

MAXIMIZING THE MARKETING VALUE OF USE OUTSIDE THE MUSIC INFRASTRUCTURE

Coordinating the timing and interaction of marketing and promotional activities within the dedicated music industry is one thing: all entities are accustomed to the schedules and other demands of a music release—the standard conventions of doing music business. But working outside the music infrastructure may involve losing the tight coordination of marketing elements that you may desire.

For example, placing your music on a television program that isn't dedicated to music puts the scheduling less under your control than if you were dealing with a music-dedicated program or network. An earlier discussion cited the case of a music-video promoter's arranging placement of Toby Keith videos to coordinate with dates and locations of his tour appearances. Music-oriented

TV productions are cognizant of their role in the music marketing mix and may work with artist representatives to optimize scheduling. Not so with non-music television. Nonmusic television stations have their own agendas, and they license music to support those agendas, not the needs of the music maker.

Consequently, nonmusic-TV use of tracks, or use in movies or in some corporation's advertising campaign, typically falls outside your short-term marketing plan. Since the nonmusic-industry use may occur independently of current touring or releasing schedules, pursuing such use can be an ongoing effort rather than a time-sensitive component of a short-term marketing campaign. Similarly, when such use occurs, your marketing task is to look for what else may be happening in the artist's activities and attempt to tie in the TV use, or to maximize its marketing value in some other way.

An example: A mature artist with no current releases hears from a TV production company that it wants to use an old track for a new program. The program becomes a hit, and attention is drawn to the song. The artist could capitalize on this positive turn of events by rereleasing the song as a ringtone or a realtone, or rereleasing the old album that featured the track, and setting up some concert appearances.

CHAPTER 9

Promoting Globally Through Live Performance

Live performance is marketing. An artist out on the road is projecting an image and sound into the public consciousness—is creating awareness. And touring different regions of the globe is one of the key ways to build audiences.

The point is the same whether the range of operation is local or global: the business of live performance is inextricably intertwined with the business of selling recorded music. Each can be conducted separately. But each reinforces the other. A strong live-performance capability can win over an audience; that same audience may then be inclined to buy a recording. A good recording, like a live show, will generate positive word of mouth, enlarging the audience. The enlarged audience means expanded territories in which to perform live, and in which to sell even more records.

FEEDBACK LOOP: LIVE SHOWS AND RECORDED MUSIC IN ASIA

Records and concerts feed demand for each other. In Asia, with its enthusiasm for both forms, the "demand loop" operates with particular intensity.

Recordings Build Demand for Live Appearances: Kids in Asia are ahead of the curve in digital technology that enables them to download entire concerts onto mobile devices. Watching it, listening to it, and sharing it with friends builds desire to see live shows.

Live Shows Build Demand for Recordings: One band from the U.K. played a show in Japan for 24,000 people. At that show, the band sold 7,000 CDs.

Live performance has always been the starting point for musical careers. Artists forge their skills on the anvil of the nightclub stage or concert hall, learning by trial and error what appeals to audiences and what does not. The exceptional artists are able to process the experiences in ways that lead to improvement in the ability to connect with listeners in both music and onstage personality. Self-confidence grows, too, and translates into forceful, sure-footed artistry.

There are exceptional cases where recording careers proceeded without benefit of live appearances. The late-career Beatles, Steely Dan, and XTC come quickly to mind. The occasional radio programmer will choose on the basis of record quality, not stage activity; the record buyer may choose due to word of mouth or written review, without ever seeing the artist perform. Yet as a general rule, live performance remains an essential factor in the music marketing equation. Even the bands cited above launched their careers with the help of stagework, building the fame that allowed them later to focus exclusively on records.

Just like local performing, global touring has three key benefits: (1) it brings in direct income from ticket sales, (2) it promotes sales of recorded music and audiovisual products, and (3) it provides an opportunity for on-site sale of nonmusic merchandise such as T-shirts. For the marketing strategist, the key issue is how to maximize touring's impact as part of the total marketing mix of record sales, live shows, and airplay.

On the global stage, apart from the vastly larger and more complex scale of the enterprise, a number of factors arise that are different from those encountered in strictly domestic operations. They relate to (1) regional differences in audience preferences and marketing opportunities, and (2) trade barriers and visa regulations that make cross-border touring difficult. Within the European Union, for example, the practice of taxing ticket sales both in the country of sale and in the artist's EU country of origin—"double taxation"—creates a situation in which it can be more expensive for EU artists to tour other countries in the EU than it is for non-EU artists to tour in the EU.

Emerging artists have extra challenges in making their way to the global stage. Fortunately, there are sources of support new artists can draw from.

Before addressing various barriers and obstacles, let's look at marketing strategy as applied to global touring.

STRATEGIC GLOBAL TOURING

Touring strategy occurs across two dimensions:

The career stage and status of the artist. An artist who is emerging or "indie" typically pursues a different strategy than that of a well-established, label-backed artist.

The geographical reach of the tour. A plan that focuses on one territory will have a different set of parameters than a plan that is fully global.

The two dimensions are closely correlated: An emerging/indie artist is more likely to focus on one or few territories, due to limitations of logistical capabilities and touring funds, lack of worldwide record distribution, and lack of a worldwide audience. That's why someone just starting out in the global market is well advised to target a single territory at first. Steadily branch out from there.

An established artist is more likely to pursue a fully global tour strategy, having already distributed worldwide and attracted a global audience. Established acts with worldwide airplay and record distribution plan global tours that are carefully structured to maximize earnings and exposure at each stop-off.

General rule for all kinds of touring: Timing is important. Ideally you should coordinate live performance dates with the release date of recorded music in the region, supported by radio play and interviews, press coverage, and advertising. Coordinated timing maximizes synergy between all marketing activities, creating a "perfect storm" of promotion and the ideal conditions for generating sales.

A timing rule of thumb is that a new release has about four weeks of "new release" promo time. Touring should fit into that same four weeks. But the life of a record can be extended by using creative touring strategy. An artist might undertake separate outings into the same territory. The first time out, the artist headlines small venues. (This is assuming the artist has recordings on the market and sufficient clout to book such venues.) The second time out, the artist could be part of a tour package that passes through the territory. The next time out, the artist might be a supporting act in a large venue. Each of these outings generates new stories to push to the media. Each keeps the name of the artist out in public. As long as publicity is being generated, buyers are more likely to think of that artist when browsing record stores. So if touring and publicity can be extended past the initial four-week retail window—months and months if possible—the sales life of a record can be stretched far.

TOURING CHANNEL PARTNERS

Thinking of touring as a form of distribution, you can extrapolate that touring requires distribution channel members, just as does record distribution. To get records to market, you need intermediaries: distributors and retail outlets. To get concerts to market, you also need intermediaries: booking agents and concert promoters.

RECORD AND CONCERT SUPPLY CHAINS

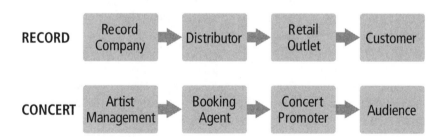

Booking agents specialize in brokering live shows and club dates. They use their knowledge of a territory's performance venues and concert promoters to make the best, most suitable arrangements for their artist clients. They choose among venues and promoters, assess the best offers, negotiate contracts, and plan the scheduling. In return they take a commission of between 10 and 15 percent of earnings.

Agents tend to specialize in territories. Part of the reason has to do with logistics. In order to communicate comfortably, within relatively nearby time zones, an agent will focus on nearby territories. Artists may employ more than one booking agency—for example, one for the United States and one for the "rest of world."

Promoters "produce" shows. They contract with an artist (or artist's booking agent) and with a venue to provide services on a given date, with the expectation that ticket sales will exceed costs and thus provide the promoter with a profit. Promoters assume the financial risk in that they take profits only after paying the artist, the venue, and other suppliers.

The intermediaries you need depends on your level of success. Booking agents, for example, are not needed by superstar acts, who have staff to deal directly with concert promoters. At the other end of the spectrum, new and emerging artists may not yet be in a position to work with either agents or promoters; they may be booking club dates through networks of personal contacts, indie labels, fellow performers, and simpatico club owners.

Whatever your stage of activity in global touring, you need sources of information. An excellent place to start is the Web site of the International Live Music Conference (www.ilmc.com), which provides a database of international booking agencies, venues, festivals, and other businesses in the live concert industry. It also provides news of the industry. The site contains many invaluable databases, and is fast on its way to being a first-rate information source. The conference from which the organization takes its name runs annually in London in early March "to pull together the key figures involved in the presentation of live entertainment around the globe." Attendance is by invitation only—meaning two ILMC members have to nominate you, or you need to be an employee of a member company.

A more established source of information about international talent buyers (concert promoters, for example) and concert venues is Pollstar (www.pollstar.com).

Another key participant in the touring process, though not a distinct channel member, is the **tour manager**. As artist management's representative on the road, the tour manager handles on-the-ground logistics. That means making sure the performers get where they need to be at the right time. It also means organizing travel and hotel arrangements, and serving as liaison between artist and concert promoter, often including settling the finances at the end of a show. Self-booking performers who are well organized and deadline driven can often serve as their own tour managers. But there comes a point when business demands on the road begin to take away from attention to the music. It is then that a tour manager becomes a necessity.

PLAY YOUR OWN MUSIC IN CONCERT

For performers, there's more money to be made by playing their own music in concert. Such uses of songs fall into the category of "public performances," with royalties payable to songwriters and publishers by performance rights organizations. In the U.K., for example, 3 percent of ticket sales are collected by the Performing Rights Society (PRS), which in turns pays out royalties to the writers and publishers.

If you perform others' music, they get the performance royalties. If you perform your own music, you receive performances royalties—on top of whatever else you earn from the promoter, of course. Be sure to keep records of your set lists for later reference if questions arise about payment.

TARGETING AND TOURING A TERRITORY

To break into global touring, start modestly. If you have been targeting a specific territory for the rest of your marketing effort—exporting or licensing CDs, for example—focus on that same country for your touring plans. As one part of the marketing plan expands to new territories, focus your other activities there, too.

The process of planning and booking foreign performances may be as straightforward as having a contact in a foreign city who invites you to come and perform. Or you might attempt a more methodical, analytical approach to targeting a country.

Basic, Do-It-Yourself Process. The most immediate, direct way to set up gigs in a specific country is to do what one U.S. singer did: She had heard that there was a good market for indie performers in Japan, and took it upon herself to book her own tour there.

She began by doing research, checking the Internet for Japanese artists who played music similar to hers. She contacted several and heard back from one, who expressed interest in her music (which was posted on the Internet) and her ideas about going to Japan.

The singer asked the Japanese performer lots of questions—about what clubs to perform in, whom to contact, how to get around Japan, what the costs might be. She wanted to get a clear picture of what the situation would be like. Then the Japanese artist offered to book the gigs and asked the singer to send CDs and promotional material. They agreed to limit the engagements to one city. If all worked out, there could be a return trip with added locations. A week's worth of shows was booked.

Another independent U.S. performer, not nationally or even regionally well known, made it an annual practice to fly to Japan for a mini-tour of small clubs. During one trip to Japan years before, she had established a small network of contacts, and they continued to bring her back year after year.

Conceivably, you could research a foreign city, learn about its venues on the Internet, choose clubs that book your kind of music, and contact the owner or music booker online, offering e-mailable music samples and photos and background material. You could complete the entire booking process from the comfort of your home Internet connection. Repeat the process for several other venues in the same general area, and you've successfully booked a mini-tour. Do well in the shows and you'll be invited back, and while you're in the country you'll be able to check out what other kinds of local venues and opportunities might be available.

This do-it-yourself scenario can be applied to a carefully timed campaign or to an open-ended schedule. That is, you can use it to set up performances during the weeks in which your music will be available in a territory's stores, or you can use it to book gigs at any time, not linked to a particular album release.

More Thorough, Business-Analysis Process. An established artist or the marketing representatives of an established artist would likely conduct a systematic analysis of market conditions in a country plus a cost-benefit analysis of doing business there before setting up live dates.

The first determination would be of the market's openness to foreign performers in general and to your music in particular. This kind of research is discussed in Chapter 2. The same criteria used for deciding where to market your recorded music can be applied to decisions about where to tour, since record sales and tours are components of the same marketing campaign.

Decision criteria include general categories such as a country's purchasing-power parity, economic system (free-market, protectionist), trade restrictions (tariffs, local content requirements), customs and beliefs, language barriers, and source effects (positive or negative view of your country).

Additional criteria include music-specific data such as annual music sales per capita, annual per capita expenditures on live music, percentage of music sales devoted to your music genre, and number and reach of media outlets.

Of course, the number and kinds of live-performance venues in a country are key to determining whether you can get access to a market. Outlets include concert halls, nightclubs, colleges, and festivals. Sources of information include online directories such as Online Gigs (www.onlinegigs.com), which lists venues, colleges, media, and festivals by U.S. state; DIY Bookings (www.diybookings.com); Pollstar's annual *Concert Venue Directory*; and individual city sites on the Internet, such as Bangkok Gig Guide, which lists and describes hundreds of local venues and the kinds of music they offer.

Another approach to finding suitable venues is to do an Internet search of clubs worldwide that feature your genre. For example, Jazz Clubs Worldwide (www.jazz-clubs-worldwide.com) enables you to choose a country and see a list of jazz clubs with brief descriptions and contact information.

Stay up to date on market news from around the world and in your targeted countries by checking the International Live Music Conference Web site (www.ilmc.com), Pollstar, and other music news sources. At this writing, for example, the following market conditions existed:

- France was experiencing an increase in its number of performance venues.
- In Asia, high demand and growing capacity signaled a ripe market for foreign touring acts. According to Denise Marsh, general manager of the Singapore Indoor Stadium, on any given night her country offered 150,000 available seats for live performance. New facilities were being built in Beijing, Hong Kong, and Taipei.
- In Japan, the concert business was on a growth curve, with the Tokyo Dome regularly selling out and even small venues doing well.
- The Ukraine live scene was hampered by a lack of venues.
- Norway was host to a healthy climate for live performance, with support for innovative music and ample coverage by the media.

As conditions change, the country that you found difficult to target last year might become more open to your sound in the near future. In the meantime, there are many others to choose from.

Once you've determined the feasibility of setting up a tour in your target country, conduct a cost-benefit analysis of the venture.

Let's assume, for example, a desired tour of U.K. nightclubs covering five cities in two weeks for a Japanese group of four musicians with a tour manager and a modest budget.

EXPENSES

Travel	
Airfare, round-trip Tokyo-London for 5	$5,000
Intercity (5 trips)	500
Local (14 days)	700
Accommodations (3 rooms × $125 × 14 nights)	5,250
Per Diem ($125 × 14 days)	1,750
Subtotal	$13,200
10% Contingency	1,320
Total Expenses	**$14,520**

Let's also assume bookings for ten nights. To break even, you would have to earn $1,452 per night. (And that's not accounting for equipment rentals.) But let's not forget about paying the four musicians and the tour manager. To cover a relatively meager payment of $150 per person per night, totaling $750 nightly, you would have to earn a total of $2,202 (that's $1,452 + $750) for each of those ten nights.

For most emerging artists the expenses would far outweigh the earnings. Yet emerging artists need to travel and perform in order to build audiences. Do this, and at some point in the future audiences will be of sufficient size to pay for costs plus provide a profit. This hypothesis is behind the concept of tour support by record companies. Recognizing the need for emerging artists to be out on the road, many record labels will subsidize early touring by paying the difference between costs and earnings and then recouping that money from record royalties. For further discussion of financial support for touring, see "Sources of Tour Support" on page 178.

TOURING WORLDWIDE

On another level, that of the established and widely popular artist, targeting one country may represent just a single block of tour dates among the many blocks that constitute a world tour. The strategic complexities of touring increase many times over when more than one country is involved. Even before dealing with scheduling strategies, marketing and promotion coordination, and contractual arrangements, any touring plan has to take into consideration regional differences in

- Language
- Customs
- Politics
- Climate and weather
- Tax laws
- Currency

In meticulously piecing together a global tour, an important market may have to be left out because the only time slot available is one in which the time of year is not conducive to travel in that country, or other events may be taking place in the region that preclude being able to attract audiences or even reserve venues.

In a choice between any two regions, you'll probably prefer the one with the most openness to international business languages, because it will reduce the chances of miscommunication and the potential for mishaps.

Some countries may have more stringent immigration and travel regulations than others. In all cases, visas must be applied for well in advance, making a global tour an administrative challenge multiplied many times over.

If a country is experiencing currency instability, you might prefer to avoid the country. If you performed there, you'd have to devote extra attention to method of payment to hedge against financial losses, and you might see it as not worth the effort. Even if currency is stable, the country's trade regulations—tax policy, for example—may make a stop-off in the country unattractive from a financial standpoint.

Political unrest, of course, creates all kinds of risks, from potential last-minute cancellations of shows to possible physical harm.

All of these fundamental factors weigh into the tour decision-making process.

One way to begin exploring global touring strategy is to look at a state-of-the-art plan devised for one of the world's most popular artist groups, the Rolling Stones. Look at it as what can be done when resources are virtually unlimited and artist popularity is universal—when you can go wherever you want. Then cut back from that to see what works for your specific artist and situation.

On September 6, 2005, the Rolling Stones released their new CD *A Bigger Bang*. The band had spent the preceding fall of 2004 and winter, spring, and summer of 2005 recording the disc, and they finished mixing it on June 28. A single featuring the two album tracks "Streets of Love" and "Rough Justice" was released to selected radio stations around the world on July 22. A world tour to support the album was scheduled to start in August 2005 with dates in the U.S. and Canada, followed by tours of Mexico, South America, the Far East, New Zealand, Australia, and finally Europe, ending in the summer of 2006. The tentative plan was as follows:

ROLLING STONES PLANNED WORLD TOUR DATES 2005–2006

May 10, 2005	Press conference, New York, NY	USA
Aug 21, 2005	Boston, MA	USA
Aug 23, 2005	Boston, MA	USA
Aug 26, 2005	Hartford, CT	USA
Aug 28, 2005	Ottawa, ON	Canada
Aug 31, 2005	Detroit, MI	USA
Sep 3, 2005	Moncton, New Brunswick	Canada
Sep 6, 2005	Saint Paul, MN	USA
Sep 8, 2005	Milwaukee, WI	USA
Sep 10, 2005	Chicago, IL	USA
Sep 13, 2005	New York, NY	USA
Sep 15, 2005	East Rutherford, NJ	USA
Sep 17, 2005	Albany, NY	USA
Sep 24, 2005	Columbus, OH	USA
Sep 26, 2005	Toronto, ON	Canada
Sep 28, 2005	Pittsburgh, PA	USA
Oct 1, 2005	Hershey, PA	USA
Oct 3, 2005	Washington, DC	USA
Oct 6, 2005	Charlottesville, VA	USA
Oct 8, 2005	Durham, NC	USA
Oct 10, 2005	Philadelphia, PA	USA
Oct 12, 2005	Philadelphia, PA	USA
Oct 15, 2005	Atlanta, GA	USA
Oct 17, 2005	Miami, FL	USA
Oct 19, 2005	Tampa, FL	USA
Oct 21, 2005	Charlotte, NC	USA
Oct 28, 2005	Calgary, Alberta	Canada
Oct 30, 2005	Seattle, WA	USA
Nov 1, 2005	Portland, OR	USA
Nov 4, 2005	Anaheim, CA	USA
Nov 6, 2005	Los Angeles, CA	USA
Nov 8, 2005	Los Angeles, CA	USA
Nov 11, 2005	San Diego, CA	USA
Nov 13, 2005	San Francisco, CA	USA
Nov 15, 2005	San Francisco, CA	USA
Nov 18, 2005	Las Vegas, NV	USA
Nov 20, 2005	Fresno, CA	USA

Nov 22, 2005	Salt Lake City, UT	USA
Nov 24, 2005	Denver, CO	USA
Nov 27, 2005	Glendale, AZ	USA
Nov 29, 2005	Dallas, TX	USA
Dec 1, 2005	Houston, TX	USA
Dec 3, 2005	Memphis, TN	USA
Jan 10, 2006	Montreal, QC	Canada
Jan 13, 2006	Boston, MA	USA
Jan 15, 2006	Boston, MA	USA
Jan 18, 2006	New York, NY	USA
Jan 20, 2006	New York, NY	USA
Jan 23, 2006	Chicago, IL	USA
Jan 25, 2006	Chicago, IL	USA
Jan 27, 2006	St. Louis, MO	USA
Jan 29, 2006	Omaha, NE	USA
Feb 1, 2006	Baltimore, MD	USA
Feb 5, 2006	Detroit, MI	USA
Feb 8, 2006	Atlanta, GA	USA
Feb 11, 2006	San Juan	Puerto Rico
Feb 18, 2006	Rio de Janeiro	Brazil
Feb 21, 2006	Buenos Aires	Argentina
Feb 23, 2006	Buenos Aires	Argentina
Feb 26, 2006	Mexico City	Mexico
Mar 1, 2006	Monterrey	Mexico
Mar 4, 2006	Las Vegas, NV	USA
Mar 6, 2006	Los Angeles, CA	USA
Mar 9, 2006	North Little Rock, AR	USA
Mar 12, 2006	Ft. Lauderdale, FL	USA
Mar 14, 2006	New York, NY	USA
Mar 22, 2006	Tokyo	Japan
Mar 24, 2006	Tokyo	Japan
Mar 29, 2006	Sapporo	Japan
Apr 2, 2006	Saitama	Japan
Apr 5, 2006	Nagoya	Japan
Apr 8, 2006	Shanghai	China
Apr 11, 2006	Sydney	Australia
Apr 13, 2006	Melbourne	Australia

Apr 16, 2006	Auckland	New Zealand
Apr 18, 2006	Wellington	New Zealand
May 27, 2006	Barcelona	Spain
May 29, 2006	Madrid	Spain
Jun 1, 2006	Brussels	Belgium
Jun 3, 2006	Paris	France
Jun 6, 2006	Bergen	Norway
Jun 8, 2006	Horsens	Denmark
Jun 10, 2006	Gothenburg	Sweden
Jun 13, 2006	St. Petersburg	Russia
Jun 16, 2006	Brno	Czech Republic
Jun 18, 2006	Warsaw	Poland
Jun 20, 2006	Vienna	Austria
Jun 22, 2006	Milan	Italy
Jun 25, 2006	Athens	Greece
Jun 29, 2006	Lyon	France
Jul 2, 2006	Paris	France
Jul 6, 2006	Zagreb	Croatia
Jul 10, 2006	Nürnberg	Germany
Jul 12, 2006	Leipzig	Germany
Jul 14, 2006	Frankfurt	Germany
Jul 16, 2006	Munich	Germany
Jul 19, 2006	Hanover	Germany
Jul 21, 2006	Berlin	Germany
Jul 23, 2006	Cologne	Germany
Jul/Aug, 2006	Rotterdam	The Netherlands
Jul/Aug, 2006	Groningen	The Netherlands
Jul/Aug, 2006	Arnhem	The Netherlands
Jul 30, 2006	Amsterdam	The Netherlands
Aug 1, 2006	Amsterdam	The Netherlands
Aug 3, 2006	Stuttgart	Germany
Aug 5, 2006	Zurich	Switzerland
Aug 8, 2006	Nice	France
Aug, 2006	Cadiz, Andalucia	Spain
Aug 12, 2006	Porto	Portugal
Aug 14, 2006	Valladolid	Spain
Aug 16, 2006	Zaragoza	Spain
Aug 18, 2006	Dublin	Ireland

Aug 20, 2006	London	England
Aug 22, 2006	London	England
Aug 25, 2006	Glasgow	Scotland
Aug 27, 2006	Sheffield	England
Aug 29, 2006	Cardiff	Wales

Note: An injury of guitarist Keith Richards on April 27 resulted in rescheduling the European tour dates.

Things you should notice about this tour schedule: It's highly concentrated in the world's biggest music market, the United States. Beyond that, it completes North and South America as one large block of the tour, during summer–fall, 2005, and winter, 2006. This makes logistical sense. An entire month is devoted to Asia and Oceania, concentrating on the most active market in the region, Japan. Finally, a full three months are devoted to Europe.

Notably missing are the world's emerging music markets, except for the single date in China. Trouble spots are also not included. The conclusion one can draw is that this is a tour to skim the cream off the most affluent, already established markets. It is not designed to break new ground. And this makes sense, since the Rolling Stones have no need to win over new regions.

For the rest of us, more modest plans require decisions about where to go and where not to go. Do you go to a familiar territory to add juice to already healthy demand? Or do you venture into a region where there's only a ripple of demand so you can boost it to a tsunami? Here are some guidelines:

1. **Go where your other marketing activities have taken you.** If you have found pockets of listeners for your brand of music in a given territory, and you have been successful in arranging exporting or licensing deals there, then the region is a good candidate for touring activity.

2. **Focus on the most lucrative markets.** Start by planning for the territories where earnings are expected to be the highest. Do cost-benefit analyses to determine this. Then book additional territories around the main money-makers.

3. **Consider venturing into emerging markets, if conditions make it attractive.** There is little point in taking your act to a distant no-man's land if there is no music infrastructure for selling recordings, little disposable income to spend on entertainment, and poor facilities for performing. On the other hand, an out-of-the-way territory may offer benefits that make it attractive: a favorable percentage for you of merchandise and CD sales at the show; the red-carpet treatment because the promoter, or the government, is determined to open up the local market to international music; a significant amount of press for being among the first artists of your kind to venture into the territory. Be open to some of these opportunities.

4. **Book tours on the basis of releasing schedules.** Unlike the Rolling Stones, who released *A Bigger Bang* at one time all over the world, you may release a record at different times according to the licensing or exporting deals you are able to set up. It could be months before your domestic album finds a willing distributor in Country Z. Schedule touring to coordinate with whatever release dates you are able to arrange. Optimally, they will be close together so that you can consolidate travel arrangements and costs rather than face setting up separate tours at disconnected times for each new market.

NICHE TOURING

In marketing, you can attempt to sell to an entire population—a strategy called *mass marketing*. Alternatively, you can target a segment of the population characterized by a more narrow set of characteristics: they like rock music, for example. This strategy is called *market segmentation*. What if you're marketing a specific brand of rock—say, a band influenced by Bob Marley? You could target an even smaller population segment, the niche that prefers reggae-flavored rock. Here you're pursuing a strategy called *niche marketing*. The beauty of targeting a niche is the precision with which you can identify the niche and the distribution channels it uses—saving you the money and effort you'd otherwise waste trying to sell to buyers with little interest in reggae.

The Rolling Stones tour of 2005–2006 can be described as mass-market touring: They aimed to hit mass audiences by traveling to as many territories as possible and playing in the largest venues available.

Artists on a budget—or artists, at least, with less universal renown than that of the Stones—can profitably apply the strategy of niche marketing to global touring. An earlier discussion of how to identify listener groups and their locations (Chapter 2) essentially outlined how to identify the niche of listeners most likely to be attracted to your music and how to pinpoint where they live. The same findings can be applied to your tour planning. Go where those niches live. By basing your touring arrangements on your album marketing plans, you should automatically be touring to your previously defined niche.

The United States is considered the ultimate music market by many countries. Its concentration of media and its cultural impact make it an automatic global bullhorn for any music it consumes that it likes. But can the U.S. be treated as one homogeneous market? Actually not. It represents a vast multiplicity of musical tastes. Those tastes may be dispersed among different regions and cities, set by local populations with foreign roots or socioeconomically dictated preferences. An artist visiting from the U.K. may find large, enthusiastic audiences in one city and only minimal interest in another. A free-jazz artist may thrive in New York and "die" in Branson, Missouri. An Afro-Cuban group may draw huge crowds in Miami and play to an empty house in Crawford, Texas. For this reason the smart tour planner should look at the U.S. as many individual markets within one national boundary. Find where the niches live, and cherry-pick those markets. Don't waste resources on the vast segments of the population whose tastes are unknown to you. Success in niche touring will bring in new listeners naturally over time, allowing you to expand the listenership as far as the music's inherent appeal will allow.

Marketers can break into a country by targeting their own expatriates and immigrants residing in that country. An example: A concert promoter set up a national nightclub tour for British Indian rapper Jay Sean. With no album released in the U.S., but with Internet distribution among the U.S. population of South Asian youngsters, the rapper played to 10,000 people in New York, Washington, Atlanta, and San Francisco, according to an article in *The Washington Post*. Another example: A concert by Juan Luis Guerra and Marco Antonio Solis, well known in Latin America, nearly filled Madison Square Garden in New York, thanks to that city's dense Latino population.

Global shifts in populations constantly create new ethnic centers, which music marketers can find and target. Typically, concert promoters advertise concerts to these groups through ethnic media, music shops, and grocery stores in their neighborhoods.

Also, successful promoters choose venues that best cater to the niche audience—that have the right seating capacity and are easily accessible to residential areas populated by the niche.

Even if the populations are several generations removed from the mother country, the Internet and broadcast have brought them in touch with homeland culture, and today there is a resurgence of youth interest in music, movies, and more from their countries of origin.

Of course, affinity for brands of music isn't limited to associated ethnic groups. Producer Larry Harlow, in a 2001 *Music Business Journal* interview with writer David Litterick, described the perception of Latin music among various national populations all around the world:

> South America and the U.S. are pretty much the same because it is about dancing and they understand the Spanish language. . . . In Europe, for example Germany, the Germans don't speak Spanish, they don't know what the song is about, but they like the rhythms and they like to dance. . . . I can't work it every day, but yet there are Latin bands in Germany that work every week, and there are a lot of Latin bands in Holland and of course in Spain, where they understand the lyrics. . . . I go to Japan every year. I play two, three weeks in Japan, and of course they don't understand a word I'm saying, but they love the music and they dance well, and they take dance lessons and Latin lessons and there are Japanese musicians that play Latin music. . . . There are [also] Latin musicians in Russia, and Estonia, and Budapest, and Bulgaria.

Through long experience, Harlow learned firsthand exactly where, how, and why his music is appreciated. That direct experience is where the real marketing research occurs. But short of that, basic research can be conducted that will point you to the pockets of receptivity for your music around the globe. Start there, and focus on the niche listeners most likely to support you.

DEALS AND AGREEMENTS FOR GLOBAL TOURING

As discussed earlier, touring involves channel partners. Beyond the promoters and booking agents previously cited are the support musicians you work with and the various intermediaries who handle ticketing, merchandise sales, and more. Every channel member and activity associated with a tour require understandings between parties regarding the division of responsibilities. Contracts are drawn up to make sure the understandings are mutually agreed upon, documented, and signed. While detailed discussion of legal issues is beyond the scope of this book, a look at some of the typical tour-related deal points can shed light on common issues you'll confront.

Basic Performance Agreement. Any transaction involving performance requires some sort of agreement between parties, even if it's just a handshake. But while oral contracts are enforceable, they can be difficult to prove. Advice: Put it in writing. And here are the fundamental issues to address:

- Dates and times of the performance
- Financial terms. Various pay schemes are possible. Play around with pay structures. Choose the one that best suits the specific scenario. Options include:
  - Flat fee (guaranteed, regardless of sales)
  - Percentage of receipts from ticket sales
  - Flat fee or a percentage of the cover charge (or "door"), whichever is greater
  - Flat fee plus percentage of receipts from ticket sales

Booking Agency Agreement. The value provided is better-quality engagements, along with expertise in negotiating with promoters. Booking agents collect payment, deduct their percentage, then pay the artist or representative. Spell out the conditions:

- Commission percentage. Typically it is 10 to 15 percent of gross receipts. Agents tend to get paid first, out of the entire "pot," before that amount is reduced by payments to others. But it is important to define the pot. What is "gross"? For example, total revenues may include payment for such extras as musicians' airfare. Should the agent receive 10 to 15 percent of those extras? And which ones? Negotiate, and write it down.
- Timing of payment to artist. Typically, it is within seven days of the agent's receipt.
- Territories of representation, and exclusivity within territories.
- Term of agreement. Six months' worth of shows is typical.
- Bookings not subject to the agreement. If you booked some concerts yourself, specify that the agent is not to receive a commission for those dates.
- Key man provision. If your personal agent switches to another agency, leaving you with a replacement who doesn't particularly like your music, you need to be free to terminate the contract.

- Approval rights over assignment of your contract. If your agency merges with another that you don't like, it's important to be able to veto any attempt to transfer your contract to the new owner.

Promoter Agreement. Higher-level performances are typically set up by a concert promoter, who finances the event, pays all participants, and (hopefully) earns a profit. The deal with the promoter, often negotiated by a booking agency, covers the following points:

- Dates and times of the engagement
- Number of shows (with an option for additional shows, if demand warrants)
- Financial terms (see *Performance Agreement*, above)
- Exclusivity within the territory for a reasonable time period prior to and following the date (to ensure against "cannibalization" by ticket sales for a nearby recent or upcoming appearance)
- Amount payable on cancellation
- Division of earnings on concession sales
- Division of earnings on merchandise sales
- Rider, covering a range of specific artist requirements that could include:
  - Reimbursement for air travel and the level of travel (business class?)
  - Level of accommodation (five star?)
  - Security traveling to and from the show. (For some acts, twenty-four-hour security may be demanded.)
  - Assistance obtaining visas
- Warranties (the artist warrants there are no conditions preventing performance of obligations under the contract)
- Insurance (such as liability insurance for equipment lost or damaged in transit)
- Electricity and voltage requirements
- Safety provisions for open-air performances

Ticketing Agreements. Tickets are often sold through third-party ticketing agencies, which charge a fee for their services. Where Ticketmaster used to dominate this sector, the Internet has since spawned competitors. (As of this writing, 60 to 80 percent of concert ticket sales are now transacted over the Internet.) In arrangements between promoter and ticketing agency, issues to resolve include:

- Fee for services. What percentage of the ticket price will the agency retain?
- Timing of the agency's release of funds to the promoter. A rate of interest may be determined for amounts held beyond a specified point in time.

Tour Entourage. Backing singers, support musicians, sound engineers, and more all need clarification of and agreement on terms. Typical issues include whether they are on first-call for your tour or whether you need to put favorite musicians on retainer to ensure their availability; the scheduling of pretour and on-tour rehearsal time; whether there will be live recording and, if so, the amount of compensation due; what happens if songs are written on the road and a musician contributes a phrase or an idea—whether payment is on a work-for-hire basis or a percentage of authorship.

Merchandise Issues. The determination of whether a concert makes a profit or shows a loss often rests on sales of merchandise—nonmusic items such as T-shirts, souvenir books, mugs, and the like—bearing the artist's logo or likeness. At one concert staged by French singer Johnny Halliday, 120 vendors were hired to sell Halliday product, which had begun to be sold on the Internet six months before the show. Doors opened early to encourage sales prior to the show.

As described in *This Business of Music Marketing and Promotion*, band merchandise can be ongoing advertising for the band as well as a source of income, which is why it is an important part of the marketing program. Issues to consider include the following:

- Who should manufacture? It can be the artist's organization, or an outside vendor can be hired. If it's an outside vendor, the percentage of gross sales retained by the artist (or other rights holder, such as a record company) has to be determined. An amount between 25 and 40 percent is not unusual.

- The concert hall typically handles on-site sales, and a commission, concession fee, or "hall fee" must be agreed upon. An amount between 20 and 40 percent is not unusual.

- Sales in nightclubs may be handled by the artist. (The Web-based indie retailer CD Baby can provide you with credit-card swiping machines that you can use on-site for 9 percent of the amount you receive.) Some nightclubs require concession fees—even a percentage of CD sales on-site. You'll need to negotiate this.

- Sales at college venues may be subject to content approval. (Language, imagery, and politics are among potential sources of controversy or dispute.) Work this out ahead of time, and put the agreement in writing.

MULTICASTING THE LIVE CONCERT EXPERIENCE

As the number of platforms for consuming entertainment has increased, so has the number of ways listeners can watch a live performance. A pay-per-view version can be offered on television. A version can be streamed over the Internet. A cell phone owner can watch a wirelessly transmitted version. Audio can transmit through satellite radio. And more. All of these platforms offer opportunities to increase the viewership of a live concert—and increase the revenues.

How does it work? Media companies partially underwrite the costs of staging an event in return for their right to offer the event to their customers. All participants benefit, hypothetically.

There is the massive-scale approach to multicasting, and there's a more modest approach. Taking the massive-scale model as a starting point, Live 8, the multicity and multi-hundred-artist benefit event of 2005, attracted sponsorship from the BBC, the mobile communications company Nokia, and AOL. Each of these entities made the concert available through its platform. As digital media executive Kevin Wall told *MIDEM* magazine in 2006, "Live 8 was the tipping point. . . . Before, people were saying that you can only get the full live experience through a TV set. But if you watch a concert via mobile streaming, that's a 'wow,' because it's so immediate. The next generation is starting now. In the U.S. alone, AOL will serve around five billion individual music video streams this year, and Yahoo! some 4.5 billion."

In addition to providing expanded audiences for the live event, multicasting generates a greater amount of press. Hypothetically, each media platform spins off stories about its programming. The artist at the center benefits from this exponential increase in publicity.

Even the modest, mid-level artist can make use of this strategy. The key is to target the media—or the particular channel on a media platform—most linked with your audience niche or broader segment. Clarify to the media executives or producers how a broadcast of your concert will bring them customers or benefit their brand.

BARRIERS TO GLOBAL TOURING

Where global touring most differs from local, regional, and domestic touring is in the regulatory barriers that make the global touring process difficult. One example: A band from outside the United States was booked to play a show in the U.S., sponsored by the magazine *Billboard*. Well ahead of time, the process of applying for work permits for each band member was put into motion. All seemed to be going well until, at the last minute, a work permit was denied one member of the band because a background check turned up a DUI (driving under the influence) conviction.

This example illustrates one kind of barrier: entry and visiting regulations. Another kind revolves around taxation.

VISA REGULATIONS

Since September 11, 2001, the process of applying for visas to gain entry to foreign countries has become more arduous. Not only is it harder for musicians to plan multicountry tours, but the new regulations have an impact on who they bring and who can earn money. As British event producer Mark Cunningham told the *Music Business Journal* in 2004: "New visa application measures . . . are expensive, complicated, and time consuming. The cost and the necessary jumping through hoops are of grave concern to many crew members who regularly tour the States. The problem is compounded by the fact that it is relatively easy for U.S. crews to work over here. Not only does that mean that U.S. bands will use U.S. crews in Europe but it could also mean that U.K. bands who tour in the U.S. will find it easier to use U.S. personnel. Naturally, the situation is very unbalanced."

Promoters who wish to use foreign artists must apply for visas months before scheduling a tour. They need to ensure that the performers really intend to return home. MTV News reported in 2000 about a non-U.S. dance troupe that traveled to California for a tour. Shortly after arrival, they dropped out of sight, presumably to repatriate. In 2003, according to an article in *The Washington Post*, a well-known Indian performer was accused of taking payments to arrange passage out of India for people whom he allowed to pose as members of his performing group. In the days of the Soviet Union, members of the Russian Ballet seemed to have a habit of defecting to other countries. Now in particular, with fears of terrorism permeating government bureaucracies, much more scrutiny is being paid to visa applications.

For prospective tour participants it means starting the application process early, expecting difficulties, and having backup plans in case visas are denied anyone associated with the tour.

And it's not just the visa that can cause headaches. Foreign performers working in Australia, according to the Web site of Newsouthfolk Tour Management, have to obtain, in correct order, a Tax File Number (TFN), an Australian Business Number (ABN), written permission from the Musicians Union of Australia or the Media and Entertainment Arts Alliance, sponsorship for their visa application (Form 148), a Class 420 Entertainment Visa (Form 147), and a Foreign Resident Withholding Variation (FRWV). The lead time for obtaining a TFN and then an ABN is approximately two months. And other countries have requirements of their own.

TAXES ON LIVE MUSIC

In global touring, you can expect to confront a range of different approaches to assessing tax on foreign performances. Many governments apply what is called a "withholding tax" on earnings of performances by nonresident artists. In the U.K., for example, the tax authority was withholding 23 percent (at press time) of the fee that an artist received. In Germany, the amount was 30 percent. Promoters or artist management can typically apply for a reduction of tax based on production costs, but the ease or difficulty of doing this varies across borders.

An artist's home country may tax earnings from foreign performances. In such cases, the artist is being doubly taxed—a situation that has caused some bitterness among EU artists touring within that trade bloc. These musicians echo the earlier claim that, because of double taxation within EU countries, it's more expensive to be an EU performer touring within the EU than it is to be a U.S. performer touring within the EU.

Detailed analysis of tax policies in different countries is beyond the scope of this book. But it's important to bear in mind the attention that will have to be paid to taxes, whether by you or, better, by your accountant or financial advisor. Before booking the tour, find out the policies of your target country and factor the taxes into your profit-and-loss calculations.

SOURCES OF TOUR SUPPORT

As the cost-and-earnings breakdown on page 165 shows, tours are expensive operations that can easily lose money, particularly at the emerging-artist stage. Yet touring is important—especially for emerging artists trying to break into new territories and intermediate artists trying to shift from nightclubs to arenas. Fortunately, financial and other support are available from a number of sectors. They include record companies, corporate sponsors, festivals, and government agencies. And marketers-artists with intelligence and creativity can find alternative ways to make touring possible—without becoming indebted to investors.

RECORD-COMPANY TOUR SUPPORT

A record company, recognizing the importance and difficulty of building audiences, may be willing to provide an artist with financial support for touring. This usually means paying for any shortfall between tour costs and earnings. Preparing a detailed, line-by-line tour budget will indicate how much this shortfall may be.

The money is not a giveaway. Record companies recoup—repay themselves—from earnings on your record sales. That's why record company support, or any other third-party financial support, should be a last resort, or at least not the first choice. The most financially sound approach is to tour modestly and prudently so that the venture pays for itself. Any inclination to accept loans—which is what record company tour support essentially is—should be carefully scrutinized to make sure that the potential for future earnings is high enough to justify going into debt now.

Record companies do not necessarily recoup 100 percent of the tour money they advance. You can negotiate it down to 50 percent. Or you can ask that it be 100 percent of earnings only from records sold in the territory of the tour. Creative, innovative deal making can often uncover new and interesting, mutually beneficial approaches to financing and repayment.

SPONSORSHIPS, INCLUDING MULTICASTING

Sponsorship and co-branding arrangements can be set up with companies targeting the same audiences and territories as the artist. The company underwrites a portion of the tour cost. In return it advertises itself as a sponsor in advertising, in-store promotion, onstage bannering, and/or other methods.

For the artist, it is important that association with the company not be viewed as a negative by core audiences. That's why the choice of company is critical. Industries that commonly sponsor tours include beverages, fashion, communications, electronics, and automobiles, to cite just a few.

As described in "Multicasting the Live Concert Experience" (page 175), partnering with a media company to widecast a performance is a good way to share costs of touring.

FESTIVALS AND MULTIARTIST TOURS

Rather than going it alone, you can exploit the collective clout of multiple artists and the collective wisdom of highly experienced concert promoters by aligning yourself with a music festival or a multiartist tour. You share the spot-light, but you also gain entry to territories that you might not be able to afford to visit were you attempting it on your own. A standout performance at a fes-tival in front of a huge audience can do wonders for an artist's career. New audiences can be brought into the fan base, building new momentum for record sales.

Research current festivals and multiartist tours by checking the Yahoo! Internet listing of "music festivals" or by doing a general keyword search of "music festivals." Visit Pollstar online (www.pollstar.com) for news and sched-ules of planned tours.

When researching festivals and multiartist tours, keep in mind your strate-gic aims. Know the kind of audience you're trying to reach, and make sure the festival can reach that audience. Choose festivals on the basis of territories that you are targeting.

Getting signed to participate in a tour requires a promotional effort sim-ilar to that needed to interest a record distributor or get radio play or get on a TV show. The tour producers want bands with buzz, that can help them attract audiences. Your job, as marketer of your services to tour promoters, is to convince them of your value on the artist roster. Your existing kit of pro-motional materials—one-sheet, artist bio, fact sheet, press clips—should already have the kind of information promoters need to see. Target the right festivals and tours, and get your promotional materials to the talent bookers as early as possible.

GOVERNMENT SUPPORT FOR TOURING

Some countries, seeing the benefit of exporting and importing culture, have programs to subsidize music performance.

The Netherlands, for example, has a program called the National Pop Institute (NPI), www.hollandrocks.com, that assists local performers with costs of international touring.

The 2005–2006 European Tour Support Program of the European Music Office (www.musicineurope.org) awarded a total of €300,000 in grants to well-established artists and upcoming talents, with the objective of "stimulating the mobility of artists and the circulation of their works in Europe." The grants supported tours of seven countries and nineteen shows on average per artist. The organization is planning to expand this program internationally.

Take a look at what your own government may offer in terms of tour sub-sidies. There may be a program for a genre or category that fits you.

CREATIVE APPROACHES TO TOURING

Ideally, a tour should be self-financing. There are ways to make this possible without resorting to subsidies, loans, and advances. Company sponsorships and co-branding, cited previously, are great ways to spread the costs of touring without having to pay back any money. Short of that option, you can focus on reducing costs and bringing in nonperformance income.

Save money by devising alternate approaches to accommodations. An "adopt a band member" program can yield stay-overs in private residences that also build fan support and loyalty. Like the indie artist who set up her own Tokyo tour, mentioned earlier in this chapter, you can contact and network with musicians in the target territory and get suggestions for the best cheap places to stay—or maybe set up stay-overs with local musicians. The main thing is to avoid overspending on the road—dispel any "superstar" fantasies that can lead to profligate use of credit cards—and keep your eye on earning, not unloading, money.

To earn extra money that can make the difference between tour surplus and deficit, sell recordings and/or other merchandise at shows. For recordings, make sure that on-site sales won't incur the displeasure of retailers or other channel members that sell your record, and make sure you've cleared the division of earnings from on-site sales with all parties who may have an ownership interest.

Promoting Globally Through Integrated Marketing Communications (IMC)

There is distribution, and then there is communication about distribution. Communication—to inform, to persuade, to remind—helps create customer awareness and interest, without which there will be no impulse or desire to buy. Distribution may stop at retail and fail to "sell through" to final customers unless there is communication to the public that the musical product is available. Communication builds demand.

Communication about music can take many forms: word of mouth; publicity and stories (news and features) in print, broadcast, and electronic media; paid advertising in print, broadcast, and electronic media; and interactive "relationship building" through direct messaging on the Internet and through other channels.

Some artists and their business representatives rely on word of mouth. A natural, street-level "buzz" is created among viewers of a live performance who feel enthusiasm about it and tell their friends. Excitement and interest may build. Demand may grow, and audiences may proactively seek out concert dates and records for sale. Still, while persuasive advertising may not be required for the highly popular artist, some kinds of communication will always be needed, even if only to leak information that a new album is on the way.

For global communications, as with domestic, the tasks are at least threefold: (1) identify your objective, (2) craft the message, and (3) choose the communication channel and mode. A fourth task, if you have chosen several modes, is to configure and schedule an effective mix of communication modes—for example, newspaper and Internet ads to build initial awareness, accompanied by press notices to provide detail and shape perceptions, followed by sales promotion to motivate short-term behavior and "close the sale," supported by direct marketing to build one-to-one relationships with customers. This mix, and the management of it to convey a consistent impression, is what is meant by the term *integrated marketing communications* (IMC).

It used to be that in any given enterprise, publicists operated on their own, ad creators operated separately, and sales promotion people went their own way. Uncoordinated and inconsistent brand messages would go out into the world, resulting in incoherent branding. Today, the focus on IMC means all the different communication functions work together so that a coodinated, coherent message, released in a configuration of media and schedules arranged for maximum impact, burns a strong brand image in the minds of consumers.

A global marketplace complicates matters. Creating the message can be difficult because different territories may be attracted to different ideas, images, and symbols. Global communication channels can be difficult to select because different territories may favor different kinds of media. Communicating territorially requires knowledge of the culture and tastes of target markets and the communication tools they use. It's simply more data to absorb than if you were just marketing domestically.

One way to approach decisions about international IMC is to break the process down into separate components. Let's call them the Four M's of global integrated marketing communications:

- **Message:** The specific information you wish to convey to induce a market response or action

- **Mode:** The method of communication, whether publicity/PR, advertising, direct marketing, or sales promotion (also referred to, by marketing theorist Philip Kotler, as the communication "platform")

- **Media:** The vehicles and channels through which the message will be conveyed, whether print, broadcast, or electronic

- **Mix:** The balanced configuration and combination of messages, modes, and media best suited to the target market and your marketing objective

In the international market, the process of planning and executing IMC may be handled by one or more of several possible parties. The domestic record company or individual artist-seller may think about and devise an integrated marketing plan for a foreign distribution campaign, relying on the foreign distributor's advice and expertise about local media, customer tastes, and business practices. The IMC plan could also be a blueprint that the domestic company hands over to a foreign licensee to use in its own local marketing, to make sure that the artist image and marketing message are communicated consistently around the world. (Without such a suggested plan, or even required guidelines, the licensee may create new messaging that complicates or damages the brand image.) IMC could be created and implemented by a local marketing firm that the incoming record label hires for its local expertise. IMC could also be developed by the licensee, taking product from another country and marketing it locally as an import.

Whoever is handling IMC needs to work with every important campaign decision makers to develop the Four M's.

MESSAGE

At any given time in the life cycle of a musical product, or of you yourself as a performer, there may be a communication point you wish to get across to an audience or potential audience. At the beginning, that message might be: "Artist A has released a debut album, and you should buy it." Later, the message might be: "Artist A's first album is still available. Buy it now for a ten percent discount." The content of the message depends in part on the life cycle stage of the product and in part on the market situation you face. For example, you may have an album out that didn't attract many initial sales, requiring you to rework your message. Thus, before you decide on your message you need to have a clear conception of your objective. Knowing the objective, you are better able to develop the actual content of the message and then to design it in the most effective and appealing way for the target audience.

MESSAGE OBJECTIVE

Messages typically have one or more purposes: to announce, to remind, to persuade, or to motivate. Put another way, the objectives may be to

- Make people aware of your music
- Instill a positive attitude about your music
- Impel an action (e.g., to buy your music)

Identifying the objective of your marketing communication can be simple; it might be to announce a new album. Or the objective might be somewhat more complicated and difficult to achieve: You wish, for example, to draw attention to the special qualities of an emerging singer–songwriter in a market saturated with singer–songwriters. In this case your purpose is, in essence, to persuade. Sometimes the objective is simple to state but difficult to achieve: You want people to buy now, and to get them to do it you're willing to offer a special incentive to create motivation.

These objectives don't exist in a vacuum. They are dependent on the environment—the market situation—in which they exist. They also depend on the target audience. To take accurate inventory of the current market situation, your target audience, your objective, and your key communication point, you can begin by preparing a planning document—sometimes called a *communication brief*. Get agreement on its content among all stakeholders before considering it final.

A communication brief typically includes decisions about the following items:

- Current marketing situation
- Marketing objective
- Target audience
- Key communication point (key message)
- Support points
- Desired response
- Tone, style
- Design, art, photography
- Media and distribution vehicles
- Timing and budget

COMMUNICATION BRIEF

MARKETING SITUATION

The Howard McGillicuddy Band's first album sold 15,000 copies domestically and received positive reviews. It continues to sell steadily.

The follow-up recording is due to be released October 15. It is expected to sell at least as well as the first album. With positive domestic reaction to this artist to date, there's likelihood of appeal to similar audiences in foreign countries. This new release provides an opportunity to start building out to foreign markets.

MARKETING OBJECTIVE

Country A has been chosen as an initial target foreign market, due to the success there of music by similar artists X, Y, and Z. The primary objective is to make sure that an initial export quantity of 2,000 sells through at retail.

TARGET AUDIENCE

A total of 200,000 customers in Country A have purchased music by artists X, Y, and Z. Messaging and promotion should aim primarily at these customers. This audience tends to be older (forty-plus), well educated, affluent, professional, Internet savvy (purchase music both online and in brick-and-mortar stores), with a preference for sophisticated music on the jazzy side. They tend to be open to new, quality music and trends.

KEY COMMUNICATION POINT (KEY MESSAGE)

People should discover and buy the record because its sound will satisfy their desire for sophisticated entertainment. Something like: "Discover the Howard McGillicuddy Band for music that stimulates your thoughts as well as your senses and rewards well-seasoned, discriminating tastes."

SUPPORT POINTS

Be on the cutting edge and be the first to discover this band and tell your friends about them.

REQUIRED INCLUSIONS

Names of Web sites and stores where the album can be purchased.

DESIRED RESPONSE

Go online or to a store to listen to and buy this album.

Tone, Style

Language that's smart, that respects the reader's cleverness, that uses interesting and sophisticated turns of phrase. The tone and style should appeal to older, educated, accomplished people.

Design, Art, Photography

Use high-end imagery that suggests qualities associated with the music: elegance, urbanity, stylishness, a touch of nostalgia, rich colors and textures. Perhaps a scene of urban nightlife, as in a sleek piano bar with windows overlooking sparkling city lights; attractive people enjoying life at its best.

Media and Distribution Vehicles

- Distribute on land through local distribution partner, via Internet and mobile through partner DMA.
- PR to target print media, radio, and Web with announcement of album and performances in key venues. Calls to editors to cover and review shows and album.
- Advertising in target alternative print media, including endorsement from Artist X.
- Sales promotion via artist signings at key retailers, with song giveaways and front-of-store displays.
- Postrelease promotion per market response.

Timing and Budget

- Live performances scheduled during fourth week of release.
- PR, advertising to start running five weeks before album street date.
- Budget to be decided; recommend strong initial push to launch band in Country A.

MESSAGE CONTENT

With a clear concept of your objective, and with knowledge of your target audience, you can move on to developing the specific content of the communication. You choose the words, tone, and structure of the communication that will be the most convincing.

Part of the message is persuasion. To persuade, you need to embed in the message words or images that capture the aspect of the music that will appeal to the target audience. Here's an example of a message that both made an announcement and offered a persuasive bit of information carefully targeted to the audience: A music producer decided to announce the release of his new CD by posting a message on an Internet newsgroup of which he was a member. The subject of the newsgroup was Brian Wilson and the Beach Boys. The producer's message first invited newsgroup members to check out his new CD on a popular Internet retail site. He added that his inspiration while producing the CD was Brian Wilson's *Smile*, a legendary production that took Wilson years of meticulous attention to complete. Mentioning that record to Wilson fans is like using code. It implies "obsessively produced masterwork" in a way that they immediately understand and that might spark their interest.

In crafting your message for maximum impact in international markets you need to think about the following factors:

- Appeal, uniqueness, and believability
- The awareness-interest-desire-action (AIDA) formula
- Whether to standardize or customize the message

The first of these items has been expressed by author–marketer Philip Kotler as desirability, exclusiveness, and believability. That is, the message should first be interesting, so that people pay attention. Then it should be unlike other messages, so that people are more likely to remember it. Finally, it should be credible, so that people don't dismiss it.

The second item, the AIDA formula, is widely recognized as a method of eliciting desired responses. It addresses the stages of response categorized as cognition, affect, and behavior—or learning, feeling, and doing. You want to make buyers aware of your product. You want them to feel good about it. And you want them to make the purchase.

Those aspects of message content are more or less universal. It's when you get into the issue of standardization versus customization that the complexities of international marketing come into play.

Your life would be easy if you could craft a clear communication and have it work for every country you planned to sell in. Your costs would be less, too. But one message may not work for all countries due to language and cultural differences and regulatory requirements.

The language obstacles are obvious: a word or phrase may have a different meaning in a foreign country, so you need to check your terminology carefully. More broadly, the tone, style, and imagery of your communication may work well in one country but have no impact in another. As with product development, discussed in Chapter 4, you might want to apply mass customization to your messaging—that is, find a basic message that will work anywhere and then refine or adjust it for different territories.

A study titled *Consumption Symbols as Carriers of Culture*, published by the Marketing Science Institute, found that some "brand personalities"—representing a set of characteristics, traits, and values—tend to have universal resonance while others are culture-specific. For example, people everywhere seem to be drawn to excitement, competence, sophistication, and sincerity. But the U.S. emphasizes toughness, ruggedness, and individuality. Japan, on the other hand, values peacefulness, optimism, and community. In Spain, meanwhile, passion, emotional intensity, and spiritualism are valued.

What you need to do is find the universal aspect of your product—say, excitement—and then either make sure the message has nothing that will repel the local audience, or refine the message to actively appeal to the local audience. Find the quality of the music that can resonate locally and then find the right words and images to make sure consumers receive the information in the way you intend.

Local regulatory requirements may force you to rethink a message concept. In China, for example, there are strict rules about how women may be depicted in radio and TV advertising. In the United States, hard liquor can't be advertised on network television. In some countries, children under twelve can't be directly advertised to—doctors in Australia condemned advertising to kids as child abuse. Before finalizing a communication concept for a target territory, thoroughly research local advertising regulations—and social/cultural conventions.

MODE

Knowing your marketing objective and the content of the communication you wish to convey, you then need to decide on a mode of communication. A mode refers not to a specific kind of media or communication vehicle but to a tactic, a particular approach to marketing communications, which may involve several media. There are many possible tactics you can take, all generally categorizable under four main modes:

- Public relations (PR) and publicity
- Advertising
- Direct marketing
- Sales promotion

Each has its advantages, and each tends to be effective in specific circumstances. An integrated marketing communications strategy may draw on several different modes for different stages of the marketing campaign or different aspects of your marketing objective.

In applying these modes to international marketing, it's important to know not only the general uses, advantages, and disadvantages of each but also the specific applicability to and usefulness in your targeted territories.

PUBLIC RELATIONS (PR) AND PUBLICITY

Public relations, the term, represents a range of related activities all having to do with making information about a subject public—as "news," not ads—through print, broadcast, and electronic media. Another name for it is publicity. As detailed in the book *This Business of Music Marketing and Promotion*, publicity is the art of attracting attention, for free, via the information outlets that consumers routinely use. Publicity is part of the lifeblood of the music marketing operation.

The tools of publicity are the media list and the media kit. The *media list* is the marketer's, or marketing PR specialist's, collected list of professional contacts in the media industry—the editors, writers, reviewers, and personalities who decide what would make a good news piece, profile, review, or feature story. The *media kit* is the presentation package of introductory information material that summarizes the artist, music, or other product, and that the marketer makes available in hard copy and on the Internet for target media people. Internet posting of the media kit, at the artist's or record company's Web site, is ideal for ease of access and downloading by members of the press.

The kit consists of current news, biography, fact sheet, press clips or quotes, photographs, and music samples. The "news" part of the package is in the form of a press release, the central tool of publicity. It's a succinct "story" about the current activity, presented according to formal conventions and written like a news piece. For details about the basics of media kits and publicity, see *This Business of Music Marketing and Promotion*.

When Best to Use PR. Publicity is an ideal mode for the introductory stage of the product life cycle. It informs and at the same time provides details. It can be directed at target audiences through print and Internet news sources to build initial interest. In combination with advertising, PR can add depth and dimension to a communications campaign. It can precede advertising to build excitement before ads hit the media. In addition to costing nothing, the advantage of PR is that it gives more credibility to a communication than if the message came from a paid-for advertisement.

PR also works as a periodic reminder after the introductory phase has passed. Any new activity on the part of the performer, from a new tour date to a guest appearance on a television show, can be the subject of a news story the publicist pitches to editors. Keeping stories flowing through the media is one way to keep a performer in the public eye and a career alive.

International Public Relations. PR is not immune to the "think global, act local" precept common among worldwide marketers of goods and services. Cultural differences often dictate custom messaging to take into account differences in cultures. But the logistics of localizing a PR campaign in a foreign country can be complex.

Challenges start with language. Although English is considered the international business language, that doesn't mean that a pitch letter sent in English to a French editor will not be at a disadvantage. If your aim is to get through to editors, to remove all barriers from accepting your pitch for a story, you would do best by communicating in the local language.

The same applies to press releases. If you want one to be read by an editor in a foreign country, you should have it translated into the local language. In addition, you should keep the press release short. Some countries, the U.S. being one, tend to produce lengthy press releases. Other countries prefer them brief. The safe approach is to keep the press release to one page.

Translation takes effort and expertise. Chances are reasonably high that record companies outside the U.S. have people capable of doing this. But U.S. companies may not. For those companies it will be necessary to find someone with local expertise. This presents a logistical challenge, an extra expense, and the risk of a poor press release. If you don't speak the local language, you won't be able to check the work of the translator without extra help.

The difficulties of cross-culture journalism came up on a regular basis in one U.S. online music publication. An Italian reporter regularly submitted stories from Italy. They were typically reviews of concerts or profiles of musicians, with musicians' comments often included. The reporter would translate his stories into English before sending them to the main office. The problem was, his English vocabulary was less than precise. U.S. editors who worked on his pieces often found themselves uncertain about the exact meaning of a phrase or a musician's quotation. Even long-distance phone calls to the writer failed to yield clarification, since the writer was no better at speaking English than he was at writing it. With his stories there was always the chance that his intended meaning would not show up in the story and that words attributed to musicians were not quite what he'd meant to convey.

A good translation of your press release is a necessity if you want to maintain control over the communication and not have the wrong impression conveyed in the media.

Of course, pitches to the local media should have local appeal. They might be linked with concert appearances in the area, for example.

To take care of all these bits of business, to publicize successfully in a target foreign market, you really need to work with someone who knows local media outlets and knows the language. Ideally you'll have a person like this for each different market you enter. Preferably each maintains a presence in that market, so that he or she is connected to local media by telephone within the same time zone—or separated by only an hour or two. (It really doesn't work to have your publicist respond to a 3 A.M. phone call from a media representative nine hours away. The publicist must be in a position to respond to media needs immediately.)

Who might this publicity person be? It could be a freelancer recommended by your distributor. It could also be someone working in-house for your distributor. If you can't find anyone local, you might have to handle foreign public relations yourself, from afar. Fortunately, the Internet and e-mail make such a do-it-yourself approach possible, if not ideal. If your story is interesting enough, or your artist popular enough, you might not have to concern yourself with such niceties as translating your press release or cutting it down to a shorter length; the media will be more than happy to prepare stories on your act.

If you do end up working with local professionals, you face the challenge of coordinating and monitoring their work. Consistency of image and message is important, even when aspects are shaded to meet local preferences and requirements. So assign one person—yourself, if there are no other people—to communicate guidelines and required messaging to the field agents. Set up a regularly scheduled conference call for getting reports from them about successes and problems in media placement.

Downside of Public Relations. In publicity, you control the message as far as the writing of the press release or the pitching of the story. But once a writer or editor takes over, you lose control. The published story may have a spin far from what you had wished for. The impression on the reader may be different than you had hoped for. It can happen. For more control over messaging (but for higher cost) you turn to advertising.

ADVERTISING

"The obvious way to promote a modern act now, would be to take out a few adverts: one in the *NME* [*New Musical Express*], one in the *Guardian Guide*, one in the *Face*—that's the normal sort of way," U.K. artist manager Phil Robinson told the *Music Business Journal*'s Ryan Cairns. "I think the best form of promotion is TV—but that is at the other end of the financial scale. . . . You just need to groom your act and drop some very key TV adverts. . . . You can plant a seed [in a popular TV show], and follow up with another advert two weeks later, in a show he/she is also watching, then it will start to work. The thing with TV advertising is that when it works, it really works."

The advertising referred to here is basic, informational, awareness-building display ads and broadcast commercials. Another kind is direct-response advertising, discussed separately in the next section, "Direct Marketing."

People will tell you that advertising has lost some of its luster in recent years. Stated reasons include the sheer number of messages currently competing for consumer mind share, the rise of new and more interactive communication vehicles, and the ability of satellite TV watchers to record programs and skip past commercials. One statistic indicated that advertisers now reach no more than 15 percent of the population with an ad in prime time, compared to 40 percent in the mid-1980s.

Yet there is still a place for advertising. It remains a preferred means of reaching a large number of people simultaneously and building awareness of, if not desire for, the thing being advertised. It's a great opportunity to control the content of the message, control the location of the message, and control the impact (frequency) of the message. Furthermore, despite widespread distrust of advertising, the sheer existence of an ad on TV or in print confers, in the public mind, a kind of legitimacy on the product.

True, advertising can be incredibly expensive at its high end: $2.3 million on average for a thirty-second commercial on the U.S. Super Bowl broadcast in 2004. But now that cable TV offers hundreds of channels and more targeted programming, it's possible to arrange a schedule of commercials on cable TV for an affordable cost.

The media options for advertising include print (newspapers, magazines, billboards, transit postering), broadcast (network, cable, and satellite TV; international, national, and local radio), and electronic (Web site ads of various types, e-mail newsletter sponsorships).

When Best to Use Advertising. Similar to PR, advertising works best at the beginning of a marketing campaign, when you want to start from scratch and create awareness of a new product among a population. Advertising also serves well when your aim is to remind the public about a product after it's been on the market for a while.

When planning advertising, you are concerned with all the message factors discussed in the "Message" section of this chapter, as well as with the media placement and schedule.

Media placement—a full-time job responsibility in ad agencies—focuses on

- Type of media
- Timing of ad-casting
- Location of ad placement

In choosing media, you're concerned with reach, frequency, and impact. *Reach* refers to how many people are exposed to the ad. It could be millions, as on the U.S. Super Bowl show or in *People* magazine, or it could be highly targeted thousands. You target the population segment you want to reach. *Frequency* refers to the number of times the target population is exposed to the ad. Related to this is strategic timing over the length of the ad run. In broadcast, you might run an ad continuously, several times a day, for a month. Or you might concentrate the ads into a short time, to get maximum attention around the time the music goes on sale. Or you could use a strategy called *flighting*, which alternates periods of advertising and no advertising, achieving extended though intermittent exposure with smaller expenditures than continuous advertising. Another approach is *pulsing*, which involves low-level continuity with "pulses" of increased advertising tied to retail activity—such as the album street date. Details of advertising options are discussed in *This Business of Music Marketing and Promotion*.

International Advertising. This faces some of the same challenges as international public relations: messages lost in the translation, logistical difficulties in localizing the process, and different media preferences in different markets. Here's how they play out in the advertising mode.

First, the international scope of advertising is indicated by the sum of global expenditures—$569.8 billion in 2005, according to a report prepared by ad agency McCann-Erickson. (Compare that to the music industry's worldwide recorded-music sales of $32 billion only one year earlier!) A large chunk of that amount goes to multinational agencies such as BBDO Worldwide, J. Walter Thompson, Grey, Ogilvy and Mather, and Publicis.

The way these agencies work indicates the challenges of international advertising: they have offices or subsidiaries all over the world with local expertise in messaging and media, easily able to convert global communications to locally appealing communications. The local offices are specialists in the kinds of local media that predominate, the media-consumption patterns of local populations, and the cultural conventions that tinge the perceptions of messaging.

This kind of local expertise is a requirement for effectively advertising beyond your domestic borders. Yet most of you won't have access to multinational ad agencies or to a worldwide infrastructure of local agents. What do you do?

As with public relations, your local distributor or licensee can be a primary source of expertise on music-related media outlets and music-consuming local audiences. These individuals may be able to work with you to customize your ad messaging for local audiences and recommend local print media, broadcast programming, and Internet sites best able to reach your target audience segment. Alternatively, these people may be able to recommend local advertising specialists to serve as your agent for ad creation and media placement.

Another source of information comprises other record companies and successful recording artists who tour and sell in the territory you're targeting. Contacting their marketing departments or artist managers may yield some valuable recommendations for how to advertise abroad.

On the Internet, the International Advertising Resource Center (www.bgsu.edu/departments/tcom/faculty/ha/intlad1.html) provides a wealth of links that can lead you to information on country-by-country media, advertising practices in specific regions, international advertising regulations, and a lot more. It's worth spending time here and at other business sites devoted to your target country to immerse yourself in the local environment you'll deal with.

Downside of Advertising. People have a well-trained distrust of advertising. They tend to view it as an imposition on their time and attention, an attempt to manipulate, and often unworthy of trust. To counteract this, make ads creative, entertaining, clever, informative, and targeted to audiences who would be interested. The ad agency McCann-Erickson has a motto: "Truth Well Told." Adhere to it, and you stand a better chance of getting and holding attention.

DIRECT MARKETING

The real action in marketing communications, especially for many small labels and emerging artists, is in the category of direct marketing. This is where marketers employ creative strategies—including those currently called guerrilla, viral, and buzz marketing—to reach consumers directly and, typically, provide a mechanism for direct ordering of products. Direct marketing is where today's predominant theory of successful marketing—that you aim for a one-to-one, dialogue-based relationship with your customer—plays out. And in international music marketing, direct marketing may be the most available and effective of the IMC modes.

Direct marketing encompasses numerous techniques. They include

- Word of mouth
- Viral marketing

- E-marketing
- Direct mail
- Direct-response advertising

These categories are not necessarily mutually exclusive. In fact, they tend to overlap. But separating them for discussion can help us begin to understand the sometimes confusing array of direct-marketing options.

Word of Mouth. Creating a "buzz" of interest that takes on a life of its own and spreads throughout a network of individuals is what word-of-mouth marketing is all about. It can be set in motion by the artist himself talking to friends, but in most cases is better handled by someone other than the artist—a person who can be perceived as having more objectivity than the individual obviously positioned to gain from the promotion.

The vehicles for word of mouth can be verbal conversation, e-mails, instant messaging, Web postings, blogs—however people communicate directly.

The channels of word-of-mouth communication can be through salespeople, independent experts (other musicians, for example), and such social networks as friends, family, work associates, clubs.

Word of mouth works best when the first people contacted are "opinion leaders"—people of influence, whose passing on of recommendations will be taken seriously by recipients.

An example: A well-respected, prominent member of several Internet newsgroups became a fan of an emerging artist. When the artist independently released a CD, the newsgroup member recommended it in his newsgroup chatrooms. Within days, four hundred hits and twenty sales of the CD were logged at an online retailer, all from newsgroup members who respected the source of the recommendation.

Viral Marketing. Newsgroup messaging is where word of mouth crosses over into viral marketing—a more strategic use of social networks to build awareness and influence opinions.

One particularly large network is MySpace.com, with more than 37 million users in 2006. People post their profiles, pictures, and preferences, including music. The site has become such a leading source of information among teenagers that musicians post their MP3s there to build a buzz. Labels regularly use MySpace to get exposure for new and up-and-coming artists. Even leading performers such as Madonna post their music on MySpace. The success of the channel led to the launch of MySpace Records, a label for unsigned artists who populate the site. Started in the U.S., the MySpace Web site launched in the U.K. in April 2006.

Viral marketing aims to subtly infiltrate target social networks via their daily routines. The marketing plan for one emerging Internet music retailer had young representatives going to nightclubs and other public venues to mention the retailer in conversations and to give away coupons for free downloads.

The Coca-Cola Company created branded lounges for young people in several shopping malls, the purpose being to create an enjoyable hangout that happy customers would positively associate with Coke.

International Word of Mouth and Viral Marketing. Word of mouth tends to begin locally. In target territories, ground-level WOM campaigns can be launched locally through professional, expert, and social networks. The U.S. singer mentioned in Chapter 9 may have triggered word of mouth through expert (other musician) channels when she contacted Japanese musicians to help her set up a tour in Tokyo; those musicians might have "passed the word." Local distributors can use their sales channels to pass word of mouth to deejays, retail representatives, and club owners.

Viral marketing reaches internationally through the Internet. Newsgroup members may come from all over the world, making it possible to globally promote an artist from the home country. For on-the-ground viral marketing, local marketing agents or your licensees or distributors can help with ideas— and with implementing your ideas.

E-Marketing. The huge subject of e-marketing is the biggest story of all in the world of marketing since the mid 1990s. The maturing of Internet business has revolutionized marketing to the point that niche marketing, one-to-one marketing, personalized marketing, and customer relationship management (CRM) have become not only achievable but core components of strategic plans. It has made these operations affordable. Since the Internet reaches all around the globe, it is also a natural vehicle for worldwide marketing communications.

E-marketing encompasses such operations as

- Web site marketing
- Online advertising
- Search-engine optimization
- E-mail marketing
- Wireless communications

Web site can be the artist's home site or product page on a retailer's site, or it can be the record label's site featuring promotion on the artist. Much has been written about the structure of Web sites and how to optimize them as marketing communication tools. The book *This Business of Music Marketing and Promotion* provides many details.

The relationship-building aspect of e-marketing is critical. A customer needn't be short-term or single-purchase. Many businesses calculate *customer lifetime value*—a figure, that, if realized, can put a value on current customer service and loyalty-building strategies—strategies that keep the customer coming back for more over the lifetime of the artist and his recordings. It's cheaper to put energy and marketing resources into keeping that customer coming back than it is to attract a new customer. Thus there is an emphasis, in marketing today, on *customer relationship management* (CRM). A Web site is an ideal tool for CRM since it offers processes and procedures for interacting with customers and creating a positive, satisfying customer experience. Do this by making your Web site easy to navigate, fun to visit, and as personalized as possible.

Online advertising can include multimedia ads in various shapes and sizes on commercial Web sites, with hyperlinks to pages where the music can be purchased.

Search-engine optimization involves paying to have your site's link appear in a high position when customers type certain keywords for searches. Google, to mention one search-engine company, allows you to buy what it calls *sponsored links* or *pay per click*. You create an ad—a headline, short message, and hyperlink—that appears in a prominent position on the computer screen when words that you choose are searched for by customers. Choose "new jazz," for example, and you can have your message come up in a high or top position when people type "new jazz" into their Search prompts. The more you pay per click, the higher your message appears.

E-mail marketing can involve a personal message sent in bulk to names in your e-mail address book. Your collected list of names can come from many sources, including CD Baby if you sell there, where every sale is revealed to you by name, e-mail address, and other information. Add these names to your mailing list, but be sure not to antagonize or impose on these people by sending them unwanted e-mail. Make sure that your first message offers the option to "opt out" of receiving future e-mails. Even better, offer an active option to "opt in" to future e-mails. Also, batch your mailing list into a single e-mail address, so that recipients don't receive an entire page-full of addresses in the "To" field of your e-mail.

Keep messages informal, friendly, and as personal as possible. Make sure you provide a link to a page where people can purchase or get more information.

The sample e-mail message on the next page can be considered news. A slightly more developed piece would add up to a full-blown newsletter, which is an interesting way to make regular—monthly, quarterly, bi-yearly—contact with fans.

Marketers often have concerns about tracking hits to e-mail messages and newsletters, so that they can determine whether readers are clicking through to buy CDs. Internet techies know that you can create special URLs to capture readers' click-throughs before redirecting them to their intended destination. Checking the records of these "redirect" URLs shows how many people click through from the e-mail or newsletter.

Wireless marketing offers an alternative messaging channel to that offered by the Internet. Text messaging has been common in territories, such as Europe, where use of cell phones and other wireless devices is high. Multimedia marketing content is certain to become more pervasive.

International E-Marketing. Important considerations in multicountry e-marketing, as with "terrestrial" marketing, include standardizing as much as possible, localizing parts that need to be localized, and paying attention to local regulations and restrictions. The following categories of activity come into play when international strategies are pursued:

- **Technology:** Web sites that are designed to be country specific, as you'll find in Amazon.com's international section, must be built to support different currencies and languages.

SAMPLE E-MAIL MESSAGE

From: "Howard McGillicuddy"
Date: Sat, Apr 1, 2006 2:30:15 PM
To: [aggregate e-mail address]
Subject: Howard's new album is out
Reply-To: [howard's e-mail address]

Hello friends,

I've been busy completing tracks for my new record, and I'm happy to report that *McGillicuddy, Strings Attached* is finally ready for you to hear.

You can get it at [online retailer hyperlink] now. The first 10 of you who buy it there will get a free T-shirt. Be sure to provide your address where prompted and copy this code—HMB1234—into the "message" field so we know you're one of our insiders.

I think you're really going to like this music. We've got some guests, including ace guitarist Warren Mitchell, and a batch of new tunes written by our piano player Ashley Pruett. You can listen to samples at www.howardmcgillicuddy.com.

Upcoming dates:

April 15: San Francisco, CA: Johnny's Jazzeria

April 20: Sacramento, CA: Fred Rhodes' Rhodehouse

April 25: Santa Cruz, CA: The Red Barn

Hope to see you there!

Howard

- **Translation:** One multinational company maintains Web sites for 110 countries and territories and supports nineteen different variations of twelve languages, including Chinese, Japanese, and Korean. Your smaller outfit probably won't be able to go to this extreme, but it is important that translations take into account regional differences of the same language. In addition, care should be devoted to translating idiomatic language so that meanings are conveyed accurately and not misinterpreted. Automated software is available for translation, but it is generally best to use human translators.

- **Design:** Develop a design template to standardize imaging and brand, to create a consistent global profile. But make the template flexible enough to accommodate local tastes in color and iconography. Also allow room for text that might run longer after translation. German, for example, tends to run 30 percent longer than English. An example of standardized design localized for different countries can be found at Amazon.com. The general buying experience is the same for all customers, but details are different to meet local needs.

- **Sourcing:** It's been said that recipients tend to respond more positively to e-mail and other electronic communications from their own country than they do to foreign messaging. Yet foreign sourcing is not immediately apparent in the incoming message windows of most e-mail programs, so there shouldn't be a source-based barrier to opening e-mail. Still, consider having e-mail campaigns sent out from local agents or your foreign distributor or licensee. Web sites run by larger, more established operations would ideally have separate Web domains for country-specific sites—for example, mcgillicuddyband.fr for France and mcgillicuddyband.uk for the United Kingdom. Forms used on those sites should conform to local address formatting.

- **Regulations:** Laws regarding privacy, taxation, and other e-commerce issues vary widely from country to country. Before proceeding with e-mail campaigns to foreign countries or Web sites that provide purchasing options, be sure to check local market regulations and laws, and then follow them.

Direct Mail. Printed pieces sent to names on a mailing list fall into the category of direct mail. Before e-mail, this was the way to reach prospective customers—or previous customers—directly, rather than through mass media.

As detailed in *This Business of Music Marketing and Promotion*, direct mail encompasses many different kinds of pieces, simple and complex:

- **Letters:** Straightforward communication, personalized to the extent possible, announcing upcoming events or products and referring recipients to a Web site for ordering, or including a tear-off order form

- **Postcards:** Attractive imagery and message on the front, details on back with purchasing information, and space left for addressing, best for promoting a new recording or upcoming events

- **Flyers and Rack Cards:** Simple one-sheet announcements with design, either self-mailing (folds over, tapes shut, addressable) or envelope-ready, like a letter, with similar response options
- **Leaflets:** Brief folding promotion pieces, usually six or eight panel, sometimes with tear-off business reply card (BRC) or order form, often used to promote programs, series, or product lines and rarely used for selling a single recording
- **Brochures:** A booklet midway between a leaflet and a catalogue, typically used to promote programs, series, or product lines and rarely used for selling a single recording
- **Catalogues:** Magazine-length advertisement for full product lines, such as a record company's new releases and backlist, with order form and contact information, and typically sent several times per year, but now largely replaced by Web site product pages
- **Newsletters:** Hard-copy counterparts to e-mail newsletters, good for older customers and when interesting design is a key feature; great for mixing news with sales and thus being perceived as entertainment as much as a sales piece

Bulk-mail rates allow businesses to get quantity discounts on large mailings, subject to size, weight, and other regulations that you need to check *before* preparing the printed piece, to avoid finding out too late that you designed the wrong size.

International Direct Mail. The cost and immediacy of the Internet have made it a preferred e-marketing mechanism to the onetime dominant direct mail, which involves printing and paper costs; incurs mailing expense based on weight, size, and distance of travel; and can take lots of time to get where you want it to go. Yet some audiences still prefer hard copy—especially in territories where Internet penetration is negligible (see "Media," page 203). And unlike in the United States, where customers tend to receive nearly one thousand pieces of direct mail per year and thus tend to think of it as "junk mail," some territories—parts of Europe, for example—tend to receive more like fifty pieces per year per address. One could argue that those countries are promising markets for well-designed and targeted direct-mail campaigns.

The international considerations for e-marketing tend to apply equally well to direct mail. Translation needs to be sensitive to the fine points of local interpretation. Prices and fees must be expressed in local currency. To ensure consistency of branding across country borders, start with a template for design and copy, then fill it in with locally applicable information and messaging. (This also reduces the cost you'd incur from designing completely different mailing pieces for each country.)

Writer Susanne Khawand, in the 2005 Directmag.com article "Adaptation Is Critical" (www.directmag.com), says, "You'll find that a U.S. self-mailer with bold colors and design may perform better in Europe if it's formatted as a business letter and provides detailed information on the offering." Why? Americans tend to respond better to short, punchy messaging and then make quick decisions, whereas Europeans have been described as preferring more discussion and deliberation before making decisions. This is where a country's cultural and communication characteristics, as discussed in Chapter 2, can really determine the form and content of the messaging you send out.

Khawand also points out the importance of using reliable mailing lists. If you obtain a list from a domestic broker or business, the reliability and currency of the foreign addresses may be suspect. Thus, you should use mailing lists assembled by entities in the country you are targeting. As with other aspects of marketing, mailing list information may be obtainable from your foreign business partners or their associates.

Postal rates and regulations vary from country to country. As soon as you know you'd like to target a foreign country for a direct-mail campaign, investigate that country's rules so that you can plan out the right design and format ahead of time.

Direct-Response Advertising. Where direct mail constitutes self-contained mailing pieces that provide response mechanisms, direct-response advertising consists of messaging through third-party media and providing a response mechanism. This type of advertising contrasts with the kind discussed in the "Mix" section on page 208, which is awareness advertising meant to, well, increase awareness across a broad swath of the population. Direct-response advertising, on the other hand, is designed to instigate immediate action, such as calling a toll-free telephone number, going to a Web site, or tearing off and mailing a reply card. DR advertising tends to be more targeted than awareness advertising, in order to reach people who may be likely to take action.

DR advertising can be in magazines or other print media, on billboards or other outdoor media, on the Internet in the form of click-through banner ads, on cell phones or wireless devices, and on the radio and TV. DRTV can include thirty-minute infomercials, but you, a music marketer, are not likely to use this option.

For music, your most likely direct-response advertising would be on Internet sites popular in target communities. The flashy, multimedia nature of Web ads suits the kineticism of music quite well, and the demographics of Internet users and music listeners converge nicely. The same is true of cell phone users. As cell phone advertising evolves, you may be looking more closely at this option, especially when trying to reach audiences in Asia.

Radio may be less effective, simply because much radio listening takes place in cars, and any toll-free number or Web site mentioned in an ad is likely to be forgotten by the time the driver pulls into a parking space. Plus, radio is expensive. Television fares better, simply because the viewer may be near a telephone or a computer and thus able to respond immediately. Cable television rates can be surprisingly affordable, if your targeting is precise.

An e-mail with a hyperlink to your sales site is a kind of direct-response advertising. (Remember I said all these categories tend to overlap?)

A valuable characteristic of direct-response advertising is its measurability. Torn-off reply cards come back to you, and you can count them. For Web addresses, you can set up what is called a *jump page* just for the ad; hits from the ad are counted there before redirecting the customer to the desired destination; toll-free phone replies can also be counted. Measuring is important when you want to quantify the return on investment (ROI) of the DR campaign: Did sales outweigh costs? Is the effort worth repeating?

International Direct-Response Advertising. The guidelines for direct mail apply equally well to international DR advertising. In countries where Internet penetration is deep, the Web may be your best medium. Web advertising with hyperlinks to your sales site also bypasses the complexities of setting up telephone relays from the local territory to your home country and gets around the expense and delays of paper mail.

Where Internet use is low, magazines and newspapers may be the media of choice. Your distributor can help arrange co-op advertising with retailers—display advertising that promotes several different artists, with costs split between participants.

The key is to research media use in your targeted country and then design advertising for the preferred media. Of course, don't overlook local regulations, customs, and cultural preferences when designing ads—as you've been reminded throughout this book regarding all your international marketing activities.

When Best to Use Direct Marketing. The elements of direct marketing are so varied and have so many uses that they can be used at virtually any phase of a communications campaign. At the beginning of a campaign, word of mouth and viral marketing can be used to create buzz. E-marketing can be used throughout the life of a product or the career of a musician to build community and loyal fans, who can then be mobilized whenever there is something new to buy. E-mail can be used at any time to remind, to inform, and to motivate. Direct mail and direct-response advertising can be used as a targeted inducement to buy, perhaps best used when general awareness has already been created via publicity and advertising.

Downside of Direct Marketing. Whether e-mail, a flyer in the mailbox, or a pop-up ad on the Web, much of direct marketing is looked upon as junk—unwanted messages foisted upon the often unwilling recipient. The beauty of Web sites and certain types of newsy e-mail, on the other hand, is that they can be used to combine entertainment and marketing, inducing visitors to come on their own volition, or leading recipients to "opt in" to receiving future messaging. The key, as with any kind of persuasive communication, is to put yourself in the shoes of the customers, imagine what they might want or like, and then provide it.

Another downside of direct marketing is its reliance on mailing lists, which can be out of date or inaccurate. When purchasing a mailing list, make sure the broker is based in, or obtains the list from, the country you are targeting, and be sure that the broker is reputable. If you maintain your own list, as you should as you build up loyal customers and audiences over time, be sure to keep it current by providing change-of-address forms in your electronic and hard-copy communications.

SALES PROMOTION

When awareness has been created, interest has been sparked, and the customer has been enticed to visit the "store"—whether it be brick-and-mortar retailer, online product page, or an ad with a response mechanism—you may still have to close the sale. The customer could be looking at the artist's CD cover with admiration but uncertainty about whether to spend money on it. For that reason, you may have to provide an extra inducement to trigger the purchasing decision. The inducement could take the form of a discount price, a free gift, a coupon for some extra item, entry in a contest, or some other value-adding offer, the nature of which is limited only by the bounds of your imagination.

This kind of offer, creating short-term incentives to attract immediate sales, is called sales promotion. It is simultaneously an attention getter, a motivator to act, and a call to act now. The strategy itself is not a communication so much as a tactic to manipulate consumer behavior, similar to using rewards to get a dog to behave as desired (not to belittle human consumers, but the analogy is too appropriate to ignore). The communication part—letting people know about the offer—is why sales promotion is considered a part of IMC.

As detailed in *This Business of Music Marketing and Promotion*, there are two categories of sales promotion. One is consumer based, focusing on the aforementioned incentives for customers to buy. The other is trade based, concentrating on providing distribution channel members with incentives to give your product special treatment so that its sale potential is improved. Both consumer and trade promotion help your product to stand out in a crowded marketplace.

Trade incentives can include deductions from what retailers owe you—or agree to pay you—in return for prominent display in stores so that the CD is highly visible to customers. (You pass on the price reduction through your distributor.) Incentives can involve quantity discounts, such as 15 percent of an order designated as free—another way of describing a 15 percent discount on a quantity of CDs. You can also offer discounts for advertising—you permit the retailer to deduct a percentage from the price of an order in return for the retailer's taking out advertising that includes your CD.

Needless to say, before embarking on a sales promotion, it's important to estimate the total cost of the program (for example, a coupon discount amount multiplied by the anticipated redemption rate) against the anticipated sales boost.

When Best to Use Sales Promotion. A consumer sales promotion becomes especially meaningful—as opposed to appearing arbitrary and maybe even desperate—when it is tied to an event, a celebration, or some other noteworthy occurrence. Tying album sales to an upcoming live concert by offering with each album a coupon toward purchase of a ticket, and offering discounts on back-catalogue recordings to "celebrate" a new release, are ways to use events to justify promotions.

Keep consumer sales promotions relatively infrequent and brief, to avoid devaluing the product in the eyes of consumers.

Some marketers put trade promotion at the top of their marketing budget, calculating that without support from channel members and some kind of differentiating treatment at the retail level, the product will have little chance of rising above the competition. If their budget allows, they turn next to consumer promotion, and only after doing what they can there do they turn to advertising. A counterargument can be made that good advertising can motivate buyers to look for the CD in a store or online, regardless of whether it has preferential display positions in stores.

International Sales Promotion. Hypothetically, you might take a sales promotion strategy that worked in your home country and work with your foreign distributor and retailer to apply the same strategy in that country. Let's say the strategy involves distributing coupons to selected customers—for example, people who bought your preceding record—by Internet and direct mail. The coupon can be presented to certain retailers for a specified discount off the price offered at the retailer.

This plan could blow up in your face, and hopefully you'll avoid having that happen by getting local market advice from your foreign distribution partners. The problems such a tactic, or any kind of sales promotion for that matter, could face have to do with a set of factors described by Kamran Kashani and John A. Quelch in a 1990 article in *Business Horizons*:

- Complex sales promotion schemes may not be able to be effectively executed by local partners. Keeping offers simple is a safe practice.
- Branding can become diluted if local channel members independently design and communicate the promotion in a way that doesn't conform to your image. Control the core parameters of any communication and strategy so that they match your brand image.
- National economic development levels play a role in whether a sales promotion can be successful. Coupons, for example, are widely used in developing countries but less so in underdeveloped countries, which tend to respond more to free samples. Research how your plan may be received before setting it into motion.
- Regulations pertaining to sales promotions differ widely across country borders, and they relate to both the kinds of promotions allowed and the manner in which they are conducted. Restrictions have been placed on the value of premiums, and on the kinds of contests that may be held. Most European countries have controls on the scheduling and permissible

types of sales promotions. Germany is known for having strict regulations. Investigate, perhaps through your distributor, what the local laws say.

The bottom line is, local sales promotion is about getting local customers to behave in certain ways. The best authorities on how to do that will be the local businesspeople with whom you work. Keep your core branding in place, but work with partners to customize communications and strategies for the local market.

Meanwhile, the International Chamber of Commerce (www.iccwbo.org) offers the following "International Code of Sales Promotion":

- All sales promotions should be so designed and conducted as to avoid causing justifiable disappointment or giving any other grounds for reasonable complaint.
- The administration of promotions and the fulfillment of any obligation arising therefrom should be prompt and efficient.
- The terms and conduct of all promotions should be equitable to all participants.
- All sales promotions should be framed in a way that is fair to competitors and other traders in the market.
- Neither the design nor the implementation of a promotion should be such as to provoke, or to appear to condone, violent or otherwise illegal or anti-social behavior, or to encourage practices contrary to the public interest.
- No promoters, intermediaries or others involved should bring sales promotion into disrepute.

Keep them in mind when devising international strategies.

MEDIA

The third of the Four M's, media, refers to the communication vehicles and channels used in the context of chosen IMC modes to convey marketing messages. The media types are print, broadcast, and electronic.

Currently, the most available media to all music participants is the Internet. In global reach, cost, and accessibility to marketers—and with user demographics similar to music's—the Internet is the first choice for many budget-challenged emerging artists. A start-up record label or an artist with a new record may create initial awareness by sending out e-mail messages to special-interest groups and including links to online retail sites for purchase. Ads and text messages on friends' and associates' Web sites can help to spread the word. Everything is done via the Internet. Cost: minimal. Downside: Some countries still have limited Internet use. Another downside: The accessibility of the Internet makes it crowded, and a difficult context in which to attract attention.

When there is a larger budget to work with, more options for media are available, from magazines to billboarding to television. How does one choose which to work with? Media choices are largely based on the following criteria:

- IMC mode
- Local media availability
- Target-audience media habits
- Message content and objective
- Cost effectiveness

Let's look at them in detail.

IMC Mode and Choice of Media

The different modes of marketing communication tend to favor particular media. Publicity, for example, makes use of news media and the tools for pitching stories to them. Sales promotion may use print ads or online messaging. So your choice of media will depend partially on your IMC mode. The following chart shows a general breakdown of mode–media relationships:

IMC Modes and Related Media

IMC Mode	Print Media	Broadcast Media	Electronic Media
Public Relations (PR) and Publicity	Media kit Magazines Newspapers Press releases	Variety programs News programs Talk shows Music programs	Media kit Music Web sites Online 'zines News sites
Advertising	Magazine ads Newspaper ads Billboards Posters Transit ads T-shirts	Television ads Radio ads	Web site ads Wireless ads
Direct Marketing	Letters Postcards Brochures Catalogues Newsletters Inserts	Radio, TV ads Infomercials	E-mail Web sites Wireless comm.
Sales Promotion	Newspaper ads In-store displays Stickers Coupons	Radio, TV ads	E-mail Web sites Wireless ads

LOCAL MEDIA AVAILABILITY

Different countries have different levels of media penetration and use. As of this writing, for example, personal-computer penetration in China is relatively low, while TV penetration there is high. (But China's population is so large that even with low Internet penetration—in percentage of population—its Internet use still makes up 10 percent of total world Internet use, as shown on the forthcoming "Top Countries" chart on page 206.) The U.S. and U.K. have large numbers of music magazines. At this writing, U.S. 'zines include *Billboard, Filter, Oxford American, Texas Music, Maxim, Rolling Stone,* and the *Believer.* U.K. publications include *Mojo, Q, Word, Uncut, New Musical Express, Classical CD,* and *Gramophone.* Among other leading markets, Japan has *J-Pop, Indies Issue,* and *Metropolis*; Germany offers *Bravo, Musikexpress, Intro, Spex, Musikwoche,* and *Der Musikmarkt*; Canada has *Access, Applaud!, Chart, Real Blues,* and *Canoe.* (This is just a sampling. Magazines come and go rapidly, so current research is always necessary before planning campaigns.) Choice of media will depend in part on what's available in the target country. (And sometimes the country you target will depend on the media available there.)

MARKETS WITH HIGHEST INTERNET PENETRATION

Territory		Percentage of Population Using the Internet (as of Jan. 2006)	Territory	Percentage of Population Using the Internet (as of Jan. 2006)
Africa		2.5%	United Arab	
	Mauritius	14.1%	Emirates	35.8%
	Morocco	11.6%		
	Reunion (FR)	25.3%	North America	68.1%
	Seychelles	23.8%	Canada	67.9%
			United States	68.1%
Asia		9.9%		
	Hong Kong	69.2%	Latin America/Caribbean	14.3%
	Japan	67.2%	Argentina	26.4%
	South Korea	67%	Barbados	56.2%
			Chile	35.7%
Europe		35.9%	Jamaica	39.6%
	Faroe Islands	62.5%	Santa Lucia	32.8%
	Iceland	75.9%	Uruguay	20.8%
	Norway	67.8%		
	Switzerland	66%	Oceania/Australia	52.9%
			Australia	68.4%
Middle East		9.6%	Guam	47.1%
	Israel	45%	New Zealand	76.3%
	Kuwait	22.8%		
	Qatar	20.7%	**World Total**	**15.7%**

Source: www.internetworldstats.com/stats.htm

Top Internet Countries in Percentage of Total World Internet Use

United States	20.0%	Russia	2.3%
China	10.9%	Canada	2.2%
Japan	8.5%	Indonesia	1.8%
India	5.0%	Spain	1.7%
Germany	4.8%	Mexico	1.7%
United Kingdom	3.7%	Australia	1.4%
South Korea	3.3%	Taiwan	1.4%
Italy	2.8%	Netherlands	1.1%
France	2.6%	Poland	1.0%
Brazil	2.5%	Turkey	1.0%

Source: www.internetworldstats.com/stats.htm

Media Habits of Target Audience

Even with high media penetration, the use of the media differs around the globe depending on literacy rates, incomes, and other factors. Wireless communications is widely embraced in Japan, which is known for being technologically ahead of the curve. Areas of low literacy rates will disfavor print media. In South America, where popular music is a key aspect of the local culture, "radio advertising has substantial appeal," according to Susan P. Douglas and C. Samuel Craig of New York University in their essay "International Advertising."

You need to select the media channels that reach your target audience. With the identification of your target audience acquired as described in Chapter 2, you then follow up with further investigation into the kinds of media these people use to get their information. One way is to do an Internet search of your music style and then note some of the publication sites that come up in the search.

Message Content and Objective

A given category of media will handle certain types of messages better than others. Daily newspapers are good for messages that demand immediate attention. National magazines work well for getting an awareness message to a lot of people, not so well for messages that call for an action "tomorrow." So your choice of media will depend partially on the nature of your message.

Message characteristics that determine media choices include targetedness, time-sensitivity, complexity, and format.

Targetedness refers to the message's degree of specificity to particular groups. It may be an awareness-building message intended for a mass audience (low specificity), in which case you would use national publications, billboards, Web ads on widely viewed sites, wireless messaging, and TV and radio if within your budget. Or your message could be intended for a niche audience (high specificity), for which you could use niche publications, e-mail, special-interest Web sites, or targeted radio and cable TV. You might have multiple customized versions of a core message, for which you would choose easily alterable and highly targetable media, such as e-mail and direct mail.

Time-sensitivity refers to the degree of immediacy of the desired response. If the message is aimed at informing or reminding in a general way with no call to immediate action, you can use media with a longer "shelf life" such as monthly publications and billboards. If you want message recipients to act quickly, you'll need to use high-frequency media such as daily newspapers and e-news sites, e-mail, wireless communications, and radio and TV.

Complexity of messaging refers to . . . well, the complexity of the message. If it's simple—"McGillicuddy's new album is available"—it can go on media that people don't tend to spend a lot of time with: radio, Web ads, billboards, and the like. More complex messages—describing the details of an artist's sound or point of view—will go in media that invite and allow closer scrutiny: print magazines and newspapers, direct mail, and Web sites.

Format refers to the graphic complexity of the communication, from simple all-text to highly visual to multimedia. All-text messaging can be articles in publications, e-mail notices, direct-mail letters, simple ads, and—in audio form—radio announcements. More-visual messaging requires print media, graphics-capable online media, or television. Multimedia messaging requires Web delivery, television, or multimedia-capable wireless.

COST EFFECTIVENESS

The ultimate value for you of a particular medium is in the number of meaningful, impactful exposures of your message it provides for your media cost. What is meant here by *number of meaningful, impactful exposures*?

First, *number of exposures* has two dimensions: *reach*, or the number of people exposed to the message, and *frequency*, the number of times they are exposed to the message, which strengthens the imprint on the memory. Second, reach and frequency are useless unless it's the right audience. Your communication about an edgy band of rebellious punk rockers might be rejected by a conservative audience. So your medium has to reach the audience you create music for. The term for this criterion of media effectiveness is *impact*.

Costs of media coverage are expressed with slightly different terminology by different media. The most common term is *cost per thousand*, which can refer to numbers of impressions (in online media) or number of exposures (print media). You want to find the least expensive cost per thousand, as long as the media vehicle reaches your target audience. The vehicle should also have an audience that pays attention to commercial messaging. For instance, readers of news magazines are less likely to pay attention than readers of specialty publications, such as music magazines.

Television advertising expresses cost as *cost per rating point*. A rating point represents the percentage of the population reached by a television program. *Gross rating points* (GRP), which are what you buy, refer to the total number of rating points multiplied by the frequency of broadcast.

Cost effectiveness is calculated differently for public relations and publicity, since the media coverage is itself free. Cost can be determined by the payable work hours put into preparing publicity materials and interfacing with media representatives. Effectiveness can be calculated based on the size and quality (appropriateness) of the audience reached.

MIX

The fourth of the Four M's, mix, denotes the balanced configuration and combination of messages, modes, and media best suited to the target market and your marketing objective. Whatever configuration you choose, the elements should be tightly coordinated to ensure consistency of message, style, and imagery. This is how you build a strong, coherent brand identity. You also create the media version of an echo chamber, in which a message heard somewhere one day is seen somewhere else on another day and thereby is reinforced even more. Eventually the message gets driven into the mind of the consumer.

The marketing communication mix will quite likely differ from country to country. That's because each country has its characteristic combination of preferred media, consumer habits, distribution channels, and trade regulations. So in configurating a communications mix you'll be working both with the country requirements and the complementary functions of the various marketing modes.

Those complementary functions become obvious as you become immersed in a communications campaign. If you concentrate on one mode, you'll soon become aware of the lack of another. To understand this, consider the differences between direct marketing on one hand and PR/advertising on the other. Direct marketing can be looked upon as tightly targeted, specific, and conducted almost person to person. In contrast, awareness advertising and publicity tend to be widely dispersed and general, and blanket mass audiences—you "let the world know" about the product. Ads and PR, in mass media, tend to create broad but shallow awareness. With direct marketing, you achieve narrower but deeper awareness.

Let's say you can't afford advertising in the launch of a product. But you conduct a direct marketing campaign that reaches targeted social contacts and special-interest groups. These customers may become enthusiastic supporters. But as their buying activity wanes, you begin to feel the vast void of public indifference that might be filled were there only more communication to the mass audience. Conversely, if you were doing only awareness advertising, you might not get the motivated purchases you'd achieve with direct marketing.

When the two strategies—mass-shallow and targeted-deep—come together successfully, they create breadth of awareness and a depth of motivation that begin to interact—the optimal sales environment. The chart below illustrates the relationship.

INTERACTION OF AWARENESS ADVERTISING AND DIRECT MARKETING

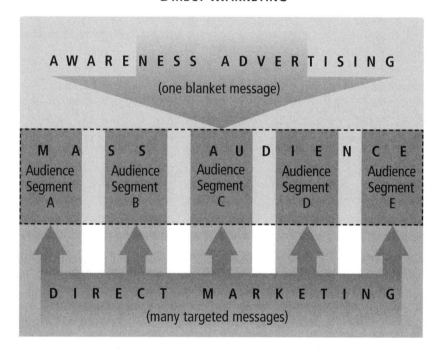

= Maximum awareness and motivation to purchase

Awareness advertising achieves broad but shallow audience penetration. Direct marketing has narrower but deeper impact. Combined, they amplify each other's effects.

What are some other methods employed by record companies? In Germany, according to the Canadian Independent Record Production Association (CIRPA), major record labels have traditionally spent most of their advertising budgets (up to 70 percent) on television advertising. In France, the major record labels spend 45 percent of their promotional budget on TV advertising, 9 percent on radio and print, and 26 percent on point-of-sale materials and gifts.

But the landscape is always changing, so the thing to do is to come up with fundamental criteria for making your mix decisions. Factors you can use in deciding upon the right marketing mix include

- Type of market
- Buyer-readiness stage
- Stage in campaign/product lifecycle
- Budget

TYPE OF MARKET

All the market characteristics of your target country play a role in your choice of communication mix.

The kinds of media used in a country are, of course, key. A highly developed, technologically up-to-date country will enable you to use the latest Internet and wireless transmission vehicles, which opens up your communication options considerably. A relatively underdeveloped country with poor Internet penetration will require you to use older, less-targeted media.

Specific media vehicles may be present in some countries and not in others. Turkey, for example, lacks music magazines. Thus feature stories about artists have fewer print outlets there. PR reps have to work around that problem.

Education levels in a market's populace make a difference. A low-literacy population will inhibit your ability to use print media or to provide complicated, lengthy descriptions. Other demographic factors, such as median age, also play a role. Younger audiences, for example, are plugged into the latest technologies. Older people tend not to be. High-affluence populations have greater access to computers and expensive communication devices than do poorer populations.

Regulations and government restrictions, as described previously, may have an impact on the kinds of messaging you are permitted to convey.

A country's distribution infrastructure also affects your IMC. In many underdeveloped countries you may find a fragmented, multimember distribution channel. The many channel members and impediments—such as inertia—may prevent the product from moving efficiently through the channel. In such countries, the fuel for channel activity is market demand. Your task will be to create that demand in order to, as author Charles W. L. Hill writes in his book *International Business*, "pull" product through the channel. The IMC modes best for this are broad awareness advertising and publicity.

Review the country data you gathered when first investigating your target territory (described in Chapter 2) before settling on a mix of message, mode, and media.

BUYER-READINESS STAGE

Your communications mix should change as your target audience passes through different stages of readiness in the purchasing process.

At the beginning, the audience is unaware of your music, so you need to emphasize awareness messaging through the modes and channels best suited for it—that is, publicity and advertising in widely read print and Web publications and widely heard and viewed radio and TV. Trade sales promotions help get the music wide distribution and prominent displays in stores.

As the audience becomes aware, you shift the mix to emphasize persuasion and providing more-detailed information. Viral marketing can help move the recommendations of opinion leaders through social networks and broaden favorable understanding of the product. Reading about the artist, noticing mentions in various media, and receiving positive word of mouth help move customers toward purchase.

To facilitate the next step, closing the sale, you add sales promotion—special purchase incentives such as coupons.

The buyer is someone you want to keep interested—for your next release—so you engage in CRM (customer relationship management) on the Internet to make the person feel like a valued member of your music community. Chat rooms, artist Web site "appearances," and V.I.P. activities all help to make this happen.

Of course, once a campaign is well under way, you will have a target audience in various different stages at any given time. So you may be issuing communications to the newly converted—say, inviting them to participate in contests and "premium customer" activities at your Web site—at the same time you are trying to bring new customers into the fold. And you'll be balancing this against the other criteria determining your marketing mix, such as the lifecycle stage of your campaign or product.

IMC MIXES FOR DIFFERENT BUYER-READINESS STAGES

| Mode | Buyer-Readiness Stage | | |
	Awareness	Comprehension/Conviction	Ordering
PR	Announcement	Bio details/ reviews/features	
Advertising	Announcement	Information with testimonials	
Direct Marketing	Announcement	Recommendation of opinion leader	
Sales Promotion	Trade incentives		Purchase incentives

Note: Strategies vary depending on many factors; each situation is unique.

STAGE IN LIFE CYCLE OF CAMPAIGN OR PRODUCT

Like living entities, products sent out into the marketplace have life cycles with beginnings and declines. They're "born" when introduced and first promoted. They experience "growth" as the market begins to accept them. They enter "maturity" when they've been around for a while and have lost the glow of their exciting youth. They begin to "decline" when other products pass them by in the competition for audience attention.

The marketing mix should shift as the product passes through these different phases.

In the introductory stage, you need to give it the royal welcome, with broadly dispersed awareness advertising and PR, and with trade sales promotion to ensure effective distribution. Using viral marketing helps to build grass-roots awareness.

In the growth stage, support audience acceptance with invitations to mailing lists and Web communities, provide publicity that fills out the picture of the artist with biographical details, and use positive reviews to pump up your media kits and get even more press coverage. Artist performance activity in support of the release should provide ample raw material for stories to feed to media producers and editors. Further word of mouth can have a viral effect and broaden the audience.

In the maturity stage, as other products begin to come on the market, provide reminders about your product—perhaps in co-op ads, citing the album as "back catalogue" in an ad for the artist's new release—along with new sales incentives to keep your product selling in stores.

The decline stage may involve an album that continues to sell in small quantities without any help, due to its reputation. Miles Davis's 1950s album *Kind of Blue* and Van Morrison's 1970s *Moondance* come to mind. Albums in this category receive ongoing publicity in the form of inclusion in music reference books and biographies, so there's not much else that the marketer needs to do other than include the older album in ads for the artist's entire catalogue when important dates or events warrant some new publicity or advertising. But the great majority of albums may find sales dropping off to a trickle. Deep discounts, along with modest reminder advertising in co-op ads, can help sell remaining stock.

The following charts show IMC plans for two different countries: the first is highly developed and technologically advanced; the second is less developed, with low Internet penetration. Both cases assume an artist to be entering the territory for the first time.

IMC Plan for Different Life Cycle Stages, Advanced Economy

IMC Mode	Product Life Cycle Stage			
	Introduction	Growth	Maturity	Decline
PR	Announcement/ bio detail (Newspaper/ Web sites)	Reviews/ tour reports (Web/print)	Stories w/ new activities (Print pubs)	Stories w/ new activities (Print pubs)
Advertising	Announcement (Newspaper/ radio/outdoor/)	Reminder co-op ads (Newspaper)		Reminder co-op ads (Newspaper)
Direct Marketing	E-mail to social networks	E-newsletter to purchasers (E-mail)	E-newsletter to purchasers (E-mail)	E-newsletter to purchasers (E-mail)
	CRM (Web site)	CRM (Web site)	CRM (Web site)	CRM (Web site)
	Announcement (Mobile phone)	Reminder (Mobile phone)	Reminder (Mobile phone)	Reminder (Mobile phone)
		Recommenda- tion of opinion leaders (E-mail)		
Sales Promotion	Incentive/ song sampler giveaways at social events		Incentive/ discount coupon	Incentive/ free items with purchase

Note: Strategies vary depending on many factors; each situation is unique.

IMC Plan for Different Life Cycle Stages, Developing Economy (Low Internet Penetration)

IMC Mode	Product Life Cycle Stage			
	Introduction	**Growth**	**Maturity**	**Decline**
PR	Announcement/ bio detail (Newspaper)	Reviews/ tour reports (Print pubs)	Stories w/ new activities (Print pubs)	Stories w/ new activities (Print pubs)
Advertising	Announcement (Newspaper/ radio/outdoor)	Reminder co-op ads (Newspaper)		Reminder co-op ads (Newspaper)
Direct Marketing	Announcement (Word of mouth/ viral marketing)	Newsletter to purchasers (Direct mail)	Newsletter to purchasers (Direct mail)	Newsletter to purchasers (Direct mail)
		Gig reminders (Postcards)	Gig reminders (Postcards)	Gig reminders (Postcards)
Sales Promotion	Incentive/ song sampler giveaways at social events	Autograph signings	Incentive/ discount coupon	Incentive/ free items with purchase

Note: Strategies vary depending on many factors; each situation is unique.

BUDGET

Any integrated marketing communications plan is contingent on having a promotion budget. Publicity, fortunately, costs very little, and when it works it is very effective. But it's only one of many tools. If your budget is extremely limited, you'll focus on Internet marketing, however you can use it. E-mailing social networks, having a media kit at your Web site for the press to look at, and making sure Web addresses of purchasing sites are posted wherever and whenever you communicate (on your recorded telephone message?) are some ways to start. You'll really have to count on word of mouth and hope you get some positive reviews to start sales momentum. And artist performances will be relied on heavily to generate purchase-inclined fans.

A common method of determining IMC budget is setting it at a percentage of sales, either past or projected. Such percentages have ranged between 5 and 50 percent of sales depending on the industry. The problem with this method is that there's no assurance that the promotion budget will be spent effectively, rendering irrelevant its relationship to some larger number.

The more-recommended method is to determine your marketing objective and then spend what it takes to achieve that objective—within the constraints of the bank account, of course. If you achieve the objective you have set, your money will have proved well spent and will be outweighed by profits.

CHAPTER 11 — Managing the Global Music Marketing Program

With any attempt to sell music in a foreign country comes a corresponding increase in the number of tasks that you need to coordinate. Part of the larger schematic is putting together the plans to successfully enter a new market. Another part is getting the physical and digital product into places of purchase and setting up performance dates. Yet another part is stirring up and maintaining local interest in the music. Finally, you respond to the outcome of your campaign, whether highly successful, moderately successful, or not successful. And then you decide where to go next.

As you launch a campaign to expand sales to foreign territories, it's helpful to have a summary or checklist of the entire marketing process nearby and easy to access. You can use it as a basis for creating whatever scheduling charts and spreadsheets you'll need in order to manage and control all your activities. The following master list of steps described in preceding chapters can help you get the right jobs done at the right times.

THE GLOBAL MUSIC MARKETING MASTER LIST

Not all the steps in this list will apply to your particular situation. If you are an independent artist, for example, you won't be concerned with setting up a foreign subsidiary. So use the items that are applicable, and keep the rest for future reference.

MARKET RESEARCH

- Define your product's style and characteristics through comparison with existing products.
- Find out where similar products have found audiences by researching sales data and examining international popularity charts and playlists.
- If you already sell domestically, and if you keep a record of e-mail inquiries, see if there's a pattern of interest in your music from particular countries.
- Prepare a list of promising foreign markets based on the data you have found.
- Research the countries on your list to determine their profit and risk potential:
  - Is there an acceptable degree of market openness and accessibility (few trade restrictions)?
  - Is there an effective music-marketing infrastructure, both land based and digital, along with robust music sales?

- Is the country attractive in terms of overall economic health?
- Are there adequate protections against piracy? Acceptably low levels of piracy and corruption?

- Research the countries on your list to determine cultural compatibility and potential conflicts, such as source effects (attitude toward your product's country of origin).
- If you're inexperienced in global marketing, choose one country to enter first, based on the results of your research. Keep the others in mind for future targeting.
- Consider entering a developing market to capitalize on novelty and being early-to-market.
- Research potential foreign business partners by identifying businesses that have worked with music similar to yours, by attending trade shows, and by conducting Internet searches.

BUSINESS STRATEGY

Consider which land-based business strategy to employ: exporting, licensing, setting up a joint venture, or operating a fully owned foreign subsidiary:

- **Exporting** tends to work better when: you want to start out small; you want to limit your commitment; you want to maintain a high degree of quality control; you want more frequent payment; foreign tariff barriers are minor; customization is not necessary or is minor; and local packaging and labeling needs are not particularly complicated.
- **Licensing** tends to work better when: you wish to avoid the complex logistics of exporting; you want to let the foreign company take the financial risk; customization would be too costly for you and better for a local record company to handle; local packaging requirements are complex and a local record company would handle the campaign more capably than you; you trust the local company's accounting practices and manufacturing quality.
- **Joint venturing** tends to work better when: you are marketing a product line rather than just one or two recordings; you want to avoid logistical hassles of exporting; you want more control than when licensing, but you want to share some risk; you're willing to make a significant investment in and commitment to the foreign market; you trust the foreign partner.
- **Foreign subsidiaries** tend to work better when: your business is large enough to warrant a foreign office; you're determined to make a long-term commitment to the foreign market; you want complete ownership of the operation and earnings.

PRODUCT DEVELOPMENT

(Except where licensee is handling product customization and packaging)

- Determine the formats best suited for the target market: CDs, digital files, cassettes, vinyl discs (most commonly, CDs and digital files).

ACTIVITIES ACCORDING TO BUSINESS STRATEGY

YOUR TASKS	STRATEGY			
	Licensing	Exporting	Joint Venturing	Wholly Owned Subsidiary
Production	F	F	Negotiable	F
Package Design	Negotiable	F	Negotiable	F
Manufacturing		F	Negotiable	F
Retail Distribution		F	Negotiable	F
Online Distribution	Negotiable	F	Negotiable	F
Publicity	Negotiable	F	Negotiable	F
Sales Promotion	Negotiable	F	Negotiable	F
Radio Promotion	Negotiable	F	Negotiable	F

Note: General guidelines only. Division of responsibility varies widely depending on individual arrangements.

- Decide what special features (if any)—local-language vocal, bonus tracks, other—to include in the foreign version of your product.
- Decide what music changes (if any)—instrumentation, mix—need to be provided.
- Decide what atmosphere, symbolism, and mood to emphasize in packaging and communications.
- Determine foreign regulations for packaging and labeling, and plan to address them in your package.
- Before preparing package design and text, find out if there are any must-avoid images, symbols, words, colors, or other communication elements.
- Establish a music release date—a "street date"—for the targeted territory. Build performance dates, radio play, and marketing communications around this date.

ADMINISTRATIVE PREPARATION

- Explore your bank's currency exchange services for businesses, such as forwarding exchange contracts and foreign currency options.
- Consider setting up a foreign bank account to optimize currency exchange.
- To ensure accurate logging of and payment for foreign public performances of your recording ("neighboring rights"), find out which local licensing agency handles that service and make sure you are registered.
- If you are the writer or publisher of compositions on the recording, make sure you are registered with your domestic performing rights society. Make sure it has reciprocal relationships with foreign rights societies and that

there is a channel for payment to you for such uses as broadcast perform-ances, digital radio performances, and concert performances.

- Consider arranging a subpublishing agreement with a foreign publisher, to ensure thorough exploitation of local marketing opportunities for your compositions.

- For payment of mechanical royalties (for uses of others' compositions on your recording, based on number of copies distributed), be prepared to include foreign copies in your accounting for payment to your local mechanical rights society. If you are licensing in a foreign territory, the licensee will be responsible for paying mechanical royalties to its local soci-eties based on the number of copies the licensee distributes.

- To ensure accurate tracking of retail sales, register with the local sales tracking organization. (In the U.S., it is Nielsen SoundScan.)

DISTRIBUTION

For Hard-Copy (CD, Cassette, Vinyl) Distribution:

- Arrange for CD and hard-copy distribution by securing an exporting or licensing deal with a foreign distributor or record label.

- Alternatively, if you're joint venturing or working out of a wholly owned local subsidiary, secure a deal with a local distributor.

- Arrange for hard-copy sale via online storefronts by opening up accounts with such retailers as Amazon.com and CD Baby.

For Digital Distribution:

- Identify digital music retailers (DMRs) that are popular in your targeted territory. These may include global online music services such as iTunes, global mobile music providers such as Vodafone, and regional counter-parts of these services.

- If you are a large label and have the needed staff, consider working directly with DMRs.

- If you are an individual, small, or mid-sized operation, identify and arrange representation by a digital music aggregator (DMA) to distribute your music to targeted DMRs.

Sales from Your Own Web Site:

- If you plan to sell from your own Web site, customize the site for foreign sales; if possible, create a special page in the language of the country you are targeting; arrange for payment in foreign currency.

LIVE PERFORMANCE

- Learn about the current political and economic status of the country before booking tour dates (probably previously revealed in your marketing research).

- Find out if there are government restrictions on foreign performers, including song content restrictions (probably previously revealed in your marketing research).
- Aim to perform in several of the leading markets (population areas) in the targeted territory.
- If not handling booking yourself, identify and engage the services of a reputable booking agent that handles the targeted territory.
- Apply for visas well in advance of tour plans.
- Book initial dates closely preceding or following the CD release date. Aim to play the most lucrative markets within a four-week time frame after the CD release, if possible.
- Consider repeated visits to the country in different performance contexts, such as headlining a small venue, participating with other artists in a package tour, or as opening act in a large venue. Each visit is an opportunity for renewed publicity and extending the life of the CD.
- Do a cost-benefit analysis of your touring plans. If the analysis indicates a shortfall, find ways to cut costs or find sources of tour support, possibly including corporate sponsorship.
- Explore potential for multicasting deals as way of enlarging your audience and sharing tour costs.

Radio Play

- Identify trend-setting programs, and attempt to get your music on their playlists.
- For terrestrial, digital, and satellite radio, identify and list stations and networks that broadcast your kind of music in the targeted territory.
- Exploit Internet-based sites like Live365 that play your music and provide a link to where the music can be purchased immediately.
- Explore additional opportunities in community radio, student-run radio, rural radio, cooperative radio, participatory radio, free radio, alternative radio, educational radio.
- Mail your promo package—cover letter, one-sheet, CD—to contact people at appropriate stations. Or e-mail a cover message with a link to your streamable song and another link to your online media kit.
- Consider the use of independent promoters in the targeted country to do the radio-contact footwork for terrestrial stations.

Integrated Marketing Communications (IMC)

- Identify/appoint personnel, if other than you, to handle local marketing communications in the targeted territory, to ensure effective localization of communications, including translation.
- Coordinate domestic messaging and strategy with local foreign marketing

personnel to maintain consistency of core communications and branding across borders.

To be overseen by designated marketing individual or team:

- Customize your basic media kit—bio, fact sheet, press clips, photos, music samples—for use in foreign country PR. Prepare both hard-copy and online versions.

- Prepare, or at least sketch out, a "communication brief" defining your current objectives, messages, and possible communication vehicles.

- Develop message content, retaining core concepts but tailoring for local audiences as necessary.

- Choose the media outlets in the targeted area most used by the target audience, and plan to use them for publicity, advertising, direct marketing, and sales promotion.

- Develop a mix of IMC modes—PR/publicity, advertising, direct marketing, sales promotion—best suited to your target market, stage in product life cycle, stage of buyer readiness, and budget.

- Plan shifting arrangements of messages, media, and modes for the different stages of the product rollout: introduction, growth, maturity, decline.

FURTHER STEPS

- Take steps to market the artist as a brand—if not as a well-known individual performer, than as a representative of a style, culture, and demographic.

- Look outside the music industry for co-branding opportunities, looking for well-financed companies that your artist's music and image could help attract new audiences. Approach them with co-branding proposals.

- Actively promote appropriate recorded tracks to producers of film, television, video games, and other entertainment media that license master recordings.

- Explore all manner of format for selling your music, including ringtones, ringbacks, and other concepts from your own imagination.

- As with domestic marketing, manufacture nonmusic merchandise to sell at shows and on your Web site.

NEXT MOVES

If all goes well in your initial venture into international music marketing, the next logical step is to expand further, if you are so inclined.

Guidelines for expansion include many of those used for your first venture: choose countries that offer the fewest obstacles to communication, cultural understanding, trade activity, geographical access, live performance, and, ultimately, realization of profits.

As you build a portfolio of foreign markets, you'll find that different countries demand different business strategies. As discussed in Chapter 3, countries with low barriers to entry and few product customization requirements might warrant exporting. Countries with high tariffs and complex packaging requirements might need licensing if you are to profit with the least effort. If you are a full-blown, committed record label you might choose to set up a joint venture in another country or open a satellite office elsewhere. Your arrangement of multicountry business strategies for CD distribution could look like this:

	Country A	Country B	Country C	Country D
Strategy	Licensing	Exporting	Joint Venture	Licensing

A more detailed arrangement of marketing strategies across several borders could look like this:

	Country A	Country B	Country C	Country D
Land Strategy	Licensing through ABC Records	Exporting through DEF Records	Joint venture with GHI Records	Licensing through JKL Records
Digital Strategy	Distribute through global DMA	Distribute through global DMA	Distribute through global DMA	Distribute through global DMA
Tour Strategy	Week 1: Headline nightclub	Week 2: Headline nightclub	Week 3: Opening act theater	Week 4: Part of multiartist arena tour
Radio Strategy	Licensee to handle	Web, satellite, local promotion to terrestrial	Partner to handle	Licensee to handle
Integrated Marketing Communications	Supply guidelines to licensee	Local co-op ads; e-mail blast; trade promotion; reviews	Supply guidelines to partner	Send ad templates; media kit for translation

Over time, as you grow comfortable with the process of exploring and venturing into foreign markets, you also accrue networks of foreign business associates. You strike up relationships with them that might last for years, and that help smooth over the inevitable bumps you encounter in trying to get your music to the global public. And eventually you find that, for all the cultural differences you encounter, the underlying impulse in all your valued foreign contacts is strikingly similar to yours. You see it at international music-business conventions when, during evening social events, participants gathered from all over the world respond with equal enthusiasm to showcased performers from different countries. You and the others share a joy in the excitement of music itself—an affinity that got you into the business in the first place, and that brought in your foreign counterparts, too. Discovering this similarity, and realizing that you're actually more alike than different, is one of the great fringe benefits of doing business around the world.

Ultimately, you might be surprised by the results that your global marketing efforts bring. The guitar-playing singer–songwriter who in her own country might get lost in the crowd of competitors could in another country be embraced as a star. Hidden pockets of opportunity and openness to your kind of music may reveal themselves: The Sumatran singer who has mastered the vocal style of Ray Charles. The American musicians who've become expert players of Javanese gamelan. The Dutch fans of Duke Ellington. The Asian fans of Joe Satriani. The more you explore and expand, the more you realize that global music marketing is not only a process of building audiences and music careers but a kind of cross-cultural adventure—with rewards that extend far beyond the realm of commerce.

It's an adventure well worth taking. And best of all, it comes with your own musical accompaniment.

CHAPTER 12

Profiting from Global Music Publishing

Somewhat tangential to the direct music-to-consumer marketing process, but important to understand nonetheless, is the sphere of music commerce called music publishing.

Music publishing revolves around activities designed to secure performances of music compositions, from pop songs to symphonic works, on stage, in broadcast, in movies, on the Internet, in video games, on cell phones, in toys, and in any other context that can be imagined. The compensation comes in the form of royalties paid to the composer and publisher, or to another owner of the music, who is said to "own the copyright" to the work.

This sphere is different from the recorded and live music marketing discussed thus far in this book. The focus to this point has been on marketing to consumers. Music publishing, on the other hand, involves marketing to businesses. Publishers actively engage in promoting the music to artists who might record it, movie and TV producers who might use it, brands that might build ad campaigns on it, and so forth. The payment comes from these businesses.

Because music publishing involves a particular, and complex, set of business practices distinct from those of selling CDs and downloads and concerts directly to music fans, a full and detailed analysis of global music publishing is beyond the scope of this book—in fact, warrants a complete book of its own. Yet a brief overview here should alert you to the basic opportunities available in this lucrative layer of global commerce, which you should explore further if you're a composer, lyricist, or someone who is attracted to the business side of these arts.

SUPPLY CHANNELS OF MUSIC PUBLISHING

As with distribution of recorded music, and with presentation of live music, the field of music publishing consists of a supply chain of participants devoted to making the product, moving the product, and providing administrative services to make everything run smoothly and productively. The chain consists of the music creators, the music publishers and subpublishers, the buyers, and "rights organizations" that coordinate collection and payment of fees. Let's take a look at them.

COMPOSERS AND LYRICISTS

The basic unit of music-publishing commerce—the song or composition—begins with the music writer and the wordsmith who create it. When the music is created, it is referred to in legal circles as *intellectual property*, the ownership of which is defined by the term *copyright*. He who holds the "copyright" to a composition is entitled to the earnings generated by the copyright, or composition. The initial writers, unless they're writing on a work-for-hire basis, are considered automatic owners of the copyright. At some point they may sell the copyright. The new owner is then entitled to the copyright's earnings. Copyrights have legal term limits, such as "the life of the composer plus seventy-five years," after which the ownership of the composition goes into the *public domain*, where it is free to be used by anyone. An owner can stop the transfer to "PD" by "renewing the copyright." You can be sure that the copyright end dates of valuable songs are tracked carefully by the owners to make sure the deadlines for renewal are not missed.

PUBLISHERS

Many writers and lyricists would probably prefer writing the composition to handling the selling of it. That's where music publishers come in. The music publisher takes care of the business of getting the composition performed, for fees and royalties.

The term music *publishing* is a bit of a misnomer in that it implies printing and distribution, like a book. Music publishing did once focus on printed music—sheet music. But the name has stayed in place even as the business has evolved, and today publishing has to do primarily with exploiting the money-making possibilities of a composition through any number of channels, most of which are electronic.

The term *music publishing* also brings to mind images of hoary old offices, with executives and secretaries and clerks and all the accoutrements of well-established businesses. Some, to be sure, conform to that image. The larger ones, such as EMI and Peermusic, function as mini-conglomerates, replete with office parties, health plans, and long-accepted ways of doing business. But the term really refers to a category of music commerce, and any music entity can opt to pursue publishing. Many composers and lyricists, in fact, choose to set up their own "publishing companies" rather than give up the 50 percent of earnings that publishers routinely retain. All you need to do are establish a business name and purchase a business license. But when you realize that getting the music to generate earnings can be a full-time job, you think seriously about delegating that task to an experienced professional.

"Those task" includes the following:

- **Administering copyrights and finances**. Publishers acquire a "catalogue" of copyrights. They keep records of those copyrights. They renew them. They may sell them. For new songs by represented writers, publishers register them with appropriate government agencies. They receive payments from various sources for uses of copyrights (a song recorded for a CD, for example), pay shares to writers, to copublishers, and, if applicable, to foreign original publishers. They keep financial records.
- **Developing new business**. Publishers take action to generate earnings. They do this by maintaining and communicating with networks of contacts throughout industries that use music, from record companies to artist

management companies to TV and film companies to multimedia conglomerates. Publishers envision how their songs might match artists and audiovisual contexts. They imagine musical arrangements, and they pay for recordings of songs using those arrangements—recordings that can be used as sales tools to prospective users. Publishers also set up relationships with foreign publishing partners—subpublishers—who may be better placed to secure uses in the territories where they are active.

Sources of Revenue

Music publishing can be a highly lucrative business, if a song catches on and becomes a "standard"—a universally loved piece that everybody wants to record. The song may generate *mechanical royalties*—payment for recording ("covering") by an artist and release on a CD—in the form of a percentage of sales income or a fixed sum per unit distributed. The song may also generate *broadcast royalties* (also categorized as *performance royalties* in some sectors), constituting payment when the song is broadcast on the radio or on TV. The song will likely generate royalties for *performance* in live-performance venues, in restaurants, and in karaoke bars. And *synchronization licenses*, for use in audiovisual works such as video and film, will bring in even more royalties. Digital royalties, for transmission over the Internet and through cell phones, are sources of yet more income. In fact, any commercial use of a composition represents a source of income—and yes, this includes the selling of sheet music.

Revenue Collection and Distribution Agencies

Many of the licenses—the grants—to use compositions are set up directly between the music publisher and the prospective user, or licensee. But a good number of uses are permitted on a "blanket" basis. For example, radio stations may play a song without dealing directly with every song publisher. Instead, they obtain what is called a *blanket license* from a music industry collection and distribution organization representing multiple publishers and writers. The organization then pays out royalties to member publishers and writers from the pool of collected license fees.

The names for these kinds of organizations include "performing rights societies," "authors' rights organizations," "licensing organizations," "copyright management organizations," and more, but they all perform roughly the same task: that of centralizing transfer of fees from numerous disparate sources to numerous disparate recipients, making life easier for all involved. Examples include ASCAP and BMI in the U.S., PRS in the U.K., SACEM in France, and JASRAC in Japan.

In some territories, different kinds of royalties funnel through different organizations. Royalties for performance through broadcast and on stage might go through one organization, while mechanical rights royalties might go through another. Typical flows of copyright revenues are shown in the following chart.

FLOW OF COPYRIGHT PAYMENTS FROM USERS TO SELLERS

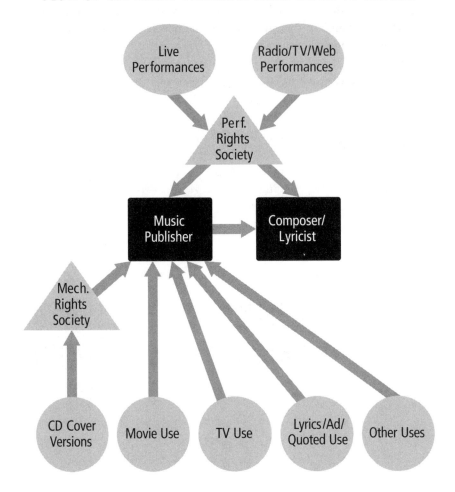

GLOBAL MUSIC PUBLISHING NETWORKS

As you might imagine, the process of doing business across borders can be quite a bit more complicated. Yet, as composer Suzanne Ciani points out in Chapter 13 (page 230), "I have always found publishing to be a more dependable part of the business [than CD distribution]. The performance societies for the most part are assiduous and well-coordinated with their American affiliates, and the subpublishers that we work with . . . are pretty straight-ahead in their royalty statements."

The key to global music publishing—or, expressed more exactly, global copyright sales—is the network of business entities that can make it all work. If you are trying to market songs in a foreign territory, you really need (to borrow a military term) "boots on the ground" in that territory to handle local business development. The way to achieve that is either to work with an international music publisher with local offices in your target territory or to establish an agreement with a local publisher—a *subpublishing agreement* in industry parlance. Ultimately your international network may consist of different kinds of arrangements in different territories—working with local publishers in some areas while working through an international publisher in others. Your multi-country publishing revenues might flow as follows:

MULTITERRITORY FLOW OF COPYRIGHT PAYMENTS FROM USERS TO SELLERS

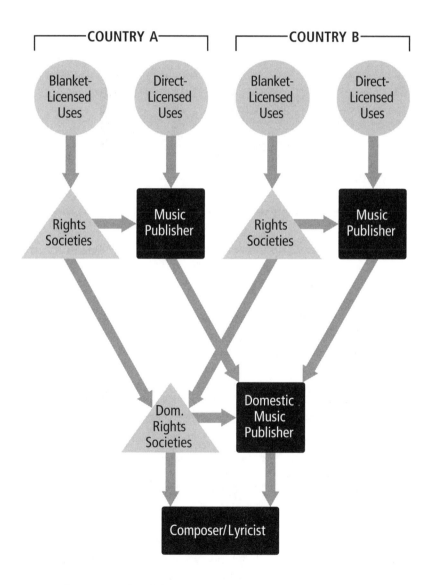

To explain: In each of these countries, blanket-licensable uses such as broadcast and live performance are payable to the local rights society. If that rights society has a reciprocal agreement with your domestic-rights society, the former submits payment to the latter. If your music is locally subpublished, the society pays that publisher, which then keeps a share and sends the remainder to your local publisher. Direct-payable uses—i.e., those that are managed not through rights agencies but rather directly between user and publisher—are payable to the publisher, which submits net earnings to your local publisher.

There are, of course, many variations on these licensing and payment schemes. For present purposes, having knowledge of the general structure of music publishing channels is the best place to start.

When venturing into marketing copyrights worldwide, you need to make sure that your network is set up effectively. Don't assume that if your song gets played on foreign radio someone will ensure royalty payments to you. Make sure your performing rights agency has reciprocal agreements with foreign rights agencies. And ensure that your music publisher—and this may be you if you're "doing it yourself"—either has effective foreign offices or subpublishing agreements with reputable local publishers.

It is the local publishers, or local offices of your domestic publisher, that do the work of scouting for local opportunities to place your music. They are the "boots on the ground" spoken of earlier.

In the context of the recorded-music marketing addressed in this book, any recording or performing artist who also composes has an opportunity to earn additional money for public performances, "mechanical" uses, and "synchronization" uses of the original music. Don't overlook this dimension when pursuing other aspects of marketing. Sign up with a home rights agency and with a publisher—or be your own publisher. Explore publishers in target territories and make deals with them to represent your music. And stay in touch with them. Check on the status of your music catalogue. Make suggestions if you become aware of any potential uses in the target zone—an artist who might want to cover your song, for example.

The music publishing side may be complex, but that's largely a result of the sheer number of outlets for music. Understand them, know how to access them, and learn how to ensure compensation for them. Then put them to work for your music.

CHAPTER 13

Comparing Notes: Interviews

Experiences in the global music market are as varied as the professional aims and personal perspectives that participants bring to the field. Yet all kinds of experiences have aspects that can be studied and learned from, regardless of your chosen sector of activity. Keeping in mind that tapping into others' expertise is an important part of any business enterprise, we turn now to a set of interviews with representatives of five different approaches to global music involvement.

THINKING GLOBALLY AS AN INDEPENDENT MUSICIAN

SUZANNE CIANI, COMPOSER, RECORD LABEL OWNER, UNITED STATES

Suzanne Ciani is a pioneer in the field of electronic music and sound design, with fifteen albums of original music in a broad array of expressions: pure electronic, solo piano, piano with orchestra, and piano with jazz ensemble. Before establishing her own California-based record label, Seventh Wave, Ciani ran a commercial production company in New York, creating award-winning music for a host of high-profile *Fortune* 500 clients. She has toured throughout the United States, Italy, Spain, and Asia.

Describe, briefly, what you do as an independent composer and record company owner.

SC: Oh my. I do it all. Basically, my function alternates between the creative and business areas. Creatively, I compose, perform, and produce the music. Next comes the album design and artwork along with manufacturing. And then I concentrate on distribution and marketing efforts. And in my spare time—just joking—I coordinate the seeking of concert opportunities.

In what ways are international business opportunities important to your business success?

SC: I have always had an eye towards international venues: my publishing company is called Musica International, formed about twenty years ago, with the express vision of connecting to a world market. The world market becomes more and more significant every minute as other countries develop an appetite for American musical trends and as technology continues to shrink the planet through digital communications and file downloading possibilities. And it's fun—I get to work closely with foreign partners and hopefully develop the business enough so that I can go to the country and perform, meet my fans, and enrich my life through contact with a new culture.

What kinds of international business opportunities do you pursue? Exporting? Licensing? Which kinds of arrangements are preferable, and why?

SC: It may seem initially that exporting is a better option—and it is a good way to open up and prime a market. It obviates the need for the foreign entity to invest in manufacturing and allows them to concentrate on marketing and distribution. However, many countries have particular packaging vocabularies and needs, and it might be better to allow licensing in order to better communicate to their buyers.

Licensing is a bit scarier in that one loses a bit of control: with an untrustworthy international partner one is not sure of the quantities manufactured. Though in some countries, like Spain, mechanical royalties have to be paid right at the point of manufacture.

But overall I think there is a big distinction between the distribution end and the publishing end. I have always found publishing to be a more dependable part of the business. The performance societies for the most part are assiduous and well-coordinated with their American affiliates (I am with ASCAP), and the subpublishers that we work with (peermusic, BMG, Warner) are pretty straight-ahead in their royalty statements. Subpublishers are also instrumental in following through on synch licensing opportunities that come up. Recently, "Turning," originally a love song, was licensed for a washing machine commercial in South Korea and the subpublisher nurtured the deal to completion.

How easy or difficult is it for an independent composer and record company owner to attract interest in foreign countries?

SC: I think it is very much a matter of timing. New Age, for example, is a "trend" that unfolds from place to place. If one catches the wave and knows when a particular country is open to a particular kind of music, then it is an easier job. Some countries never seem to open up to a particular kind of music. Fortunately, there are many possibilities, and it is best to concentrate on the ones that are ripe than to despair at not making any inroads. The biggest issue is that it is time consuming to nurture many separate deals.

Are some countries easier to do business with than others? Which are easier? Which are more difficult?

SC: In the independent world, we are frequently talking about relationships with smaller, indie-style labels and distributors. It never seems easy, really. The general sparsity of communications due to differing time zones and language differences make the process seem less tangible and more distant.

I think it really helps to physically go to the country. I love working in Asia: they are so media savvy, energetic, and professional. France has been difficult for me. Italy is frustrating even though I go there twice a year and speak the language. Germany easier. And so on.

What are the biggest challenges you face in doing overseas business? How do you handle them?

SC: Language is a problem, although I speak about five (badly). I frequently use a translating program for communications. Asian countries, rather than European ones, are more prepared to do business in English.

We have a European bank account for accepting payments in euros, which can be more favorable than dollars. One of my pet peeves has been the foreign taxes: large chunks of royalties are withheld. Presumably you can get these refunded, but it requires going through hoops with the IRS here and then chances are still small that the foreign country will refund. Better to take a deduction, I've found.

When you attend the MIDEM international music-business convention, what are your aims? What do you hope to get out of the conference? Does it work for you?

SC: My main aim at MIDEM is to meet people. It is a rare opportunity to actually be face to face with a distant business associate. It is like going around the world in three days. It takes a lot of preparation and a lot of follow-up to nurture new contacts, but the opportunities are there for the taking.

Any advice for independent musicians who want to begin doing business in foreign countries?

SC: Well, look at your performance royalty statements (ASCAP or BMI or SESAC) and see if your music is being played in a particular country. This information might steer you toward a place to start focusing.

Use the Internet to do research, of course. Check out the music you like in a foreign country and see who is publishing and distributing it. Contact them.

Go to MIDEM.

Make subpublishing deals if you can and then get the support of these companies to recommend other business partners in licensing and distribution.

Keep your Web site up to date; it is your international calling card.

Anything else you'd like to add?

SC: Never give up your publishing.

DISTRIBUTING MUSIC IN A GLOBAL MARKET

ROB KUILBOER, CEO, ASTRAL MUSIC, THE NETHERLANDS

Astral Music, founded by Rob Kuilboer, is a wholesaler and distributor of physical products, including CDs, DVDs, vinyl records, and other merchandise.

How did you get into the distribution business?

RK: I have always been influenced by music. As a youngster I spent all my allowance and earned money on attending live concerts and collecting records. I was intrigued by the music business but never thought it was something you would do as a job, unless as a musician, which I was definitely not. After finishing Dutch pre-university high school in 1983 I didn't have a clear vision on what to study, and after several temporary occupations, including being an autodidactic sculptor and painter, traveling from town to town and making stage props for theater performing groups, I was asked to play records and fill in for somebody in an indie bar in 1985—something that I enjoyed doing for ten years in several clubs under the alias of DJ Robson. From 1987 I also found employment during the day at an Amsterdam import shop and later moved on to work as a buyer and salesman for a Dutch wholesaler-distributor called Boudisque and later as a manager of the dance department at Roughtrade Benelux. In '95 I started Astral Music, as a van service selling records from the back of a truck.

Talk a little about what you do and what Astral Music does—especially in working with artists and record labels from outside your country.

RK: As the CEO of Astral Music, my task is to clarify the overall goals of the organization and to focus resources on those goals. A great deal of my day is preoccupied with monitoring and managing the use of the available resources. I consider myself a hands-on type manager, and I work from a desk in the sales and logistics office, a desk in a separate office, and one from my home. Working in the hectic dance music industry with nearly 250 new unique titles to choose from each week means staying in shape and in touch with club and radio deejays 24-7.

Astral Music is a wholesale and distribution company of physical products like vinyl, CD, DVD, and merchandise. We are based in Europe and import and export from all over the world and have exclusive distribution deals with some of the most prominent European dance labels.

We offer artists and record labels distribution based on three deals: sales and distribution, manufacturing and distribution, and pressing and distribution.

With the S&D deal the label delivers finished products in our warehouse. The label is responsible for payment of royalties, artwork, manufacturing and packaging, mechanical rights, and promotion and is the owner of the product.

With the M&D deal, Astral Music takes care of payment of mechanical rights and manufacturing and packaging. As these costs will be deducted from sales statements, the label remains the owner of the finished products.

With the P&D deal, Astral Music pays for manufacturing and packaging, mechanical rights, and promotion and is the owner of the product and has the right to press and sell the physical products. An override is paid to the label above five hundred units sold. In this deal Astral Music also manufactures an amount of eighty white labels for promotion.

In all the above-mentioned deals the sales are captured in monthly statements, which are paid thirty or sixty days end-of-month, depending on the format (vinyl, CD, or other). Labels receive a login to our site and can monitor all stock movements in real time. Labels can also monitor to which country items are being sold and they can select any date range they like. The system we use is transparent and very useful for both marketing and financial purposes. As a label partner you are able to keep track of the expected revenue statement during the course of our monthly sales cycle.

A license partner of the label located in a foreign country can be alerted by the label when we are seeing good sales of a title of the label's catalogue in this country. This usually generates more license income.

Who determines the price you pay for a foreign label's product? You? The foreign label?

RK: We try to agree on a buying price together with the label, which enables us to place the product in the market for a PPD (published price to dealer/retailer) that suits the market best and enables us to maximize sales. The higher the price, the more difficult it will be to sell quantities. Quantities are necessary to be able to average [attain economies of scale] for the high initial costs for masters and lacquers.

Please describe, in general terms, the markups that are added to that price. What costs are calculated into the final price to the customer in the store? Distributor percentage? Retailer percentage? Freight? Tariffs? VAT?

RK: The price structure on sound carriers like vinyl or CDs is complex. For instance, the vinyl format—already, in manufacturing, there are choices to be made, like whether to use full-color artwork, inner sleeve, and 3mm spine outer sleeve, or go for black-and-white labels and a disco bag. Even 33 rpm or 45 rpm can adjust the pricing, since mechanical rights payments differ. When the record is being distributed, the distributor will charge a fee according to the pertaining service levels—whether the release is only accompanied by an e-mail with the specific details of the item; or whether the service includes promotion and mailing of links to sound files, pack shot [picture of the artwork], telesales, a sales representative on the road, freight included in prices, and allowing high discounts to customers. When the label allows the distributor to give high discounts, the distributor will find that the fee needs to be adjusted to a higher level as a small percentage on a low price may be insufficient to cover for the costs involved in distribution. A distribution fee can vary from 18 to 26 percent.

Some distributors choose to work with a fixed price and pay discounts and extra service levels out of their own pocket, which means that the difference between the fixed buying price and the PPD could be higher than a 26 percent distribution fee.

There is a difference in percentage added by a physical retailer who owns a shop and a retailer who owns a Web shop. The physical retailer adds 60 to 80 percent before VAT on top [of the PPD] and the Web shop adds 35 to 65 percent before VAT on the PPD. Both retailers calculate their markup on top of the actual buying price—put concisely, the price they pay, minus discounts but including freight costs. [*Editor's note:* Distributor payment calculation practices vary widely.]

Obviously, the Web shop still has to take the costs of freight to the consumer into account. When the shop is located in a different continent from where the distributor is located, often tariffs or import duties have to be taken into account, which need to be paid at customs before the goods are cleared for landing. In most cases this tariff is a fixed percentage on the value of the shipment and varies from 3 to 10 percent, which the shop will also add to the price.

Although the sales tax in the U.S. is between 5 and 9 percent, in Europe the VAT can vary per country from 15 to 25 percent, which turns a consumer product like a CD immediately into a well-thought-over investment. In the Netherlands for example: a book is charged with 6 percent VAT; the movie DVD and the soundtrack CD of the same book is charged with 19 percent. As you can imagine, the high tax on sound carriers opposite to the low tax on books has been a hot topic with retailers over the past years.

Who pays freight, tariffs, and other costs of doing foreign business?

RK: The receiver, or company that buys the goods, usually takes care of all costs that arise from the moment that the seller tapes up and closes the shipment. Sometimes the seller has a better deal with a freight forwarder and takes care of payment of shipment and includes freight charges on the invoice to the customer.

Are your export deals usually for a fixed number of units—say 2,000, with options for reorder? Are your payments made to the foreign label periodically, after 30, 60, 90, or 120 days?

RK: Most of our export deals involve a minimum order, a "returns" percentage with a deadline, and free product; in some cases we offer consignment, when we feel this would be necessary to generate sales. We try to negotiate on realistic numbers as we'd rather receive reorders than returns. We do not discriminate against foreign labels. Our payment schedule is, in general, thirty days for vinyl releases and sixty days for CD releases, after statement.

Are 100 percent of unsold goods returnable by the retailer to you, as in U.S. domestic distribution deals?

RK: We offer up to one-year return right on initial orders on CDs and DVDs only, and three months return right on initial orders on vinyl records. We do withhold a percentage [or payment due] for returns, but only in cases when there is no new product from the label to be expected.

Are the export deals done in the exporter's currency or in euros? Or is this negotiable? If you must pay in the exporter's currency, how do you protect against changes in currency exchange rates?

RK: Astral Music has a flexible setup regarding currencies. We are able to invoice in U.S. dollars, euros, and British pounds. As we buy a lot from U.S. and U.K. suppliers, we are always in need of these currencies. This and the fact that we adjust the exchange rate every month, keeping it on the safe side of the euro, minimize the risk of currency exchange fluctuations. Nothing to do with currency, but equally as important when it comes to narrowing the goalposts of risk threats, is the credit insurance on accounts with payment terms.

Tell us a little about volume discounts—or "free goods"—you may get from the exporter.

RK: Every record company is allowed to reserve a percentage of stock for promotional purposes. The label does not pay mechanical rights and royalties on this part of the stock. Exporters usually reward higher volume orders with free product.

How do channel advertising and promotion work? Does the exporter offer you a discount, which you pass on to the retailer for in-store promotion? What is a typical discount percentage?

RK: In order to generate awareness on new releases and to convince retailers to take in product, a certain amount of promotion must take place and reach effectiveness by creating a pull in the market. This is the ideal situation. The money spent on promotion must be used wisely. As promotional budgets are tight and there are a lot of options, choices must be made. Free publicity like reviews and interviews in printed and online media, and prizes and giveaways at radio stations, are easy to organize and only cost postage and packaging and a few phone calls. The exporter usually offers promotional samples or finished products to start up promotion and a percentage of five to ten percent on the initial order for retail job racking. Sometimes Astral Music contributes a small part of its markup to match the required discount level needed by shops to advertise the release in their newsletter.

How does the foreign label handle advertising and promotion for its goods in your country, apart from channel promotion? Does the label, on its own, contact local media for coverage and place local ads? To whom does the foreign label go for help with local advertising and publicity?

RK: We advise the label in whom to contact within this territory when there is an interest and budget to do more promotion. As soon as we have made introductions with media we leave it to the foreign label to set up an interview or press day [press conference] in addition to the already planned concert. Sometimes the artist's management is involved in the promotion of the album.

We arrange ads and banners, as we would like the foreign label to benefit from discounts we have with these media types within this territory.

About radio: Is there any opportunity for exporters to get radio play in the Netherlands? Are there local content requirements that limit how much airplay can be devoted to nondomestic music? Who handles local radio promotion? The distributor?

RK: Domestic labels, let alone foreign labels, find it extremely difficult to enter national radio in the Netherlands. Radio stations' airplay formats do not allow the radio deejay to enter more than a few personal choices. This and the lack of change limits the number of new entries and leaves hardly any space for an exporter to penetrate. In other countries, like France, there are also other rules, like the predominant French radio format that allows only French-produced and French-spoken songs. We use an independent radio promoter in the Netherlands and basically coordinate all radio promotions. We charge a fee for this, and often this fee is implemented in the quantity of free goods.

Do you ever request that the exporter alter any aspect of a CD to make it more saleable in your market—for example, delete or add a track, or change the packaging?

RK: Only a few exporters use secondary A&R [artists and repertoire] across territories regarding the say in track listings. However, it is advisable to consider every aspect of the product thoroughly. Simple changes can make a big difference in sales. We have advised exporters from non-Anglo countries to change their domestic language on the cover to English. When we feel that a release would do well in Japan, we would ask the label to add a sticker in Japanese, explaining about the content. Obviously this sticker must be easy to be peeled off, as it is much cooler for somebody in Japan to possess an imported album. Packaging matters and must be right. It must appeal and it must immediately say something about the quality of the product. When the packaging looks cheap, it is hard to charge a high PPD. When the packaging is a special laminated multicolor carton DigiPak with foldouts and special metallic details, both consumer and retailer are willing to pay more. The CD looks more like a present, something unique. We always take the full presentation into account when we advise and when we buy goods.

Is there anything important about exporting/importing that you would like to add? Or about the Netherlands or EU music market?

RK: The Netherlands is well known for its high standard of transportation and services. Being based near Schiphol Airport and only forty-five minutes' drive from one of the world's biggest harbors, the port of Rotterdam, certainly has its logistical advantages.

As the world is turning into one centralized global marketplace, causing music markets to change fundamentally, the business model of distribution of physical products will have to change inevitably as well. In the past, distributors were dealing with distributors. Today distributors need to be able to deal with numerous distributors, with retailers across borders, and even direct with consumers at the same time in order to be able to grow or sustain as an operation. Tomorrow, distributors will need to handle downloads as well, as part of their setup, whether they like it or not, either on a nonexclusive basis or as an aggregator, and by offering downloads to retail or to the consumer direct. The sky may still be the limit in the music industry, but you have to realize that you need to reach much higher to be able to see it.

We decided to start innovating through technology at Astral Music in 2001 when we turned our operation into a B2B-based Web model that enables our customers to enter orders, search the catalogue, pay online, check available quantities, listen to sound files, find release info, track and trace, upload complete order files, monitor financial status, check pack shots, supply content as XML, and make use of other out-of-the-box solutions. We also serve our labels and suppliers with several options in Web shop fulfillment and the capability of uploading and correcting data, monitoring sales in real time and by any given date range, checking open orders, checking quantities sold to specific territories, reviewing previous statements and financial status, and so on.

As downloading has become more user-friendly and fast Internet has become more available in Europe, we have completed our download platform, in order to improve our service to labels, artists, and retailers.

How do record companies from outside the EU—for instance, the United States—find out about and get in contact with Astral Music?

RK: Record companies can find us on the Internet at www.astralmusic.com, where we are happy to answer any questions regarding distribution possibilities.

The labels we distribute include our details and logo on the records and CDs, which makes it easier to find us. Other than that, we do attend or have representation at conventions like the ADE, MIDEM, Popkomm, Sonar, and the Winter Music Conference.

MARKETING DIGITAL MUSIC WORLDWIDE

DANIEL CHEUNG, HEAD OF ORCHARD ASIA, HONG KONG

The Orchard is a leading international distributor of digital music. Orchard Asia, headquartered in Hong Kong, focuses on new digital media content, the next generation of applications and devices, and the new business opportunities they will create. Daniel Cheung is a seasoned digital media executive with more than twenty-five years' experience in telecommunications and global information technology. Before starting up Orchard Asia, Cheung held senior technical and management positions with Bell Laboratories, AT&T, and Cable & Wireless.

First, a little about you: How did you become involved in the music business, and digital music in particular?

DC: My involvement in the digital music business is a carefully planned transition and not a chance engagement. After Y2K, telecommunications faced a number of industrywide challenges, including deregulation and major changes in market dynamics, and the industry was searching for ways to migrate from a low-margin infrastructure business to a value-added services-oriented business with higher profit potential. I was leading a number of efforts at the time in this paradigm shift, and digital music/media was one of them. The process brought me in touch with The Orchard in 2004. I recognized the unique positioning of The Orchard in the global digital music-media industry and, more importantly, their corporate commitment to the development of the global digital music-media space. I joined The Orchard earlier this year [2006] and took on the responsibility of developing the Asian markets for The Orchard.

What does The Orchard do? How does it fit into the digital music marketplace?

DC: The Orchard is the world's leading digital distributor of music and a marketer of digital music/media. The Orchard believes that every independent label and artist deserves the opportunity to make their music available through-out the world.

The Orchard provides the entire value-chain of digital music and is fully integrated into the digital music marketplace. We supply music to over one hundred digital stores around the world, including iTunes, eMusic, Napster, Rhapsody, and Sony Connect. We distribute labels like Lookout!, Fierce Panda, Saregama, Shanachie, SST, Laugh.com, Delicious Vinyl, Epsa, and hundreds of others. We distribute artists like Ray Charles, Green Day, Afrika Bambaataa, Ravi Shankar, Black Flag, Public Enemy, John Legend, George Carlin, Coldplay, and over 22,000 others. Furthermore, we aggressively pro-mote and market music to digital stores and secure feature placements for our labels.

The Orchard has been a key driving force in the digital music market-place and our mission is to be a truly global player in this space and contribute in a significant manner to the development and growth of the global digital music/media industry, which is still in its early stages of development.

How is digital music distribution—downloads, streaming, mobile music—changing the global music business? What opportunities does it offer to artists and record labels that were not available with standard brick-and-mortar distribution?

DC: Digital music distribution, with its direct and virtually instantaneous access characteristics, has fundamentally changed the way music is being deliv-ered, marketed, and purchased by consumers, and at some stage in time will change how music is being produced. It has also created new business models, such as à la carte and subscription.

This offers tremendous opportunities to artists and record labels, particu-larly the independent ones, in terms of much broader and faster access to mar-kets that traditional physical distribution simply cannot match.

What is your view on the future of the hard-copy CD? Will tangible music products such as CDs remain a significant factor in music sales? Or are they due to disappear as today's young digital-friendly audiences mature and replace older CD buyers?

DC: The question on physical versus digital distribution now is "when will it happen?" instead of "will it happen?"

It is safe to say the cycle for digital products to overtake physical products will be longer than the replacement of vinyl records by CDs. However, wireless will accelerate the pace and will eventually overtake the online sector.

What are the chief challenges in marketing digital music worldwide?

DC: The distribution and hence marketing of digital music worldwide is cur-rently limited to a handful of major stores in developed U.S. and European markets, which need to be broadened into other markets (Asia, for example) and channels (such as wireless) for the healthy and sustainable growth of the industry.

A major challenge in terms of marketing Asian digital music worldwide is the labeling and categorizing of "world music," which isolate Asian music; and not promoting the important crossover aspect of the music. However, a corresponding challenge is balancing crossover with the desire to retain key ethnic identities.

How can emerging artists and small labels best use digital channels to reach audiences outside their own countries? Should they work with digital music aggregators?

DC: Digital distribution is the ideal channel for emerging artists and small labels in reaching global audiences, with its relatively low overhead and a much shorter time-to-market cycle. The quality of music will always be a key element for success; however, marketing will be the determining factor.

Artists and labels should choose and work with reputable digital music aggregators that have the requisite marketing capability and a passion for and commitment to the digital music movement.

The Orchard has been opening offices all around the world. How does this fit with The Orchard's overall business strategy?

DC: To be truly global is an integral part of The Orchard's strategy, and these offices are actually "centers of excellence" spearheaded by individuals who are leaders and subject-matter experts in their respective territories or markets. These offices, working in tandem with The Orchard U.S., provide a global platform for independent artists and labels that also appreciates and under-stands cultural differences and the wide range of market dynamics in various regional and local markets.

What are the goals of The Orchard's Hong Kong operation?

DC: Asia is home to a number of major markets in the world (e.g., China, Japan, and South Korea), which represent a consumer base of mega propor-tions and a vast pool of music talent. Asian markets and content will be key driving forces of the global digital music/media industry going forward.

The Orchard established Orchard Asia in 2006 to focus on the develop-ment of Asia into a major content-provisioning center for the world and a key distribution channel for non-Asian content. Asia is a centerpiece of The Orchard's global strategy.

What about music business in general in Hong Kong? How much activity is there in local music? In music from elsewhere?

DC: In Hong Kong, China, and the rest of Asia, the music business continues to be plagued by piracy. The tide is now turning, with China entering into the WTO and the IFPI intensifying its fight against piracy in key markets world-wide, including Hong Kong and Singapore in Asia.

Greater China (Hong Kong, China, and Taiwan) and Asia in general are dominated by local repertoire. Non-Asian or Western repertoire only accounts for a small percentage of the overall market. However, digital distribution will change this landscape and allow consumers greater access to music from the U.S., Europe, and other parts of Asia.

For foreign record labels that want to do business in Hong Kong, what are the chief opportunities? The biggest obstacles?

DC: Hong Kong is now a special administrative region of China, and together they represent the largest consumer market in the world with over 110 million Internet users and more than 400 million mobile phone subscribers and growing—an extremely large addressable market for digital distribution, with a low penetration of foreign labels.

The biggest obstacles are: understanding local market characteristics and business cultures, which are vastly different from the Western markets, and working with local partners with established relationships, international experience, professionalism, and integrity. These obstacles are typical throughout Asia.

For Hong Kong artists and labels wishing to do business elsewhere, what are the main hurdles?

DC: The hurdles are similar to those faced by foreign labels wishing to do business in Asia and differ only in magnitude. There is a large pool of Asian expatriates in non-Asian countries, which allows Asians to have relatively closer and wider exposure to Western cultures. However, finding a trusted global partner with the required distribution and marketing capabilities remains the main hurdle.

Finally, what general advice would you give to indie artists and record labels that would like to begin selling their music in foreign countries?

DC: Digital distribution provides unprecedented distribution opportunities for indie artists and record labels, and yet exacerbates competition. Consumers can compare music virtually in real time by previewing sample clips—a standard offering with digital stores. Music from indie artists and record labels will be competing in a much larger playing field as compared with the physical distribution and traditional marketing environment.

Good music is the sword and a good distribution partner is the shield—you need both to venture out.

Is there anything that you would like to add about the global music market?

DC: The global music market is currently at a watershed. A number of factors—such as when digital formats will overtake physical formats to become the mainstream, the development of wireless into a key music distribution platform, and the challenges in establishing Asia as a major market player in the world—will have significant implications to its future course.

The Orchard, Orchard Asia, and other like-minded entities worldwide are dedicated and committed to the development and long-term growth of the global digital music/media industry, and the horizon looks brighter and better as we march forward each day.

INTERNATIONAL MARKETING
IN A SMALL RECORD COMPANY

MARY JUREY, DIRECTOR OF MANUFACTURING AND INTERNATIONAL OPERATIONS, NEW WEST RECORDS, UNITED STATES

New West Records is an independent record label based in Los Angeles and Austin, Texas, featuring Americana, southern rock, roots, gospel, folk, country rock, and indie rock.

How about a little background on you?

MJ: I went to Duke University, in North Carolina. My degree is in public policy and Middle Eastern foreign policy.

What does your job at New West entail?

MJ: I am like a mini-label inside the label. I handle all the international aspects, selling our products overseas.

Which countries are you working with currently?

MJ: We deal with Spain, the U.K., Italy, France (which actually falls under the U.K. for us), Scandinavia, the Benelux, Australia, New Zealand, and sometimes Japan and Germany.

How do you go about finding and choosing foreign business partners or initiating business in foreign markets?

MJ: It's sort of a "feel" situation. It's trial-and-error—people you've had success with in the past. The people who pay their bills, those are the people you stick with.

How do you decide whether to export or license in a given country?

MJ: That is a tough one. In the majority of cases we tend to export. It tends to be more lucrative. Sometimes, if a host country, so to speak, is really game for licensing, we'll do it, depending on the money. We analyze each release and then decide. But in most cases, in general, we export. In all the time I've been doing this, we've licensed two records.

How do business arrangements with foreign distributors differ from arrangements with domestic distributors?

MJ: It's sort of a smaller scale for us. We go through a major distributor in the U.S. It's different, but there are also a lot of similarities. The U.S. distributor is bigger, it has more reach.

—in size of fee or commission paid to distributor—

MJ: That's about the same.

—in timing of payment to the record company—

MJ: We're paid more immediately by the foreign distributor. In this case, our terms are net sixty.

What considerations go into deciding on an export price for a foreign market?

MJ: The power of the dollar, although our prices haven't changed that much—they're pretty much at cost-price. Currency fluctuations don't affect us that much. If you tried to change your prices every time the dollar changes you wouldn't be able to keep up. You pick a price and then stick with it. Then, over time, if the dollar goes up, or down, you adjust it. But I don't think you should try to compete with it.

What role are digital formats—downloads, streaming media, and so forth—playing in your international marketing strategy?

MJ: Digital marketing is extremely important for each release. The international communities are in many cases more digitally savvy than the U.S. is.

Do you alter or customize music or packaging for any foreign markets? If so, what kinds of things do you do?

MJ: Sure. In Japan, they like for us to just ship them the discs. They make their own packaging. It's also lighter to ship just the CDs. The art is kept essentially the same. The distributing company there, though, may add their own logo. We make a lot of our products in DigiPaks. Sometimes they will change those into jewel cases.

How do you handle promotion in foreign countries? Radio? Publicity/PR? Advertising?

MJ: Mostly, I oversee all of that. In some places, we have publicists. So, they help. They do PR and radio work.

But the queries for major interviews, for example, come back to your office?

MJ: In most cases, yes.

What are the biggest challenges you face in doing business internationally?

MJ: The most obvious is, you're not there. You hope that everything you're asking people to do—or they say they're doing—is actually happening.

How do you communicate with your various contacts?

MJ: Mostly by e-mail. Occasionally, a phone call.

Any other points you'd like to add?

MJ: Really, this is selling records by long distance. In general, I am interested in people who are interested in the kinds of music we have to offer. If they are fans, there seems to be a better relationship.

GENERAL OBSERVATIONS ON GLOBAL MUSIC PROMOTION

PETER FOSSO, FOUNDER/PRESIDENT OF NETMUSIC AND GLOBAL MUSIC PROJECT, UNITED STATES

Global Music Project (GMP) is a nonprofit organization that provides support for global humanitarian and environmentalist charities through the talents of the world's musicians and other artists. Its mission is to better the world through music by bringing financial support and increased awareness to select globally oriented organizations.

A little about you: How have you been involved in the global music marketplace?

PF: I started out by playing in various rock groups during the 1980s and 1990s and have always looked for ways to support other artists. I then started a local record label in Seattle, called Insight Records (www.insightrecords.com), which supported local artists and released a number of compilation CDs, some of which benefited charitable organizations. Around that time I also founded NetMusic (www.netmusic.com), a company that started off as a directory of music sites and later evolved into being an online retailer for independent artists.

The idea for Global Music Project (GMP) came to me in 2002, and the site was launched during that same year. We were fortunate enough to begin receiving strong interest from artists around the world right out of the gate. Independent artists tend to be very focused on ways they can get exposure for themselves and their music, and GMP of course offered them that opportunity, and it remains a primary focus of the organization today.

What are the major differences you see between marketing domestically and marketing globally?

PF: Well the most obvious, of course, is that you're dealing with a much larger palette. I believe that, although it can be more complex dealing in multiple territories, it can also offer an organization—especially one such as ours—some great opportunities. The development of technology-driven countries such as Dubai, plus the proliferation of the Internet, widens our reach and continually presents new possibilities for partnerships, new customers, and overall growth. And fortunately for those of us who are English-speaking Americans, communicating with many of those in the other various countries around the globe is not a problem, as English tends to be so prominent. And Internet translation software has been improving significantly.

But a company needs to be sensitive to how you might be perceived in other countries as well, so as to not offend, and so you can direct your message and brand to communicate with the target audience. Monetary sensitivity is also a potential factor. We are currently discussing how we might structure pricing for each of our downloadable songs differently in some countries than in others, based on the strength of their economy.

Given that CDs still represent the bulk of recorded music sales, what are the relative pros and cons of the current standard business strategies for selling them abroad?

PF: Well, of course, shipping has always been a fairly large part of the cost, although this is usually, in the end, something of which the consumer has had to bear. Downloadable music has only a fraction of that cost for its distribution over the Internet, and the consumer can, of course, enjoy it immediately after purchase. Plus there's no limit to its supply.

What are the chief challenges in marketing digital music downloads, streaming, mobile music, ringtones worldwide?

PF: The greatest challenge, and usually that which is the most labor and revenue intensive, is simply getting the consuming public to know about the artist, song, or music service. Once that leap has been made, the goal then is simply to make the sale. Marketing globally, as mentioned previously, has the added challenge of multilingual communication plus one's marketing message ringing true with the audience. There also may be issues with computer-software compatibility and slower Internet connections—each a contributing factor driving a potential new customer toward continual use of CDs. This, of course, is not limited to other parts of the globe and is a challenge to doing business in the U.S. as well.

What are your thoughts about the difficulty of getting on foreign radio due to local content quotas?

PF: I believe it's a good thing that countries allot a certain amount of airtime to support their own artists. I personally strive toward supporting a country's own culture and do not necessarily want to take anything away from that. And with the advent of new types of radio (such as Internet radio), I'm sure that we'll all be sharing more and more the great music each country has to offer.

How important is global touring? What are the chief benefits? Challenges?

PF: Even with all of today's technology, there's no substitute for being somewhere in person. There are many, many artists all over the world who are making great music but do not have the means to record it. This music is part of their culture. Global Music Project's first initiative is to visit the artists in countries whose culture is threatened by globalization, and go in and preserve this culture. There is so much great music being made, and so much that disappears each day. We intend to preserve this music that is threatened never to be heard again and allow others to discover this great music being made around the world. This is our "tour." But the challenge we have is a financial one. We're looking to everyone we can to make a financial contribution to us so that we may accomplish this important work.

What kinds of customization of music content and packaging do you see in global marketing?

PF: At this time, we are not customizing any music content for foreign markets. Downloadable music carries very little "packaging" per se, so our focus is more on the ability to translate that tiny bit of information that might affect purchasing. We utilize a translation service on our Web site; however, we believe our visitors are primarily English-speaking, though many as their second language.

Music downloads tend to be less about the packaging and more about the music. After all, there's really nothing "physical" about music. There never has been. Music is a collection of sounds. Although they tend to be stored in some fashion, it's all about the aural experience. The packaging is usually to hype or to inform.

What are the greatest challenges of global music marketing?

PF: The single greatest challenge is the communication of your marketing message across diverse cultures that utilize a variety of different languages. The other challenges might be based around e-commerce, like receiving payment from any country around the globe, or interacting with a non-English-speaking customer.

To what extent does music piracy in a country dissuade you from doing business in that country? How do you protect against it?

PF: We do not restrict anyone from doing business with us. Our catalogue consists primarily of independent artists, and they tend to believe it's better to get their music heard than to restrict others from hearing it—even if it means that it might be pirated.

Finally: Do you have any advice for first-time global music marketers?

PF: Don't forget about the nonprofit sector. Partnering with an organization like Global Music Project can be a good way to jump-start your marketing, get some great exposure, plus help a worthy cause. Whether it's producing an event or the release of a new CD, making it a benefit for a nonprofit organization can bring increased exposure, greater sales, and heightened awareness of you along with the organization you support.

Most importantly, the advice I offer is: Learn all you can, but jump in before you feel you know it all, 'cause you never do. And reading this book is a great start!

Regional categories in this section follow the guidelines of the U.S. Central Intelligence Agency's reference maps.

The "Distributors" category in the country-by-country listings includes companies that may engage in one or more of the following activities: distribution, import/export, licensing, digital aggregation. Research the company for details.

The list of distributors is necessarily limited to some of the larger businesses. For complete lists, consult some of the local music trade organizations cited in the country-by-country information below.

INTERNATIONAL

ECONOMIC AND FINANCIAL INDICATORS AND COUNTRY DATA

Corruption Perceptions Index. www.transparency.org. This list ranks 146 countries according to the degree to which they are perceived to have corrupt public officials and politicians.

The Economist. www.economist.com. Print weekly and Web site on international business. The Web site offers current commentary on world trade along with "backgrounders" on countries and topics plus current market data. A must for those involved in global trade.

International Monetary Fund (IMF). www.imf.org. Offers country financial and economic information.

Organization for Economic Cooperation and Development (OECD). www.oecd.org. Carries out analytical work on trade. The Web site posts statistics, papers, and briefs on a variety of trade topics.

United Nations Conference on Trade and Development (UNCTAD). www.unctad.org. Promotes integration of developing countries into world economy. Web site offers related analysis and data.

U.S. Central Intelligence Agency World Factbook. www.cia.gov. A set of country profiles that provide data on population, government, infrastructure, communications, and trade.

U.S. Department of State. Background Notes. www.state.gov/www/ background_notes. Information on geographic regions and entities.

World Bank, www.worldbank.org. Includes data on people, environment, economy, technology and infrastructure, trade and finance, and more.

World Trade Organization (WTO). www.wto.org. Provides trade statistics, economic research, and information on a wide range of trade topics.

TRADE PROCEDURES AND RESOURCES

Basic Guide to Exporting. www.unzco.com/basicguide.

Business Culture Worldwide. www.businessculture.com.

Currency Converter. www.xe.com/ucc. This site allows you to compare values of any two world currencies.

Export911. www.export911.com. Information on export-import marketing, management, letters of credit, export cargo insurance, shipping, logistics, manufacturing, purchasing, bar codes, and more.

Freight World. www.freightworld.com. A professional guide to worldwide freight transportation and logistics.

Import Regulations of Major Countries. www.tdctrade.com/sme/ir/index.htm.

International Business, 6th Ed. Charles W. L. Hill. New York: McGraw-Hill/Irwin, 2006. Leading textbook, used widely in M.B.A. programs.

International Business Center. www.internationalbusinesscenter.org. General resource with information on culture, logistics, marketing, trade, and travel.

International Business Etiquette and Manners. www.cyborlink.com/besite/Default.asp.

International Chamber of Commerce. www.iccwbo.org.

Marketing Management, 11th Ed. Philip Kotler. Englewood Cliffs, NJ: Prentice Hall. Leading textbook on all aspects of marketing, emphasizing theory.

World Clock. www.timeanddate.com/worldclock. A guide to time zones, calendars, and clocks for all regions of the world.

World Public Holidays. www.tyzo.com/tools/holidays.html. Information on more than 100 countries focusing on public holidays, but also covering phone dialing codes, electricity requirements, embassies, and more.

Worldwide Business Reports. www.worldbiz.com. Country-specific reports on business practices, business customs, cross-cultural communication, negotiating, international etiquette, business entertainment, and more.

MUSIC INDUSTRY

All You Need to Know About the Music Business, Rev. Ed. Donald Passman. New York: Simon & Schuster, 2000. Engaging look at how the music business works.

Alliance of Artists and Recording Companies (AARC). www.aarcroyalties.com. U.S.-based organization that distributes Audio Home Recording Act royalties to artists and record companies around the world.

BIEM. www.biem.org. Membership organization of societies that administer mechanical rights.

Billboard. www.billboard.com. The international newsweekly of music, video, and home entertainment. Includes popularity charts.

Billboard International Buyer's Guide. New York: VNU, annual. Listings of record labels, music publishers, wholesalers and distributors, raw materials manufacturers, and companies by country.

Canadian Independent Record Production Association (CIRPA). www.cirpa.ca. Provides music industry data on countries with most music activity; covers media, retailers, market characteristics, record labels, music styles, exports, and business practices.

Global Music Industry: Facts and Forecasts. London: Informa Media Group, 2002. Provides statistics on the major music markets throughout the world.

International Confederation of Societies of Authors and Composers (CISAC). www.cisac.org. Provides forum for coordination and standardization of practices of member societies.

International Federation of the Phonographic Industry (IFPI). www.ifpi.org. Represents a membership of record producers and distributors in over seventy-six countries. Priorities include improving copyrights, coordinating international antipiracy activities, and global market research.

International Live Music Conference. www.ilmc.com. Web site lists booking agencies, festivals, venues, and more.

Pollstar. www.pollstar.com. Information on international talent buyers and concert venues.

This Business of Music, 9th Ed. M. William Krasilovsky, Sidney Shemel, John Gross. New York: Billboard Books: 2003. Overview of the music business with an emphasis on legal issues.

This Business of Music Marketing and Promotion, Rev. Ed. Tad Lathrop. New York: Billboard Books, 2003. Covers essential procedures for selling music.

World Intellectual Property Organization (WIPO). www.wipo.int. Promotes respect of intellectual property throughout the world.

WORLDWIDE MUSIC STYLES, CHARACTERISTICS, AND PREFERENCES

AllMusic. www.allmusic.com. Database of music artists, recordings, genres, and styles, with options for exploring related music by country, mood, influences, and other parameters.

Charts All Over the World. www.lanet.lv/misc/charts. Search by Artist to find out what countries an artist is charting in.

MTV International. www.mtv.com/mtvinternational. Entertainment and playlists for more than twenty countries.

Worldwide Internet Music Resources. http://library.music.indiana.edu/music_resource. Links to country-by-country music sites, newsletters, and other resources.

CONFERENCES AND SEMINARS

ADE. www.amsterdamdanceevent.nl. Annual dance music event.

CMJ Music Marathon. www.cmj.com. Annual convention in New York City showcasing new music.

MIDEM. www.midem.com. Annual international music industry trade show held in Cannes, France.

MIPTV Featuring MILIA. www.MIPTV.com. International trade show for the audiovisual content industry.

Popkomm. www.popkomm.com. Annual international trade show for music and entertainment, held in Berlin. Attended by labels, distributors, publishers, and other kinds of businesses.

Sonar. www.sonar.es. Barcelona-based conference devoted to "advanced music and multimedia art": electronica, advanced rock, hip-hop, electronic pop, digital concretism, electronic folk, and experimental jazz.

SXSW Music and Media Conference. www.sxsw.com. Austin-based music event showcasing hundreds of musical acts from around the globe.

Winter Music Conference. www.wmcon.com. Miami-based annual dance music conference, attracting artists, DJs, and industry pros.

ADVERTISING AND MEDIA

Asociación Mundial de Radios Comunitarias (AMARC). www.amarc.org. Association of international community radio broadcasters.

International Advertising Resource Center. www.www.bgsu.edu/departments/tcom/faculty/ha/intlad1.html#mc. Lists information sources useful to international advertising researchers and practitioners, in such categories as global media and international communications.

Kidon Media Link. www.kidon.com/media-link. Links to 18,000 newspapers and other news sources from almost every country and territory in the world.

Live365 Internet Radio. www.live365.com. Links to Internet radio stations.

Media Links Now. www.medialinksnow.com. Links to international magazines and newspapers.

Non-Commercial Radio Stations Around North America and the World. www.gumbopages.com/other-radio.html.

Radio Locator. www.radio-locator.com. Links to worldwide radio stations.

Word Advertising Research Center. www.warc.com.

MOVIES AND TELEVISION

European Film Exhibition Industry Report. www.factbook.net/wbcee.htm.

Hollywood Reporter. www.hollywoodreporter.com. Offers listings of U.S. and international film and TV projects that are in preproduction, preparation, and development.

Television Business International (TBI) Yearbook. London: Informa Telecoms & Media. Lists broadcasters, channels, producers, ad distributors, and more in Europe, North America, South America, Asia Pacific, Africa, and the Middle East.

AFRICA

GHANA

Distributor: Medtrade Ent

Record Industry Association: Association of the Recording Industry of Ghana. E-mail: citirock@africaonline.com.gh.

NIGERIA

Distributors: Gerald & Gerrard Ltd., Ronis Investment Nigeria

Record Industry Association: IFPI Nigeria. E-mail: aaponmade@yahoo.com.

Author, Publisher Rights Organization: MCSN

SOUTH AFRICA

Distributors: ASP Records, Boomerang Music, David Gresham Record Co., Electromode Music, EMI Music South Africa, ENT Entertainment, Essential Distribution, Gallo Music Group, Great Value Music, Just Music, Kurse Music Distribution, Mobile Music Trust, Next Music, Nu Metri Media Stores, Phase 2 Music, Select Music, Sheer Music, Smug Music, Sony BMG Africa

Record Industry Association: Recording Industry of South Africa. www.risa.org.za.

Author, Publisher Rights Organization: SAMRO (Southern African Music Rights Organization). www.samro.org.za.

Mechanical Rights Organization: SARRAL

ASIA

CHINA

Distributors: Bandu Music, Modern Sky Entertainment, PoloArts Entertainment, Rock Mobile Corp., Xintiandi Entertainment

Author, Publisher Rights Organization: Music Copyright Society of China (MCSC)

HONG KONG

Distributors: Beaver Music, Dreamtime Entertainment, Evolution Ltd., Karrex HK, Master Music, Music Gallery, The Orchard Hong Kong, Shun Cheong Record Co., Silk Road Music Co., Sui Seng Trading Co., Toco Asia

Record Industry Association: IFPI Hong Kong. www.ifpihk.org.

Author, Publisher Rights Organization: CASH (Composers and Authors Society of Hong Kong)

INDIA

Distributors: Freespirit Entertainment, Hungama Mobile, Music Gallery India, Music Today, Rhythm Corner Alaknanda RCA, Times Music, Worldwide Records

Record Industry Association: The Indian Music Industry (IMI). www.indianmi.org.

Author, Publisher Rights Organization: IPRS (Indian Performing Rights Society)

JAPAN

Distributors: Ahora Corp., Area B, Arights Ltd., Avex Marketing Communications, Blues Interactions, Cool Inc., Cybird/Coolsound, Disk Union, Dreamtime Entertainment, Elmo Co., Eugene Music/Flavour Records, Foreal Co., Hip Land Music, Howling Bull Entertainment, Japan Publications Trading Co., Keep Co., King International, Lexington Ltd., Listen Japan, Mikasa Tsusho Ltd., Music Airport, Music Wave, New World Records, Pop Group Recordings, Premium Life, Quake Records, Rambling Records, Sony Corp., Third-Ear Jpn, Tokyo M-Plus, Tower Records Japan, Ultra-Vybe, Uscita Inc., Ward Records

Record Industry Association: Recording Industry Association of Japan (RIAJ). www.riaj.or.jp.

Author, Publisher Rights Organization: JASRAC (Japanese Society for Rights of Authors and Composers). www.jasrac.or.jp.

Japan Association of Music Enterprises. www.jame.or.jp.

Music Publishers' Association of Japan (MPAJ). wwwmpaj.or.jp.

SOUTH KOREA

Distributors: Ales Music, Aulos Media, Bridge Media, Chili Music Korea, CJ Music, C&L Music, C-Sharp Media, Just Music, Kang & Music, K-Beat Music, Manine Media, Musicmine Records, N3 Co., Saem Energy Co., Sedona Media Co., Sky Music Entertainment, S.M. Entertainment, Widerthan, Winds Communication, Wiz Communications

Korean Association of Phonogram Producers. www.kapp.or.kr.

TAIWAN

Distributors: Aurora Music International, EQ Music, Ewise Digital Multimedia, Falomi Digital Media, High Note International Multimedia, Jingo Digital, Linfair Records, Magnum Music Entertainment Pan China, Rock Records Co., Sunrise International Entertainment, Underground Records, Wind Music International

Record Industry Association: IFPI Taiwan. www.ifpi.org.tw.

Author, Publisher Rights Organization: MUST (Sony BMG Music Entertainment (Taiwan)).

SOUTHEAST ASIA

INDONESIA

Author, Publisher Rights Organization: KCI (Karya Cipta Indonesia).

PHILIPPINES

Author, Publisher Rights Organization: FILSCAP (Filipino Society of Composers, Authors, and Publishers).

SINGAPORE

Record Industry Association: Recording Industry Association (Singapore). www.rias.org.sg.

Author, Publisher Rights Organization: COMPASS (Composers and Authors Society of Singapore). www.compass.org.sg.

National Arts Council. www.nac.gov.sg.

THAILAND

Record Industry Association: Thai Entertainment Content Trade Association (TECA). E-mail: ifpithai@asianet.co.th.

OCEANIA

AUSTRALIA

Distributors: AIM Trading Group, Australian Music Marketing Abroad, Colossal Records of Australia, Creative Vibes, Dimension Entertainment Aust., Fuse Music Group, HHO Multimedia Australasia, Intertia, Jazz Coordination Association of Western Australia (Jazzwa), MRA Entertainment, Payless Entertainment, Rajon, Red Eye Records, Riot Entertainment Australia, Shock Entertainment Group-Exports and Distribution, Stomp Pty.

Record Industry Association: Australian Record Industry Association. www.aria.com.au.

Author, Publisher Rights Organizations: AMCOS, APRA (Australian Performing Rights Association). www.apra.com.au.

Foreign Trade Agency: Australian Trade Commission. www.austrade.gov.au.

AIR—Australian Independent Record Labels Association. www.air.org.au.

Jazz Coordination Association of Western Australia. www.jazz.org.au.

West Australian Music Industry Association. www.wam.asn.au.

NEW ZEALAND

Distributors: Border Music Ltd., Elite Imports NZ Ltd.

Record Industry Association: www.rianz.org.nz.

New Zealand Music Industry Commission. www.nzmusic.org.nz.

EUROPE

AUSTRIA

Distributors: Balloon Records, Couch Records Music Production, Edel Musica Vertriebs, Gramola, Hoanzl Vertriebsges M.B.H., IMZ-International Music & Media Center, In and Out Records-Mathans & Kopanakis, MCP Sound and Media, Polyglobe Music Austria, Preiser Records, Rebeat Music International, Sony DADC Austria, Soul Seduction Distribution

Record Industry Association: IFPI Austria. www.ifpi.at.

Author, Publisher Rights Organization: AKM

Mechanical Rights Organization: Austro-Mechana

Austrian Music Council. www.oemr.at.

Austrian Music Export. www.musicexport.at.

Music Information Center Austria (MICA). www.mica.at.

BELGIUM

Distributors: 2 Brains Entertainment Group, AMG Records, Audiopolis Group of Companies, CNR Records, Codaex, Fassiphone Belgium, Hysterias, LC Music, Mausoleum Records, N.E.W.S. NV, Pavane Records, Super Music

Record Industry Association: IFPI Belgium. www.ifpi.be.

Author, Publisher Rights Organization: SABAM (Societe Belges des Auteurs, Compositeurs et Editeurs) www.sabam.be.

European Music Office (EMO). www.musicineurope.org.

Independent Music Companies Association (IMPALA). www.impalasite.org.

CROATIA

Distributors: Croatia Records, Dancing Bear

Record Industry Association: Hrvatska Diskografska Udruga Croatian Phonographic Association. www.hdu.hr.

Author, Publisher Rights Organization: HDS

CZECH REPUBLIC

Distributors: Curepink Distribuce, GZ Digital Media, Panther A.S., P&J Music

Record Industry Association: IFPI Czech Republic. www.ifpicr.cz.

Author, Publisher Rights Organization: OSA

Central European Music Agency, S.R.O. (CEMA). www.cema-music.com.

DENMARK

Distributors: Alliance Records Copenhagen, Bach Pack, Best Price Exports, Elap A/S, Foreign Media Group Scandinavia, Licensemusic.com, Phonofile, Scanbox Entertainment, Silverport Records

Record Industry Association: IFPI Denmark. www.ifpi.dk.

Author, Publisher Rights Organization: KODA (Denmark Music Copyright Organization). www.koda.dk.

Danish Artist Union. www.artisten.dk.

Danish Musicians Union. www.dmf.dk.

Danish Songwriters Guild. www.dpa.org.

Music Export Denmark. www.mxd.dk.

ROSA—The Danish Rock Council. www.rosa.org.

ESTONIA

Distributors: Goldenclub Records, Records Hulgi

Record Industry Association: IFPI Denmark. www.ifpi.dk.

Author, Publisher Rights Organization: EAU

Association of Estonian Professional Musicians. www.estonianmusician.com.

Estonian Classical Performers Agency. www.artistandagency.net.

Music Export Estonia. www.estmusic.com.

FINLAND

Distributors: Blue Magnum, DD Records, Hitmedia Int., Poptori OY, Securycast OY, Sulake Corporation, Teliasonera Finland, Tezoma Solutions

Record Industry Association: IFPI Finland. www.ifpi.fi.

Author, Publisher Rights Organization: TEOSTO (Finnish Composers' Copyright Society). www.teosto.fi.

Finnish Music Information Centre (FIMIC). www.fimic.fi.

Finnish Music Publishers Association. www.musiikkikustantajat.fi.

Music Export Finland. www.musexfinland.fi.

FRANCE

Distributors: 123 Multimedia, Abeille Musique, Advestigo, Airtist, Arion SA, Atoll Music, Club Dial, Compact Disc Mail, Coop Breizh, Cyber Production, DG Diffusion, EMA-CD/DVD, Fairplay, FGL Productions, FNAC, France Televisions Distribution, Francis Dreyfus Music, Fremeaux & Associés, Ghost L.A., Harmonia Mundi, Heat Distribution, Integral Distribution, J-Music Distribution, Keltia Musique, La Baleine, L'Autre Distribution, Le Maquis, Loudeye France, Multiwaves/IDCD, Musica Latina Europe, Musiwave, Naïve, Neolab Production, New Service/2 More Music, O'CD, Orkhestra International, Osmose Productions, Penelope Music, Productions Speciales, Redstar Entertainment, Sarl Records Mania, SBBS, Season of Mist—Soundworks, SFR, Socadisc,Top Link, Vicious Circle Records,V. Music, Warm Music, Warner Music France, XIII Bis Records

Record Industry Association: (SNEP) Syndicat National de l'Édition Phonographique. www.disqueenfrance.com.

Author, Publisher Rights Organization: SACEM (Société des Auteurs, Compositeurs et Éditeurs de Musique). www.sacem.fr.

Mechanical Rights Organization: SDRM (Société pour l'administration du Droit de Reproduction Méchanique) (via SACEM). www.sacem.fr.

Neighboring Rights Organization: SPRE (Société pour la Perception de la Rémuneration Equitable). www.spre.fr.

Club Action des Labels Independants Français (CALIF)

French Music Export Office. www.french-music.org.

SESAM (Société civile chargée de gérer les droits des auteurs des sociétés membres, pour les programmes multi-media). Multimedia rights organization. www.sesam.org.

UPFI (Union des Producteurs Phonographiques Français Indépendents)

GERMANY

Distributors: 24/7 Musicshop, Alive AG, AMCO Tontraeger Vertriegs, Arvato Mobile, Bellaphon Records, Bob-Media, California-Sunset Records, Cargo Records, Century Media Records, Collectors Mine, Connect Europe, Contnet AG, Coremedia, DA Music/Pallas Group, Discomania Musikvertriebs, Drakkar Entertainment, Edel Classics, Edel Distribution, Farao Studios, Fenn Music Service, Finetunes GMBH, Flex Media Entertainment, Gebhardt Musikvertrieb, Groove Attack, H'Art Musik Vertrieb, In-Akustic GMBH, Indigo MusikProduktion & Vertrieb,

Intergroove Tontraeger Vertriebs, Jumbo Neue Medien und Verlag, Klassik Center Kassel, Materna GMBH, Mconnexion, MDM Mutualism, Membran International, Metal Blade Records, Music2deal.com, Music Just Music.com, Musikverlage Hans Gerig, Musikwelt Tontraeger, Neuton Meiden Vertrieb, Nuclear Blast GMBH, Ring Musik, Rough Trade Distribution, Silenzio Music Germany, Sonopress GMBH, Soulfood Music Distribution, Speakers Corner Records, SPV GMBH, Sunnymoon Distribution, TMI Top Music International, Unlimited Media, Word and Sound Medien, Zebralution GMBH, ZYX Music

Record Industry Association: Deutsche Landesgruppe der IFPI. www.ifpi.de.

Author, Publisher Rights Organization: GEMA (Gesellschaft für Musikalische Aufführungs und Mechanische Vevielfaltigungreschte). www.gema.de.

Mechanical Rights Organization: GEMA. www.gema.de.

Foreign Trade Agency: German Office for Foreign Trade. www.bfai.com.

Association of Classical Independents in Germany. www.class-germany.de.

DMV (Deutscher Musikverleger-Verband). www.dmv-online.com. Music publishers association.

German Association of Independent Record Companies. (VUT). www.vut-online.com.

German Sounds AG Music Export Germany. www.germansounds.de.

HAMM (Handelsverband Musik und Medien). www.hamm.ev.de. Music retailers association.

VUT (Verband Unabhängiger Tonträgerunternehmen). www.vut-online.de.

WOMEX—The World Music Export. Festival, concert organizer. www.womex.com.

GREECE

Distributors: A.S. Penguin Ltd., Direct Club, FM Records, Heaven Music

Record Industry Association: Association of Greek Producers of Phonograms. www.ifpi.gr.

Author, Publisher Rights Organization: AEPI

HUNGARY

Distributors: CLS Records, Hangveto, Musicdome KFT, Record Express, Stereo KFT/Periferic Records

Record Industry Association: MAHASZ—Magyar Hanglemezkiadók Szövetsége www.mahasz.hu.

Author, Publisher Rights Organization: ARTISJUS (Hungarian Bureau for the Protection of Authors' Rights). www.artisjus.hu.

Music Export Hungary. www.mxh.hu.

ICELAND

Distributors: 12 Tonar, Ardegi EHF

Record Industry Association: IFPI Iceland. E-mail: icc@chamber.is.

Author, Publisher Rights Organization: STEF

Foreign Trade Agency: Trade Council of Iceland. www.icetrade.is.

Iceland Music Information Center. www.mic.is.

IRELAND

Distributors: Atom Music Ltd., Beaumex Ltd., CMR Records, Cosmic Sounds Ltd., Dara-Dolphin Records, Dreamlines Entertainment, Intersound Distribution, Online Music Store.com, Promosound Ltd., RMG Chart Entertainment

Record Industry Association: IRMA (Irish Recorded Music Association). www.irma.ie.

Author, Publisher Rights Organization: IMRO (Irish Music Rights Organization). www.imro.ie.

Mechanical Rights Organization: MCPS (Ireland). www.mcps.ie.

Recorded Artists and Performers Ltd. Performance rights collecting society run by performers for performers. www.raap.ie.

ITALY

Distributors: 1st Pop/1st Groove, Abraxas SRL, Andromeda Distribuzioni, Audioglobe, Butterfly Music, CDyourself SRL, Deltadischi, Duck Records, Energy Production, Enrico Castoglione Arts, Family Affair Distribution, Fanzines SRL, Franton Music, Giucar Services, Global Net, Halidon, Hitland, IMS SPA, Interbeat SRL, It-Why Distribuzione, Jupiter Distribuzione, Level One SRL, Loudeye Italia, Mobile Music SRL, Self Distribuzione SPA, Societa Italiana Della Musica, TJ Net SPA, Universal Music Italia, Venus Distribuzione

Record Industry Association: FIMI (Federazione Industria Musicale Italiana). www.fimi.it.

Author, Publisher Rights Organization: SIAE (Società Italiana degli Autori ed Editori). www.siae.it.

Associazione dei Fonografici Italiani (AFI). www.afi.mi.it. Italian independent record producers' association.

IMAÏE (Institute for the Protection of Performing Artists' Rights). www.imaie.it.

LATVIA

Distributors: Microphone Records, Riga Recording Studio

Author, Publisher Rights Organization: AKKA/LAA

Latvian Music Information Centre. www.lmic.lv.

LITHUANIA

Distributors: Baltic Optical Disc Group, Bomba JSC, Prior Records

Author, Publisher Rights Organization: LATGA-A (Agency of Lithuanian Copyright Protection Association. www.latga.lt.

Lithuanian Music Information and Publishing Centre. www.mic.lt.

LUXEMBOURG

Author, Publisher Rights Organization: SACEM Luxembourg. www.sacemlux.lu.

NETHERLANDS

Distributors: Astral Music B.V., Bellarti B.V., Bertus Distribution, Digital Media Power, Disky Communications Europe, Galaxy Music, Mid-Town Records, Munich Records B.V., Music Products B.V., Roughtrade Distribution, Rounder Europe, Solo Music Benelux, Toco Europe, Weton-Wesgram B.V.

Record Industry Association: Nederlandse Vereniging van Producenten en Importeurs. www.nvpi.nl.

Author, Publisher Rights Organization: BUMA/STEMRA. www.buma.nl.

Neighboring Rights Organization: SENA. www.sena.nl.

Conamus. www.conamus.nl. Foundation promoting the performance of Dutch Music.

NORWAY

Distributors: Artspages, Kjell Bjoerge Engros, Musikklosen, Musikkoperatorene AS, Tuba Records, Upnorth Discs, Voices Music & Entertainment

Record Industry Association: IFPI Norway. www.ifpi.no.

Author, Publisher Rights Organization: TONO. www.tono.no.

GramArt (The Norwegian Recording Artists Association). www.gramart.no.

Music Export Norway. www.musicexportnorway.no.

Music Information Center Norway. www.mic.no.

Norwegian Music Publishers Association (NMFF). www.nmff.no.

NORSK Artistforbund/Norwegian Artists and Songwriters Association. www.noart.no.

POLAND

Record Industry Association: Zwiazek Producentów Audio-Video. www.zpav.pl.

Author, Publisher Rights Organization: ZAIKS

PORTUGAL

Distributors: 2 Dance, Abilio Silva and Semanas, By the Music—Producoes Musicais, CNM—Companhia Nacional de Musica, Dargil—Sociedade Comercial Limitada, Difference Music, Farol Musica, K Par K Editions—Caparca Publishing, One Records, Sabotage—Registos Fonograficos, Zona Musica

Record Industry Association: Associação Fonogràfica Portuguesa. E-mail: afport@mail.telepac.pt.

Author, Publisher Rights Organization: SPA (Portuguese Authors Society)

ROMANIA

Distributors: Alma Artex, Cat Music, Electrecord, Mediapro Music, Roton

Author, Publisher Rights Organization: UCMR-ADA

RUSSIA

Distributors: Familia Entertainment, Fono Ltd., I-Free Ltd., Landy Stars Music, Lilith Ltd., Megaliner Records, Melodiya-FSUE-Firma Melodiya, Music Ltd., Riton, RMG Records, Soyuz Music, X-Media

Author, Publisher Rights Organizations:

NAAP (The Independent Agency of Authors and Copyright Holders). www.naap.ru.

RAO (Russian Authors Society). www.rao.ru.

Classound Russian Federation. www.classound.com.

Eastern Europe Music Convention (EEMC). www.eemc.tv.

SLOVENIA

Distributors: Matrix Music, Nika

Author, Publisher Rights Organization: SAZAS

SIMIC—Slovene Music Information Center. www.sigic.si.

SPAIN

Distributors: Arco Iris Latin Disc, Avispa SL, Bit Music, Blanco y Negro Music, Blue Moon Producciones Discográficas SL, Brixton Records, Cat Music SL, Coda Music, Digital Vision Disc, Discmedi, Discos Lollipop, Distribuciones Miyad, Diverdi SL, Divucsa Music SA, Dock Entertainment SA, Edel Music,

Envidia Producciones, Eurogyc, Filmax Music, Fundación Albéniz, Goimusic SLL, Indigo Records, JRB Producciones y Comunicacion, Karonte Distribuciones-Nuba Records, K. Industria Cultural, Locomotive Music, Long Play Records, LR Music, Mastertrax SL, Metropol Records, Miralan's Distributions 2005, Música Global Discográfica, Open Records, The Orchard, Picap SL, Popstock Distribuciones, Resistencia, Rosazul/Music DLD, Rosevil Productions, Sonifolk SA, Transdisc Music, Tumbet Music, Vampisoul/Munster/Distrolux, Ventilador Music

Record Industry Association: Promusicae. www.promusicae.org.

Author, Publisher Rights Organization: SGAE (Fundación Autor). www.sgae.es.

AEDEM (Asociación Espãnola de Editores de Música). www.aedem.es.

SWEDEN

Distributors: Bonnier Amigo Music Group, Border Music, CDA/Compact Distribution, Dicentia AB, Next Stop Distribution, Showtime Distribution, Sound Pollution AB, The Music Company Nordic

Record Industry Association: IFPI Sweden. www.ifpi.se.

Author, Publisher Rights Organization: STIM (Swedish Music Performing Rights Society). www.stim.se.

Swedish Music Publishers Association. www.smff.se.

EXME—Export Music Sweden AB. www.exms.se.

SWITZERLAND

Distributors: 234 AG, Altrisuoni, Dancing City Entertainment Star Search Group Europe, Dinifan SA, Disctrade, Disques Office SA, Guild GMBH, Musicora AG, PBR Records SA, Recrec Medien, RTSI Multimedia, Sirup Music GMBH, TBA AG, Turicaphon AG

Record Industry Association: IFPI Switzerland. www.ifpi-schweiz.ch.

Author, Publisher Rights Organization: SUISA (Swiss Society for the Rights of Authors of Musical Works). www.suisa.ch.

Swiss Music Export. www.swiss-music-export.com.

TURKEY

Distributors: A.K. Müzik Yapim, Degisim Kultur Sanat, Logizmo

Record Industry Association: Mü-YAP (IFPI Türkiye Milli Grubu). www.mu-yap.org.

Author, Publisher Rights Organization: MESAM. www.mesam.org.tr.

UKRAINE

Distributors: Astra Records Ltd., Odyssey, Winner Records

UNITED KINGDOM

Distributors: The 24 Ltd., Acrobat Music, Air Music and Media Sales, Amato Distribution, Apace Music, Avanti Records, Awal U.K., Cadiz Music, Carbon Music, Chrome Dreams, Classic Rock, Completely Independent Distribution/Talents, Consolidated Independent, D.A. Recordings Limited, Decca Music Group, Deluxe Media Services, Discovery Records, Document Records, Eagle Rock Entertainment, Enterprise Records, Essential Music & Marketing, Europa Worldwide Logistics, Fat Cat International, HHO Ltd., Indie Mobile, Kelso Entertainment, Kudos Records, Lasgo Chrysalis, Lost Moment Records, Loudeye U.K., Marathon Media International, Metronome Distribution, Music Factory Entertainment Group, Music Inc., New Note Distribution, New World Music Ltd., Nimbus Records, The Orchard, Ozmo Music Group, Passion Music, Pegasus (a division of Eagle Rock), Pickwick Group Limited, Pinnacle Records, Plastic Head Music Distribution, Prism Leisure Corporation, Proper Music Group, P&W Partners, Route 1, RSK Entertainment, SBI Global Limited, S. Gold & Sons, Shellshock Distribution, Soundlink Music, SRD Ltd., Time Music International, Timewarp Distribution, Total Home Entertainment, Uploader Music, Westway Music, Wienerworld Limited, Windsong International

Record Industry Association: BPI (British Phonographic Industry). www.bpi.co.uk.

Author, Publisher Rights Organization: PRS (Performing Rights Society). www.prs.co.uk.

Mechanical Rights Organization: MCPS (Mechanical Copyright Protection Society). www.mcps.co.uk.

Neighboring Rights Organization: PPL (Phonographic Performance Ltd.). www.ppluk.com. Collects and distributes airplay and public performance royalties on behalf of record companies and performers.

Foreign Trade Agency: U.K. Trade and Investment: www.uktradeinvest.gov.uk.

AIM (Association of Independent Music). www.musicindie.com.

British Academy of Composers and Songwriters (BACS). www.britishacademy.com.

Music Publishers Association (MPA). www.mpaonline.org.uk.

Video Licensing: Video Performance Ltd. (VPL)

MIDDLE EAST

IRAN

Distributor: Soroush Multimedia Corporation

ISRAEL

Distributors: BNE Records, Logia-Cellcom, The Orchard, Teta-Making Music

Record Industry Association: IFPI Israel. E-mail: nili@ifpi.co.il.

LEBANON

Distributors: Byblos Records, Music Master

UNITED ARAB EMIRATES

Distributor: Vanilla Music LLC

Author, Publisher Rights Organization: Arabian Music Rights. www. arabianmusicrights.com.

SOUTH AMERICA

ARGENTINA

Distributors: Af Music, D.B.N. Srl, Distribuidora Lef, Epsa Music, Leader Music S.A.C.I.M., Music Brokers/PMB Music, The Orchard, Random Records

Record Industry Association: CAPIF—Cámara Argentina de Productores de Fonogramas y Videogramas. www.capif.org.ar.

Author, Publisher Rights Organization: SADAIC

BRAZIL

Distributors: Azul Music Multimídia, BM&A-Brasil Musica and Arts, Building Records, HPI Brasil, Imusica S/A, ST2 Music

Record Industry Association: ABPD—Associação Brasileira dos Produtores de Discos. www.abpd.org.br.

Author, Publisher Rights Organizations: ABRAMUS (Associação Brasileira de Música e Artes). www.abramus.org.br., SBACEM, SBAT, SICAM, UBC (União Brasileira de Compositores). www.ubc.org.br.

Associação Brasileira da Música Independente (ABMI). www.abmi.com.br. Independent music association.

Associação Brasileira de Gravadoras Independentes (ABGI). www.abgi.org.br. Independent labels association.

Brasil Música e Artes (BM&A). www.bma.org.br.

Brazilian Music Publishers Association (ABEM). www.abem.org.br.

COLOMBIA

Distributors: Discos Orbe, Forum Discos, Tower Records Colombia

Record Industry Association: Asociación Colombiana de Productores de Fonogramas (ASINCOL). E-mail: webmaster@asincol.org.co.

Author, Publisher Rights Organization: SAYCO

VENEZUELA

Author, Publisher Rights Organization: SACVEN (Society of Authors and Composers of Venezuela). www.sacven.org.

CENTRAL AMERICA AND THE CARIBBEAN

CUBA

Distributors: Bis Music, Egrem-Empresa de Grabaciones

Author, Publisher Rights Organization: ADCAM

JAMAICA

Record Industry Association: IFPI Jamaica Group. Tel: +1 876 968 6572.

Author, Publisher Rights Organization: JACAP

MEXICO

Distributors: Discos Continental, Mas Label Mexico, Multimusic S.A., Quindecim Recordings

Record Industry Association: Asociación Mexicana de Productores de Fonogramas, A.C. E-mail: claudial@amprofon.com.mx.

Author, Publisher Rights Organization: SACM

NORTH AMERICA

CANADA

Distributors: A&R Records, Cafesonique.com, DEP Distribution Exclusive, Direct Source Special Products, Distribution Fusion 3, Distribution Select, Entertainment One, F.A.B. Distribution, Isotope Music, Justin Time Records, Magada International, Maplemusic Recordings, Outside Music, PHD Canada Distributing, Sonic Unyon Records, SRI Canada, Statik Distribution

Record Industry Association: Canadian Recording Industry Association (CRIA). www.cria.ca.

Author, Publisher Rights Organization: SOCAN, Society of Composers, Authors and Music Publishers of Canada. www.socan.ca.

Mechanical Rights Organizations: CMRRA (Canadian Musical Reproduction Rights Agency Ltd.). www.cmrra.ca., SODRAC (Société du droit de reproduction des auteurs, compositeurs et éditeurs au Canada). www.sodrac.com.

Neighboring Rights Organization: NRCC (Neighbouring Rights Collective of Canada). www.nrdv.ca.

ADISQ (Association québécoise de l'industrie du disque, du spectacle, et de la videó). www.adisq.com.

AVLA (Audio Video Licensing Agency Inc.). www.avla.ca.

Canadian Music Publishers Assoc (CMPA). www.musicpublishercanada.ca.

CIRPA (Canadian Independent Record Production Association). www.cirpa.ca.

UNITED STATES OF AMERICA

Distributors: Allegro Corporation, Alternative Distribution Alliance, Amalgam Entertainment, Apple Computer iTunes Music Store, Big Daddy Music Distribution, Big Fish Media, Caroline Distribution, CD Baby, Digital MusicWorks International, Digital Rights Agency, Fontana Distribution, Forte Distribution, Gracenote, Hep Cat Records & Distribution, Independent Online Distribution Alliance (IODA), Iris Distribution, Koch Entertainment, Legendary Music, Loudeye, Lumberjack Mordam Music Group, Malaco Music Group, MSI Music, Musicrama, Navarre Corporation, The Orchard, Premiere Music Distribution, Razor & Tie Entertainment, Red Distribution, Redeye Distribution, Rounder Records, RykoDisc, Sidecho Records, Sony BMG Music, Studio Distribution, Super D/Phantom, Tommy Boy Entertainment, Warner Music Group

Record Industry Association: Recording Industry Association of America (RIAA). www.riaa.com.

Author, Publisher Rights Organizations: American Society of Composers, Authors and Publishers (ASCAP). www.ascap.com., Broadcast Music Inc. (BMI). www.bmi.com., SESAC. www.sesac.com/home.asp.

Mechanical Rights Organization: Harry Fox Agency/National Music Publishers Association (HFA) (NMPA). www.harryfox.com

Digital Rights Organization: SoundExchange. www.soundexchange.com.

American Composers Alliance (ACA). www.composers.com.

American Federation of Musicians. www.afm.org.

American Federation of Television and Radio Artists (AFTRA). www.aftra.com.

American Guild of Musical Artists (AGMA). www.musicalartists.org.

Country Music Association. www.cmaworld.com.

Export.gov. www.export.gov. Internet information portal for U.S. exporters.

Live Music Venue Directory. www.onlinegigs.com

National Academy of Recording Arts and Sciences (NARAS). www.naras.org. Sponsors of the Grammy Awards.

National Association of Recording Merchandisers (NARM).www.narm.com. Members include retailers, wholesalers, and distributors.

Songwriters Guild of America (SGA). www.songwritersguild.com.

U.S. Copyright Office. www.loc.gov/copyright.

Tad Lathrop is the author of *This Business of Music Marketing and Promotion*, a widely used text on all phases of selling music to the listening public. Lathrop has written and edited music and marketing materials for a variety of media and a host of companies, including Billboard Publications and MTV's Sonicnet, and he has worked in music publishing, music performance, and performing-rights licensing. He produced and co-wrote *Jazz: The First Century*, nominated in 2000 for the Jazz Journalists Association Book of the Year, and the book/CD compilation *Cult Rockers*, and he has developed dozens of other books on music and the performing arts. Lathrop has taught music at New York City Technical College of the City University of New York and lectured on music-business topics in San Francisco State University's Music Recording Industry Program.